MÓNICA BUTLER

Migrant Dreams

A STEEP PRICE

AquaZebra™
Book Publishing
Cathedral City, CA

First hardcover edition January, 2025

Library of Congress Control Number: 2024922608

ISBN 978-1-954604-14-8 (hardcover)

Cover photo by Rayhanbp / stock.adobe.com

Book design by AquaZebra

AquaZebra™
Web, Book & Print Design

Published by AquaZebra

AquaZebra™
Book Publishing

35070 Maria Rd
Cathedral City, CA 92234
mark@aquazebra.com

Dedication

To Gianni, Pierre, Aria, Ronin, Florence, Callum,
and all future Butlers who join our clan.
May you always be proud of your heritage,
and mindful of all sacrifices endured by your brave ancestors.
Miss you always. Love you forever.

Sincere Thanks To
Kirt, Alicia, Norma, and Claudia.
Your support in my writing journey has meant the world to me.

Heartfelt Gratitude To
Mom and Dad, and Grandma María.
For my treasured childhood, exceptional memories,
and valuable lessons.
I know you're spinning tales behind them pearly gates.
I envy the angels you entertain today.

Acknowledgments

Diego F. Porciello
Automotive Enthusiast – Published Author & Journalist

Lucía Ploper
Sustainability Manager, Renault Argentina
Communications Manager/Ad Interim/Renault Argentina
Executive Director, Fundación Renault

On Sensitivity

It took a couple of years to gather up courage to bring to public light what in its beginning had only been meant as a family history for my descendants. Then, seeking to go public I discovered that to avoid censure, my memories would require cycling through alterations (until probably unrecognizable), before deemed acceptable for -and by- all audiences, if such is even possible in today's world. But then, they wouldn't really be my memories anymore, would they?

As we live in a culture inclined to take offense and find fault, I will more than likely be judged—if not condemned—for daring to express my opinion. But I am still entitled to it.

I opt to live and let live, allowing my fellow brothers and sisters to act of their own accord. No questions asked, as long as their conduct is discreet and falls within the boundaries of the law. No offense taken either, as long as their views aren't forced upon me. In return, I expect my actions and choices are respected in the same manner, and to the same degree. Mutual tolerance is indispensable to coexistence.

Even in instances where history may be inconvenient to today's chosen behaviors, or unkind to one's present line of thinking, historical facts should not be subjected to manipulation in order to soothe scars. Just as there is no erasing what has been, we cannot be expected to delete from our minds nor from our own stories what some of us physically witnessed.

While ensuring the wrongs of the past are prevented from reoccurring, we have a responsibility to remain true to ourselves, to our past, and to our posterity. And so, my truth should be told, not muzzled to silence ghosts of the past.

Respectfully.

Preface

As historically documented, between the late 1800's and the mid 1900's, over 2,300 vessels carrying immigrants docked at the Port of Buenos Aires. Some ambitious incomers were only trying their luck abroad; but most were escaping the ruin and despair brought on by the European conflicts.

My maternal grandparents and great-grandparents were among these arrivals. This account of events is not intended to embellish their adversities, but to convey a fair portrayal of the circumstances surrounding their departure and journey.

The Morenos, the Lenos, and the Portas did not descend from nobility. They did not occupy extravagant staterooms on the upper level of vessels crossing the high seas. Rather, they sold and handed to their localities all entitlement and custody over their humble homes and businesses, farms, and cattle. Some even signed promises of payment for years to come to secure passage to the New World.

Their dreams made it all worth it.

* * *

I fell in love with books at a young age. The scent of ink and the rustle of drying pages held a special meaning and feel. In my older years, I regret the fact that Mom, Dad, and my maternal grandparents were not immortalized in diary volumes nor family videos. I've the certainty my little granny in particular, would have broken ratings for any publisher or filmmaker. The big screen would have loved her. In truth, our entire family had the stories and an array of important characters to support any director no matter his or her skill. I know in my heart and mind that given the opportunity, the whole lot of them would have been superb at it. And I feel a strong duty to bring them to you in their deserved glory.

I am grateful for having lived an interesting life. Grew-up closely surrounded by immigrant relatives and neighbors, and ultimately spent my entire adulthood as an immigrant myself. And having learned much along the way, there is a great deal I'm eager to share. Above all, my great love for family.

I will be forever grateful to my little Grandma María Ascención Moreno Leno de Porta—quite a long name for such a small statured person. She sowed within me the early seeds of wonder, an appetite for a good story, her -perhaps to some-uneducated prose, and the importance of vibrancy, depth, and passion in the magic of storytelling. Her anecdotes colored my life and dreams. Acknowledging that all life comes to an end, I consider her legacy and her ingenious tales too precious and unique to carry with me to the grave.

This work is based on events my dear relatives and I have lived through. Most of the writings represent a personal point of view of the world, often but not always from a relatively young or naïve perspective. In the absence of extensive documentation and of information from relations -though there have been pleas for contribution- the net bringing it all together is a high-spirited - period-fitting - narrative, not intended as a political statement but as an eye opener to past and current events. All in all, it is a fusion of historical facts, anecdotes, and personal expe-riences; a mesh of passionate and entertaining memories and observations acquired through innocent eyes, untrained ears, and young—eager—minds.

The year 2020 was unique in personal and global circum-stances. The unprecedented solitude and fears lobbied on to us translated into the best time yet to put pen to paper. Or more accurately speaking, arthritic fingers to keyboard.

The recollections depicted herein have been in my mind for decades; they were scribbled on notepads and lose logs -piles of which I collected for what felt like centuries. I fully credit the pandemic for giving me a final reason and unlike opportunity to organize my thoughts and materialize the work.

The compilation was mostly assembled by the 110th anniversary of my Grandma María's embarkation -as a toddler- on the Conde Wilfredo sailing vessel, which departed Cádiz, Spain, in March of 1910, on its odyssey towards the Americas.

Grandma, together with her mother Cipriana and her eldest brother Gregorio, arrived in Buenos Aires, Argentina, on Saturday the 2nd of April, 1910, as confirmed by their documentation of record. A precocious and overly inquisitive child, she had been wise beyond her years from early on. And also from early on, she'd possessed the gift of gab, paired with a remarkably fighting spirit. She was my primary inspiration for these writings.

But memory is not always a blessing. It can also be a curse. And so, revisiting childhood events led me to cry a river of tears. In truth, in instances it felt more like a masochist crusade. Now that it is all down, I've freed myself of my anxious need to express everything that needed said and told. What a huge relief it has meant.

As copyrights limit my ability to share some material, there are only a handful of citations throughout the storyline -all of a musical nature- to enhance the sentiment I intend to evoke. These pieces are very dear to me, and their talented authors, owners, and performers have my most humble respect and credit for their work. I fully encourage the reader to use his/her favorite platform to locate further details, and images, to create a more vivid backdrop to the stories I recount, and to further immerse him/herself in the realities of place and time.

I've affixed a handful of family portraits and photographs and what little I have access to in the form of actual documentation pertaining to my family's archives. I have translated most foreign terms and phrases for the reader's convenience. And I have shared personal notes which I hope won't break the flow of the story, but instead complement its meaning.

I am hopeful the combined sum of all these elements will fill the reader's heart with the warmth of ancestral love, and with the emotion and longing they do mine.

M.B., November 2024

Old Immigrant Hotel (1888-1911). Buenos Aires. Argentina.
National Archives, Argentina. Public domain.

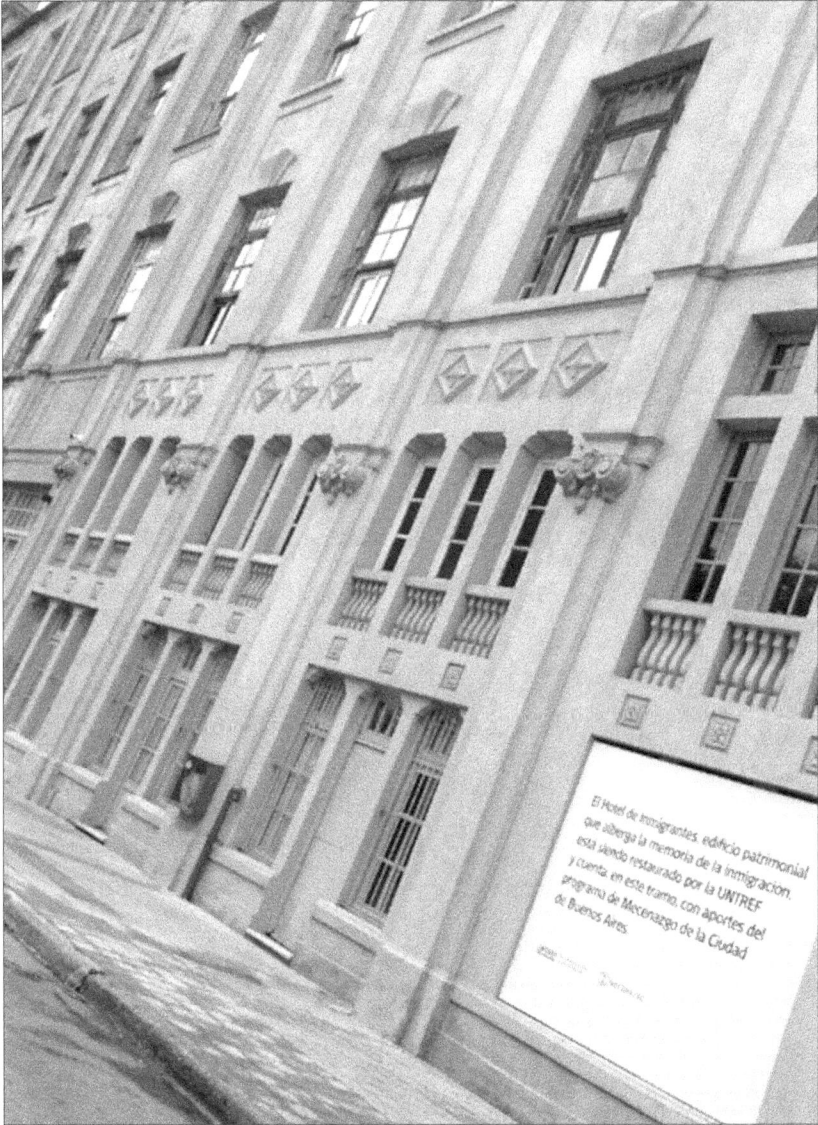

Front façade, National Immigration Museum. March 2023.
(Immigrant Hotel, 1911-1954). Buenos Aires. Argentina.
Photo courtesy of Claudia Alexandra Vera.

Waiting halls (top), sleeping quarters (bottom),
National Immigration Museum. March 2023.
(Immigrant Hotel, 1911-1954). Buenos Aires. Argentina.
Photos courtesy of Claudia Alexandra Vera.

Gallery, National Immigration Museum. March 2023.
(Immigrant Hotel, 1911-1954). Buenos Aires. Argentina.
Photo courtesy of Claudia A. Vera -photographed-
(niece residing in Tucumán, Argentina).

Table of Contents

Introduction

July 1776. The Second Continental Congress unanimously approves R. H. Lee's Resolution for Independence, declaring the legal separation of the thirteen North American colonies from Great Britain. Immediately following, Spanish King Carlos III busies himself with the creation of the Viceroyalty of the Río de la Plata - the fourth and last Viceroyalty of the Spanish Empire in the Americas. Its territory was comprised of areas presently known as Argentina, Bolivia, Chile, Uruguay, and Paraguay; and its main -but not sole- purpose was to create a stronger presence over the Spanish-controlled lands south and west of Brazil, and deter Portuguese encroachment.

***

When Great Britain began losing control over its North American dominion, the Spanish Crown had felt it imperative to protect its own conquests to the South, both from the now anxious British, as well as the menacing Portuguese. But the Brits had already made their interest well known since the early 1700's – the vast Río de la Plata could be invaluable as a colonial trading base. And, they'd also announced their intention to take over the Falkland Islands.

Spain succeeded at delaying a conflict, but as expected, when the opportunity presented itself, Britain moved forward with two successive -and unsuccessful- attempts to seize control of the two cities most accessible from the river: Buenos Aires (present day Argentina) and Montevideo (present day Uruguay). Worth mentioning is that these events coincided with preparations, by Napoleon, for the Peninsular Wars—a time when Spain and France negotiated in coalition. And so, the British thought of these attacks not just to upset the Spaniards, but to also burden the French.

In 1806 British forces opted to occupy Buenos Aires, but had been expelled shortly after. Then, they'd moved on to Montevideo, an occupation which had lasted months. While still ongoing, a third British force attempted to take Buenos Aires a second time (by then 1807), but had been met yet again by a ruthless local militia (with very little help from the Spanish colonial army).

Britain was forced to recoil, at least temporarily.

These attempts by the British, added to the continued lack of support from Spain, set in motion the independence movement in Argentina, which lasted a decade, until in July 1816 the country declared itself autonomous from Spain under the initial name **The United Provinces of the Río de la Plata.**

***

The first census in Argentina was held on the 15th, 16th, and 17th of September of 1869 under the presidency of freemason Domingo Faustino Fidel Valentín Sarmiento y Albarracín. Sarmiento, Ambassador to Chile and Perú and a recognized intellectual, was best known to his supporters as a newspaper writer born to a humble family of fifteen siblings in San Juan of The United Provinces.

Per the collected data, the total number of inhabitants was estimated at 1,877,490, including Argentinians traveling abroad for leisure, as well as those fighting in foreign lands, namely, La Guerra de la Triple Alianza. Figures indicated less than one individual every two square kilometers, though it must be noted that data for certain territories was only estimated (this referred to regions mostly populated by natives - not yet under the jurisdiction and control of the national government).

The breakdown looked more or less like this: There were over 262,000 residences (though less than 5500 individuals were landowners); and as far as population, approximately 900,000 were males. Also, approximately 315,000 were children under the age of six, and 376,000 were children between the ages of 6 and 14 (though some records argue this last number to be about 415,000). Those of voting age added to approximately 300,000 (note that women were not included in this figure - in Argentina women only acquired the right to vote in 1947, under President Perón). Two-hundred thirty-four individuals were above the age of 100 (though many-a-folk had specifically indicated they were unsure of their actual birth date, and lacked documentation to validate any estimate); about 90,000 were widows or widowers, and about 385,000 were married.

In regards to professions, there were approximately 9,602 military, 8,653 farm workers, 2,307 school teachers, 1,781 miners, 1,442 higher-ed professors, 1,047 healers, 439 lawyers, 438 degreed doctors, 240 architects, 191 engineers, and about 360 individuals were employed in the prostitution field, with a matching number of characters specifically appointed by the local Marshalls to ensure the residents' observance of the law. The remaining number was made up of jewelers and leather craftsmen, seamstresses and launderers, cooks and bakers, fishermen and coachmen, cigar makers, and shoe shiners.

Although at the time immigrants hadn't yet arrived in masses, about 15% were foreign born, and they already displayed majority tendencies in the eastern provinces of Santa Fé, Entre Ríos, and Buenos Aires. Also, contrary to common belief, these foreigners were mostly Italian, not Spanish, though Argentina's first European settlers had been Spanish born.

The most highly populated *province* was Buenos Aires (still the case in modern times), which registered about half a million inhabitants, nearly half of which in the *city* of Buenos Aires itself. [Note: there was a province named Buenos Aires; and within said province there was a city also named Buenos Aires -the country's capital. In 1880 however, the city of Buenos Aires was declared autonomous from the province].

Most Spanish immigration into Argentina had taken place during the colonial occupation between the 16th and 18th centuries. In the late 1800's however, native Argentinian workers made up less than a third of the desired and required work force. Immigrants were wanted and invited in. Such is how, by 1914, more than two million migrants had arrived from Italy, followed by 1.4 million Spaniards, 170,000 French, 160,000 Russians, and a combined 50,000 Austrian, German, and Dutch citizens, among other smaller groups.

It should be mentioned that many of the arrivals from France and the Russian Empire were Jews. This initial group paved the way for many more to join later from Central Europe, particularly during the 1930's, in their escape from Nazi persecution. They mostly settled in agricultural colonies, and although several left for Israel during the Argentinian military dictatorship of the 70's and 80's, Argentina still today has the largest Jewish population in Latin America, third largest in the Americas after the U.S. and Canada, and the worlds' seventh largest outside of Israel.

***

The 1876 Immigration and Colonization Act of Argentina, approved under President Nicolás Avellaneda (hence aka Ley de Avellaneda), intended and accomplished the birth of a period referred to as "the era of mass migration" -fifty years during which the country experienced a steady flow of arrivals, slowed only by the start of WWI.

It had been promoted abroad as Law N°817 (specifically: Part I, Chapter V, Article 12). It established in clear detail who shall be considered a legal immigrant, with limitations on age and handicap, professional qualifications, criminal conduct of record, and arrival requirements (the latter meaning: the vessel that delivered them to its shores; who had covered the monetary cost of their passage; and in what class they traveled).

It is estimated that between 1882 and 1930 (particularly in the years immediately preceding WWI), millions of Spaniards crossed the seas in search of a better life. Seeing its population figures quickly decline, and after such deliberate proposition by the Argentine government, Spain eventually responded with their own law (a retort, really), harshly categorizing migrant hopefuls, and attempting to discourage a rampant exodus (Law of Migration, 21 December, 1907).

Meanwhile, the Argentinian decree of 1876 succeeded in offering immigrants:

- free food and lodging at the *Immigrant Hotel* for up to 5 days following debarkation (note: the stay could be extended for free, as necessary, due to illness; it could also be extended by personal request, in which case the extension cost was that of ½ peso p/day p/person 8 yrs. of age and up; and ¼ peso p/day p/child aged below 8 yrs.);

- assistance to find work after a brief training in agricultural and housekeeping equipment operation, and in the latest manufacturing trends;

- a free train ride to a final destination within the country's borders (this, based on offer of employment; to join/rejoin their families; or simply to start a new life); plus 10 days of free room and board once reaching such final destination. Beyond the 10 initial days, the boarding cost was similar to lodging at the Immigrant Hotel in Buenos

Aires. The rail lines—easily identifiable as 'Ferrocarriles del Norte', 'Ferrocarriles del Sur', and 'Ferrocarriles del Oeste' provided a feasible way to get them safely on their way to a family reunion, or to a future of success.

The Argentinian government had initially assigned a smaller facility to accommodate incomers. Though primitive, it operated from 1888 until 1911 and served the arriving masses well.

The government eventually built a larger version which began its operation in 1911 and ceased in 1954. Both locations specifically housed arrivals lacking private sponsorship upon entrance. No matter the migrant's origin, another clause protected them: the free housing period could also be extended in case of lack of employment offers. But this would hardly ever become the case because laborers were in high demand, hence not many migrants could justify leaving Customs or the hotel premises without a solid offer of employment.

The hotel housed up to three thousand migrants. Its dining facility accommodated up to one thousand guests per sitting, serving three meals per day, in three sittings each (at full capacity that meant nine thousand meals per day – a lot like a cruise ship these days, though lights out was set for 7 p.m.) The initial facility, as well as its replacement, operated -on site- its own expansive kitchen, bakery, and butcher shop. Plus a free, oversized, laundromat.

But the expansive newer version which inaugurated in 1911 also housed and supported a business complex that included all services required to ease the migrants' transition into Argentine society: a storage facility, a branch of the national bank for easy currency exchange, a translator's office, a post office, a career center, and an exhibition hall where the latest agricultural equipment was offered for display and for training purposes. And last but not least, it also hosted its own hospital wing where ill incomers were treated, though it should be noted that, unlike in other countries welcoming migrants, Argentina did not quarantine arrivals ahead of presenting symptoms.

The sum of these incentives made Argentina a desirable destination for migrants. And made the prospect land no longer only attractive to poor southern Europeans, but also to their brothers of Central Europe, as well as Asians and Arabs. And so, by 1930, the number of arrivals seeking permanent refuge exceeded 6.5 million. But unlike in other regions open to accepting migrants during this period, the effect of these mass arrivals to Argentinian soil had a much greater impact, because the proportion of newcomers far exceeded the country's existing population (native and not), and their arrival generated unplanned and unmeasured changes to a culture still in infant development. The character of the local culture began noticeably shifting and molding itself after the most prevalent groups.

During the early 20th century, both the U.S. and Argentina were the two most common destinations for **Italian** migrants. But their experiences as immigrants in each of these countries differed broadly, mainly due to the 1911 Dillingham Commission Report, which set severe U.S. entry quotas and restrictions for certain nationalities. Also, despite higher literacy levels and the language advantage, Spaniards in Argentina did not outperform Italians in earnings nor in access to home ownership. This became yet another invitation for the Italian masses to continue their sea-journey below and beyond the North American shoreline.

Italians arrived in Argentina in quite large numbers between 1857 and 1920, though not all remained. Many were part of 'la clase golondrina' (the swallows). They arrived seasonally in 3rd class in the dense heat of South American Decembers to work the readying crops. Then returned home to Southern Italy by the beginning of May to share their riches and retake employment in the European harvest season.

But most did stay. It is worth noting the Italian migration process started before the Unification of Italian States (in common terms: before Italy became Italy). The masses arriving into Argentina mainly originated in the Kingdom of the Two Sicilies—a fusion of the Kingdom of Naples and the Kingdom of Sicily. Because Italy's Unification would not occur until the 1860's, the initial waves of migrants into Argentina had been Kingdom subjects rather than Italian citizens. Regardless, the arrival of the humble "Tanos" (loving Argentinian short term for "Napolitanos" and for Italians in general) totaled 44.9% of the entire postcolonial immigrant population -more than from any other country (including Spain, at 31.5%).

***

The second Argentinian Census took place the 10th of May of 1895, under the presidency of José Evaristo de Uriburu. The new totals revealed a population of 4,044,911, with one out of each four residents being foreign-born. Between the ages of thirty and fifty-nine there were now more foreign males than native.

Overall, in twenty-six years, the figures had more than doubled, and the number of children being schooled had tripled, though two thirds of school-aged children weren't yet registered for the freely offered and obligatory education. Still, the open-door policy was beginning to pay off.

The 1914 census revealed the population total had reached 7,903,662. And by 1947 it had doubled again, reaching 15,893,811.

In 1996, the population of Argentines of full or partial Italian descent numbered 15.8 million when Argentina's population was approximately 34.5 million. Today, the country has over 30 million Argentines with some degree of Italian ancestry in an overall population of 46 million.

Being that per Italian Law - and with entire disregard for place of birth - those born with the smallest trace of Italian blood are considered no less Italian than FBIs (Fully Blooded Italians), Argentina is considered more than two-thirds Italian. This fact can't be contended if the reader will look at population registries at any moment in time—Argentinian school records, sports team rosters, etc. are unarguable illustrations: half or more of first and last names are Italian.

Argentina is considered the country with the largest Italian *colony* in the world. Such is the reason there is no Little Italy within its borders -where could such boundaries be set for it, when throughout its confines Spanish is already spoken unlike anywhere else, mimicking Italian melodies? [The language spoken in Argentina is *Castellano* (Old/formal Spanish), with Neapolitan intonation]. Also, a great portion of Argentinian lingo is Italian.

CHAPTER 1

The Crossing
(Based on the Moreno and Leno Sánchez Archives)

Episcopal Palace. Cáceres, Extremadura, España. 2009.
Photo courtesy of Andrea Fabiana López de Artero
(first cousin residing in Barcelona, Spain).

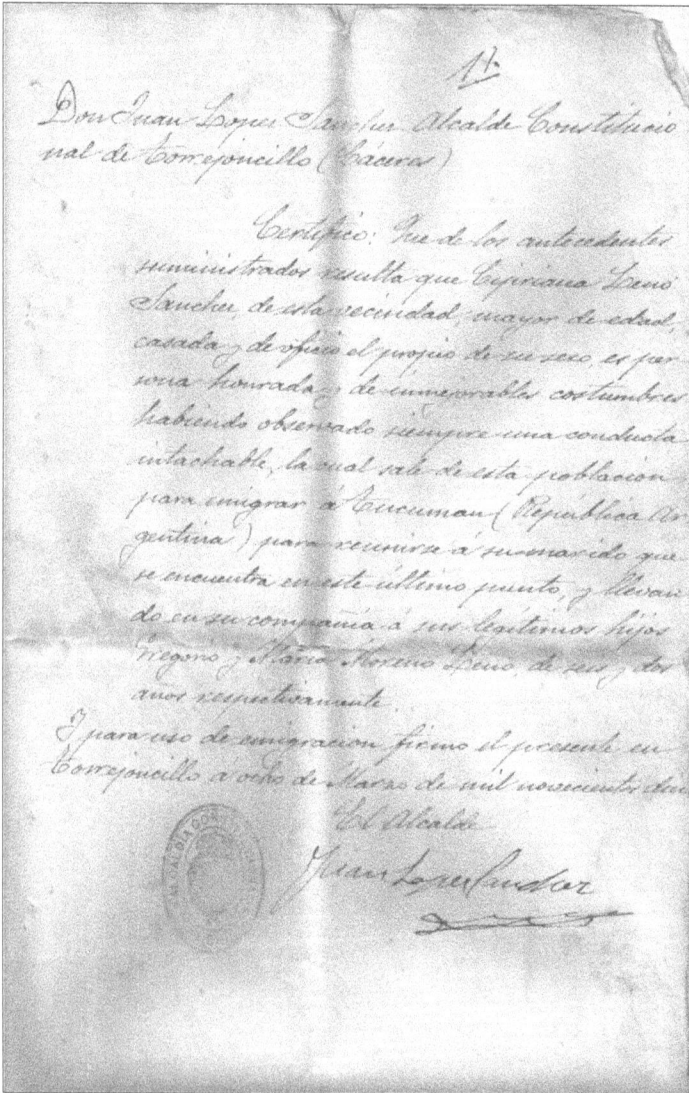

Exit permit issued by the Constitutional Mayor Don Juan
López Sánchez, on behalf of Cipriana Leno Sánchez de
Moreno, and children Gregorio Moreno Leno (6 years old) and
María Ascención Moreno Leno (2 years old – my Grandma María).
Torrejoncillo, Cáceres, Extremadura, España.
Tuesday the 8th of March, 1910.
Record extracted from family archives.

Spring. Year of Our Lord 1910. Somewhere in the Atlantic...

"¡Pues coño, ven p'cá niña!! ¡Vente p'cá!!" (Darn child, come on over here! C'mon!)

That was Remedios calling her close. Her Mama's new-found friend.

María's marveling eyes stared through the portholes. Tippy-toed over a makeshift ladder of burlap satchels filled with potatoes, she gaped into the dense darkness. Her vivid imagination murmured stories of creatures appearing without warning; blinking their displeasure at her through the thick-n-grimy green glass. Both fear and excitement bursting in her curious young mind.

The voyage was endless. Perhaps so in reality, or perhaps only given her few and immature years on this, our Holy Earth. All María knew for sure was that the confined, dark and foul-smelling space felt gloomy and scary. And didn't begin to resemble their tight but neat accommodations back home in Torrejoncillo.

Weeks before María's own departure, her Papa (*Tacio*, as her Mama lovingly called him) had embarked on his own adventure, having left behind his temporary occupation keeping burial chambers and selling flowers at the village cemetery. And his adored Priana and two *chiquillos* (little ones).

Her Mama had noticed with sadness Tacio's excitement as his decayed-looking liner prepared to set sail, headed to a faraway destination. Quite a bit ahead of her and the children, to secure employment abroad before the bulk of the family's arrival in the new land. In truth, he'd been relieved at leaving the old job behind. "Barely pays the bills" he'd frequently stated.

Priana had often sensed his upset at the inability to secure a better paying job locally. The misery taking over the village had been overwhelming. There was no worthy employment to be had -lavish hopes of a future had vanished. And many were now being drafted and sent to the northern Moroccan front line under a lengthy commitment that cared not for family, nor personal or professional obligations when there had been one or the other. Or even both.

Numerous villages had started rising in turmoil, and humble families with sons of any and all ages, had begun trading in their wealth (no matter how limited) for shanty quarters on any available and promptly departing ocean liner. And so, after many tearful discussions, Priana had finally agreed to join him on the long journey south.

He'd undoubtedly looked forward to the prospect of better opportunities and familiar faces awaiting him. His closest relatives, the Morenos, had long earlier left their native Spain and anxiously anticipated his arrival in a distant land -a land which held a promise of progress for all those who dared, afforded, and somehow survived the long and arduous passage.

But María's Mama had been the first of the Lenos to depart Europe in search of a better, safer future, leaving all her beloved relatives behind. And although Tacio's recent letter had filled her with joy at the prospect of reuniting soon, never-ending tears had streamed down her reddened cheeks the first days of the voyage. And as said tears had finally given rest, little María and brother Gregorio had grown preoccupied. Their Mama seemed sick all the time, her face ashen.

It'd all started as soon as they'd reached the embarkation point and had raised the scary, steep metal stairs, to meet the doctor waiting at the end of the line. This all, prior to being guided to the dark quarters below, that had seemed too crowded well before the bells had started blaring, signaling the start of their long journey.

The callous doctor had used the buttonhook to lift her Mama's eyelid to check for disease—the illness of easy women with fast skirts. Everyone had seemed cheerful before the stern man had subjected them to the examination. Many women had nearly fainted at his hand, and her Mama had come close, but held up strong.

***

A few days into the open sea, and already there wasn't sufficient food, nor enough warmth at night, or fresh air to disguise the acid stench of human waste and illness. The trip, met at first with such excitement, seemed now as interminable as the slow-moving waters had appeared when María had first set foot onboard and loosened her tiny hand from her mother's callused one, running to the side boards and gasping at the massiveness of blue; below, and far beyond.

There were doctors above deck also making the journey for reasons much different than those of María's family. But the lodgings below the water line were not a desirable setting for the affluent. The higher paying passengers were kept away from the penurious migrant quarters. And as the captain had warned upon departure: a doctor would only be summoned down-ship if symptoms threatened to spread.

Few children had joined during embarkation. And they'd seemed even fewer as the voyage progressed. And now her Mama's health appeared to worsen rapidly—the vessel's motion making matters worse. Each time the crew piled more coal into the *caldera* (boiler), the ship jumped softly and bounced over the foamy swells that approached; and the sails whistled loudly, and revered in excitement. And each movement made her Mama sicker.

Early on, her Mama had recognized one of the crewmembers from Papa's long-gone days working at a fishing pier, and she'd pled with little Gregorio to find him, and procure help. After long hours waiting while sitting in the humid slats, a doctor had appeared, producing considerable revolt in the sweaty air of their shared berth. Stocky, impeccably suited, and mumbling unrecognizable words under a dense mustache, the Catalonian had spilled a lengthy list of recommendations to Mama's friend. Of which María and Gregorio only caught the words *"bebé"* and a condescending *"pagaron por tré, el cuarto viene gratis"* (they paid for three, the fourth comes along for free). Their Mama was expecting. Surrounded by filth and disease.

***

Days and weeks passed, long and slow…

Since the Doctor's visit, Gregorio—almost seven—did his best to claim and clear room for *us* to rest somewhat comfortably each approaching sunset. He'd sit his skinny self in place for hours on end, blocking space near the big barrels of wine and water, normally left untouched during the dark hours. The area behind them was much coveted for quietness and privacy. Regardless, mother had a hard time of it, and often when her stomach overwhelmed her and took over her delicate frame, her new friend stepped-in to assist.

Mama and Remedios had become fast acquainted. Remedios, pale, thin, and barely older than Mama, came from a neighboring town and was also making the journey spouseless, surrounded by half-dozen *críos* (children) of her own. She herself did not appear healthy enough for the voyage. But they'd stayed near each other, often talked and laughed, and also often held hands and shared Mama's yellowing rosary while they closed their eyes in prayer during long days of rough seas.

***

At a first and only—unplanned—stopover during our long mar-itime journey, and just shortly before reaching our intended destination, we'd not been permitted to disembark even briefly. Mama had wanted to stretch her legs for a bit. Brazilian ports were also receiving migrants, but the country had found itself in active dispute with various European governments allowing said migration, as reports had surfaced about Italian arrivals sent to plantations to work in semi-slave conditions.

Shortly after, we'd finally arrived in Buenos Aires, barely in time for our new sibling to be born. The ship's loud horn and sirens had blasted deafeningly many-a-time as we stood holding hands, in awe at the new glimpse of earth emerging in the horizon. Its sprawling shore already alive in the stale pastels of dawn.

It was a bitterly crisp morning. Papa had left work in a hurry and rushed breathlessly to welcome us into his new—now *our* new—hometown. Rain had fallen, freezing and steady. And now a thick mist turned silvery upon touching the ground made for a slick run. But Papa hadn't minded. He'd been a bit late, but there had been enough time, after all. Enough indeed to think, humbly pray, and to be grateful for all blessings poured on his modest being as of late.

He'd waited eagerly at the opposite end of the pier, smiling broadly as the ship made its final push towards the shoreline. Then at its imminent approach, he'd excitedly waived his arms and hurried down the dock calling out our names, bumping relentlessly against other expecting welcomers to open way, his eyes scanning the swarm of waving hats, scarves, and hankies above and along the crowded approaching gangway.

And at first sight of our worrisome faces, he'd rushed to meet us, his advance attempts unsuccessful against that of the enthusiastic mob. Then he'd laughed out loud and been teary-eyed when he'd seen Mama walking slow, shrinking her nose as we reached the rotten-smelling pier. And her oversized round belly, which she'd held gently as they'd lovingly locked eyes for a moment in the closing distance.

Gregorio was thrilled and pushed his way through, running down to meet and hug him, shouting all along, with boundless delight. But I'd stumbled a bit and held tight on to Mama's hand, my short legs no longer accustomed to stable ground as the ship swayed in its graceful dance.

Mama's belly was quite large and she'd needed help to complete the last few steps. And loyal Remedios had been there again, a steady arm around Mama's waist. But the wind and waves had been wild the last two days and she'd been terribly ill; her abdomen having grown substantially in the last weeks, the life within now pressing insistently to be let out.

And once on firm land, Mama and Remedios had embraced tenderly, and emotions overtook them as they'd said their good-byes and wished each other health and prosperity.

And Papa had also expressed his heartfelt gratitude to teary Remedios and had waved his index finger as he warned her children to behave and care well for their young mama.

***

We were safe now, and ecstatic to have successfully reached each other. But we had yet a long way to go to reach Papa's relatives. Our family would be delayed in the city until further funds could be procured to continue inland. It would take a while yet. Papa had earned employment at the docks only days before our own arrival, and made enough to provide us temporary yet comfortable beds, sufficient food, and all we may need for the time being. But there wasn't much money left to save. Gregorio had asked whether he'd also be allowed to go to work each morning, and both Mama and Papa had held him tight and told him that Papa had it all under control.

***

Our first night together Papa had been happy but exhausted from work and ill-worries. He'd stated that after having received Mama's last letter from a few days before our departure, he'd been anxious for her and the babe in her belly, especially after his own experiences on the trip down. He was grateful we'd all made the journey in one piece, but the concerns about Mama were still in his mind. He'd been afraid the babe would be born onboard under harsh conditions. By now its debut time had surely arrived. And concerningly, it had even passed.

As Gregorio and I frolicked and explored the rooms while preparing for bed, Mama had cried intently while holding Papa's hands, attempting to explain something she'd made sure Gregorio and I could not overhear. And Papa had hugged her, kissed her tears away, and in loving tone had replied: "You can now rest and get well, *mi niña*. Anything else can wait." And he'd caressed her face longingly, hiding his own emotions.

Gregorio and I had looked at each other, wondering why Papa had seemed so worried.

With time things got better, although when the doctor was called to our humble lodgings one late night shortly after, there hadn't been a new baby after all. After the visit, Papa had talked long with the soft-spoken man while Mama laid down, weeping softly. And then Papa had sat at the dark doorway, partly looking out onto the quiet waters, and partly holding his head in his hands, sobbing in earnest. He looked so sad; just as Gregorio had been after his little toy soldier had broken, back at home. But when Gregorio had approached him and asked what was wrong, Papa had only responded: "I should have stayed and come along with you." And then Gregorio had put his thin arms around Papa's shoulder and whispered in his ear that he'd taken good care of Mama during the sailing. And they'd hugged and mourned in silence.

I was too young to understand what their sorrow had meant, but Mama's belly had remained swollen for a while, so I grew anxious and one day I'd seen her sad eyes and thinking to cheer her up I'd asked how much longer 'til I could cradle the babe in my own arms. But, her voice breaking, she'd responded: *"Sus almitas han vuelto a Jesús, María"* (their little souls have returned to Jesus). Souls. Plural. And once again, I had not understood. But each night since, Mama had held tight onto the little holy script her own Papa handed to her as Gregorio and I made our way up the ship's ramp... far, far away, the day we'd left Mama's *querida España* (dear Spain).

Eventually, we all got used to the new, bustling city. Papa had shown us where he stayed upon his arrival. He said the people at *La Rotonda de Retiro* (the Old Immigrant's Hotel) had fed him and helped him get a job. And although most newcomers rushed to leave the big city, and onto their new lives, he had stayed while he awaited our arrival. It hadn't been easy, but he spoke about them with great warmth and appreciation.

And we'd been stunned each time Papa had taken us for walks. Most everything was newer and louder than the quiet dusty fields we were accustomed to, but some big buildings had also looked quite as they had at home.

Most people here seemed in a hurry. Perhaps they all had somewhere else to be, but I wasn't sure what could be so important, so I just waved at them as I'd been taught *en el país viejo* (in the old country), as Papa called it. Only the tired and dirty arrivals seemed to notice and reciprocate my gesture though.

While lodging near the port, Papa walked to work every day. And once Mama started feeling better, he'd encouraged her to walk us further and further down the docks, selling her deliciously homemade *galletitas extremeñas.* And to chat with the *paisanos* awaiting the big ships and walking by. Papa had known what Mama needed most. She'd needed *su propia gente* (her own people).

The years passed. Day in and day out we saw so many people arriving into the city, I'd started to fear that, should we change our minds and decide to return to be near my *Abuelita* en España, there would be no one waiting to welcome us back home. And unable to rid the idea from my mind, one evening at dinner time, I'd told Papa my worries, and he'd said: "Home will always be there for us, even if everyone is gone, and even if we never get to see it again." And I don't think it had been his intention, but this had made Mama cry for a long, long while.

***

Things improved slowly, and eventually we felt an integral part of the environment surrounding us. The large number of Europeans arriving and remaining in the city made it feel quite like home, and most progress -both economic and infrastructural- made the capital also resemble the big European cities my parents had been fortunate to briefly see before leaving the old continent behind.

And the winter of 1916—six years after our arrival—as we finally prepared to leave Buenos Aires on our trip inland, we joyously partook in the city-wide celebrations held to commemorate a hundred years of Argentina's Independence. This day Gregorio and I had waved the Argentinian flag as we walked to a nearby park to join-in one of the numerous parades; and laughed as we ran to reach the platform where a military band played *Avenida de las Camelias.*

Mama and Papa's chests had swelled with pride at the privilege of early contribution to our adoptive nation's growth. A nation which had so far delivered well on its potential of progress. And fulfilled its promise of peace.

This had been another day when emotions ran high.

CHAPTER 2

The Northern Provinces
Communal Life in Argentina

Buenos Aires

During the mid to late 1800's, wealthy settlers (mostly -though not exclusively- Spanish nobility and Welsh aristocrats) built elaborate mansions within the large patches of land gifted to them by the government to help populate and modernize the city. The compounds were massive and pretentious, with excessive sitting rooms and guest and service quarters flanking each level and stairwell. Here, the rich customarily held large parties and hosted important visitors from their homelands.

South of the city (near today's *Plaza de Mayo*) the fancy facades lined block after block in today's boroughs of San Telmo and Montserrat.

But at the start of 1871, the Argentinian troops returning from war in Paraguay *(Guerra de la Triple Alianza)* had brought along yellow fever which, in the era, ran rampant in the coastal areas of Brazil. The decease took root locally and eliminated almost ten percent of the Buenos Aires population, sending two thirds into hiding. About a fourth of the wealthy population got infected and perished. A few survivors fled their expensive quarters in the *casco antiguo* to the northern part of the city -today's snobby Barrio Norte and Recoleta- further from the harbor and activity which had brought death to their doors.

The once decadent homes were abandoned and vandalized, but eventually given a new purpose as *inquilinatos* or *conventillos*, leased for peanuts in as-is condition, to the hundreds of families debarking daily from the numerous ships that lined the docks endlessly. The reason behind the thoughtful enterprise by the rich had served no other purpose than that of finally making money from the -by then- dilapidated residences.

The poor migrants craved low rents, but literally got more (or rather further less) than they'd bargained for. And such was how the most expensive period homes became *palomares* (bird cages) with caved-in roofs and collapsing floors, molding walls and falling plaster, and missing doors and windows.

***

Personal supporting note from the author.

When in my early twenties I made my way to Bs.As. for the first time, for a visa interview at the U.S. Embassy, I'd been unaware that my aunt and uncle—with whom I would be staying for a couple of weeks—resided downtown in a converted compound (aka commune, or conventillo). And although the settings' reputation was well known and questionable, on this—my first trip into the Argentine capital—I felt a thrill and a curiosity I hadn't expected to experience.

On simple approach, I learned why Italians love Argentina as they do their own land: Bs.As. is and has always been nothing but Italy away from Italy; only missing from the real one are glorious imperial ruins. The remaining infrastructure was and is still to this day, identical.

I must add that later in life, and through numerous travels and walks into the poor neighborhoods of Italy—particularly in Naples—I curiously experienced the same nostalgic feel and sounds I had as a child each time I visited my grandparents' home and neighborhood. And talking to locals, I confirmed a long-known feeling of mine...that while Italians in the U.S. consider themselves immigrants, Italians in Argentina consider themselves at home.

For those fortunate to visit Bs.As., as a true example of living style and conditions for the immigrants then, I would recommend a quick stop at a popular establishment in the San Telmo borough, which I briefly visited in the early 2000s. Prior to 1871, it had been built as the official residence for the aristocratic Ezeiza family from Genova. The lodgings were extensive, including multilevel open patio areas as well as service quarters. The property, located on Pasaje de la Defensa, had been abandoned for many decades, beginning at the height of the Yellow Fever Epidemic. Then in 1930 it was transformed into a conventillo, beginning its rental existence without repairs.

The property was eventually also used as a school for deaf children. Today, what once was individual migrant family residences within the complex (and initially used as individual guest rooms for the visiting aristocracy) is leased to tourism-focused businesses. Renovation is ongoing.

***

Tucumán

The province was a land locked, small, and not so booming metropolis, compared to the big and highly populated port cities. A few conventillos here were also large older homes turned into communal space. Otherwise, they were built specifically to function as shelter for the overwhelming number of migrants arriving frequently, after exhaustive journeys.

Afterschool hours, evenings, and weekends allowed for gatherings in the assigned common areas. Folks reminisced of old days and shared bits of wisdom and exquisite yet scarce replicas of delicacies from their far away homelands. One or another paisano played the mandolin or the accordion, and the sweet delights of *tarantella* (Italian tunes) or *jota* (Spanish folk music) would often break the air, marking a happy occasion or nostalgic moment.

Just as in the larger Argentinian cities, gangs were not prevalent, and though the locals were fortunate not to count among themselves characters like *Lucky Luciano*, at times there was a general feel of unease roaming the streets. Maintaining a curfewed schedule was smart for safety-sake and simultaneously served to keep young boys away from luring by the Camorra (Spanish for quarrel...Italian for mafia).

Demographically speaking, the population was mainly made up of a few wealthy families (old European money), tradesmen enroute to and from the northern Andes, and many poor immigrants escaping Buenos Aires in search of less crowded settings and more profitable farming communities.

In the outskirts of the city center, boroughs were built with rows of small communes surrounded by white-washed tall and thick walls. The compounds were filled within by small, precarious bedrooms built around a grand patio, a water fountain or well, and an occasional central flower bed with an imposing regional tree. Not uncommon were courtyards flanked by abundant fig and orange greenery. Everywhere the ground was fertile. Seeds defiantly grew, even when discouragingly stomped over.

The typical home of impoverished immigrants, all conventillo rooms opened to the common space, and were all connected by doors identical in size and location, which facilitated the formation of larger or smaller dwellings, as needed by the generally large migrant family units. Bathrooms were scarce and rudimentary, shared by a set number of family residences. Limited cooking and washing stations were available, hence also shared (as was the fetid air inside the stale spaces, which primary reason for being was that of shelter. Nothing more).

The compounds, two and three levels high on occasion, were gloomy and humid, yet a respite from troubled Europe. Offering sought-after low rents, they housed throngs of immigrants mainly from the Mediterranean region. A few Russian, Jewish, and Polish clusters completed the mix, with predominant languages being Italian, Castellan Spanish, and Catalonian.

***

Back to María's story…

We'd traveled long and far to reach Papa's relatives in north-western Argentina. Though only briefly on foot, our journey had been exhausting; and Papa's encouragement crucial to our focus on the final stretch. The lot of us had taken turns lifting and often dragging the extent of our family's belongings in small trunks that now threatened to give up on us at any turn. Still, our walk had felt pleasant in the cool night hours.

But early morning was starting to set in, crisp air and weak sun beams sneaking softly between and above the sugar cane tops, way over in the horizon. Though we'd tried, it was hard to judge the surroundings under the still somewhat dark blanket of the hour. There'd be time for it once we were settled -the end of the journey was near.

Papa's family awaited our arrival. Their letter said it wouldn't be long after crossing the town's imposing entrance arch. And just as stated, we'd reached the address, not far beyond the town's train station.

Noticing movement inside, one soft clap of the hands was all it'd taken. Even given the late (or rather early) hours, there had been a large number of welcomers come out to receive us and free us of our travelling load. At first, Gregorio and I thought them neighbors renting rooms from the landlord; but on rapid reassessment, they'd all displayed familiar features that matched Papa's own. These were relations.

The obvious introductions completed, and many affection-ate smiles later, we'd been welcomed into an ample residence of generously sized rooms, for as long as needed, or wanted. Quickly, a food and drink tray had been assembled and promptly presented to us. We were starved—they could see it, and though we tried, we could not hide our relief at the offerings.

We sensed they'd expected us and wished us there for a long time—they were all quite happy to see Mama and Papa. They were an interesting combo of happy and humble, a special kind of loving folk. And a few steps above the lower classes it could be said, though their privilege had not been a consequence of birthright. They were an extensive family with many young men of working age, all employed, all hard workers, and all eager to lend assistance to whomever met their aid with genuine appreciation.

They'd received us well and warmly, with truly open arms. And anxiousness now aside, we felt safe and welcomed. And we'd stayed and saved, with hopes to secure a permanent and affordable place for our growing family.

But bordering the south American winter of 1918, the home-owners had received yet more traveling acquaintances, some who'd brought along news from home across the sea; and scary stories of a deadly decease widely spreading in the motherland. Fearing the recent arrivals would have also packed and brought along the ailment, Papa was quick to find us permanent shelter where we could, hopefully, keep to ourselves. Which in our fast-growing colony couldn't really be the case, now. Could it?

***

The family settled within the small town of San Miguel, founded during the mid-1500's, the feel and look of colonial life still very much alive. Inside its urban heart, dusty fields abounded and dirt roads rutted by horse-drawn farm equipment lined most of the metropolitan area, still in early stages.

They took modest lodgings.

News about the ailment (Spanish flu) now reaching each corner of town, no sooner than settled in their new rooms, a doctor and local healers had rushed into the various compounds to get folks warned and trained on disease prevention in the widespread quarters housing the humblest of families with a myriad of young-aged children.

***

There weren't many schools around. Having come from a land rich in convent life, María was finally set to start attending a nunnery as a means of formal education. And perhaps one day, to take on the habits herself. Her brother Gregorio, four years her senior, teased her relentlessly. Each time she approached he performed the sign of the cross while repeating the Trinitarian formula. He swore the saints would tumble off their niches the day María entered the holy building.

And María was tired of it. *Sick-and-tired* of it. Her Mama needed to remind her repeatedly to control her temper and her urges to discipline her siblings. But how could she not? Little criminals Gregorio, Juan, and América always got away with murder.

Truth be known though, it was María who by now had become notorious for her astute pranks, making her parents anxious at the thought of her roaming unsupervised at a nun-run institution.

María would also be older than her classmates -not a matter of cleverness though. What she lacked for in size, she made-up for in intellect. "So, let it be known!" she often remarked while pointing her right index up, that she'd been bright and ready in her earlier years, but at the time her parents had struggled and traveled—both done too far and too long. Without a steady domicile nor money to spare, she'd been kept home, as most girls her age, to help-out with the often-numerous younger siblings to raise, and house chores to complete in the double digits, while her mother washed and ironed clothes for the male workers arriving weekly without spouses, nor extended families. The male population seemed to quadruple by the day and were quick to fill positions and work long days at the diverse merchant shops and factories springing up all over town. Fortunately, María's father had already obtained gainful—secure—employment.

Things were starting to fall into place.

***

María thrived at scholastics the first few months in attendance, although her discipline, well...it often left much to be desired. Also, in no time she'd made many friends -acquaintances who, regrettably, were her little culprits and encouraged her mischief.

And so, one ordinary day during breaktime, María and a classmate found themselves at the core of a raging confrontation. Each, and their respective posse, differed in opinion as to whether nuns kept a full head of hair under their habits. Solving the mystery would require a thorough investigation for which they had no time, nor patience. Rather, they set a betting pool and staged a game of chase. Such is how while running, María clumsily clung onto an old nun's headpiece, innocently yet harshly ripping off coif, wimple and veil altogether, to reveal an entirely bald head as the nun spun around in hysterics.

María had won the bet and bragged about it loudly. And this was the drop that filled the glass, bringing María's school days to an end. The nuns had had enough.

The persistent *Madre Superiora* had summoned her Mama *only to cause trouble* -in María's opinion- and had also sent for María, who sat waiting in the hall, facing an intricate crucifix hanging on the Madre's door, while her own mother was lectured inside. Meanwhile, María thought she could see actual blood shinning on the cross, and had dared approach to reach up and touch it as a means to verify, only to be scared witless as the door suddenly gave way and opened wide.

And upon her entering the gloomy office lit by one candle itself ready to be read its last rites, the nuns had thought to approach this case a bit differently. The savvy Madre had asked: "María, tell us, dear, why are you here?" The woman had expected she'd freely incriminate herself, yet María's reply had been: "Why, you tell me. You had me called in!"

The Madre Superiora had then re-arranged herself on her lofty high-backed chair and asked María specifically to provide her version of the story. And had then interrupted her many times during her elaborate narrative.

Tired as María was at the Madre's lack of respect, and being the lippy little thing that she was, she'd found it appropriate to finish her argument by telling the old nun: "You surely preach about patience and humility, but I fail to see your own. I dare say I'm not the only one who needs to address personal devotion."

And they'd been politely—yet royally—kicked out.

Upon returning home, Mama had told Papa that María's chances at the nunnery had been exhausted. And María -not included in the conversation, mind you- had added that she felt "Herself exhausted." Her Mama was a saint and would never have had a ready come-back for such comment. But her Papa was not amused and had proposed that she attend another school.

María, tired of structure, had asked to remain at home, offering to learn on her own *while helping Mama*. And so, it was. Her father no longer willing to be summoned if -no…not if, but *when*- she got herself in trouble once again.

And such is how María learned from that point forth. And learn she did. She learned how to play cards, how to read palms, and how to defy authority. None of these from her Mama, but from other little rascal residents of the conventillo.

***

María excelled at numbers, crafts, and cooking. But she was a magnet for trouble, and a genuine actress when the time came to disguise and justify it. She ultimately recognized (to herself only) that keeping out of mischief proved too-big-a-challenge. She never became a devout servant of our Lord Jesus, but she prayed fervently and frequently...yes siree...each-and-every-time she got herself into trouble (which was often). And so, it was only done for much needed forgiveness. Like the time she had gone along with Mama to purchase fresh produce, and as they'd turned the corner, they'd come face to face with the fast skirts that planted themselves in the dark streets and sweet-talked the men returning from work into their own filthy quarters. Having observed them at work from an upper window inside the compound, María had determined she was thoroughly disgusted with their kind. She (kinda?) understood their line of work, and how industrious the devilish femmes could be -as the saying went: "no money, no honey." The astute older ones clutched brainless males as they walked home at day's end with pockets full of hard-earned money. This secured them another month's rent while the fool men then returned home without sufficient cash to support their waiting offspring.

And so that morning while Mama hurried and avoided locking eyes with the hussies, María had stuck her tongue out and then spat at their feet. Yes, she needed redemption for her inability to overlook other people's weaknesses. Lord knew she was herself a sinner of a (much milder) kind.

***

Conventillo life was complex, and not for the faint of heart. It made folks tough. And it encouraged gossip. And the formation of cliques...

For some weeks most of the children in the complex had grown terrified of a tall matron who'd recently moved in. It was said she was a tough specimen from Naples, bringing along half dozen children, all older than María. The youngest, a teen already.

The Portas had the pity of all folks in the compound. Many adults, and children alike, had entered in disagreement with the unhappy giant and could barely withstand her shrieks and scorns.

Latest victims included María's sister América, and little brother Juan, two saints (but only when compared to herself). And enough being enough, María's amusement and patience had come to an end. "We must push the *Napolitanos* out of the conventillo," she'd thought one night as sleep approached. She had the reputation and the guts to move forward with her plot, and Lord help us all, she counted with the support of the local urchins, all itching to assist in her endeavor.

But little she knew about Napolitano stubbornness...

***

Let's remark that María always associated with younger children because everyone assumed she was younger than her actual age. It was a matter of size. And as such, also, anytime she did something that would normally warrant a belt to the bum, she got away with it because she looked and acted younger than her real age. Which summoned sympathy. And she knew it.

Most everyone allowed some of her shenanigans, fully believing she was still unable to distinguish right from wrong. Plus, if you asked María, she was fully certain she never went searching for trouble -rather, it entangled itself right in her blameless path.

This day the woman had spent hours hanging clothes in the line near the dirt patch, the children's newly chosen spot for a game of *rayuela* (hopscotch). As Doña Josefa worked, she'd noticed the menacing imps eyeing her. Particularly the squatty Spanish devil who never got what she deserved.

María and her collaborators had sat in the main circle, snacking on oranges from a nearby tree, awaiting an opportunity. The hanging of clothes was paused while the oversized matron retrieved more washing; and the little gang organized a game at the ready, unaware their plan would come to fruition far sooner than expected.

The hooligans got to it and before long, it was María's turn. Small and quick, she was fast as lightening. A total pro, it could be said. But she was also suddenly losing her proud Spanish poise, and falling. And in her balancing act, María stretched her short limbs and quickly grabbed a hanging sheet. The children went mute as the line began to pull and one end dropped on the loose dirt just as the giant re-emerged from her chamber.

The woman screamed, the walls shook, the rascals scattered, and María broke into the run of her life. Her legs weren't long but they were fast, thank heavens. Sole and cement met rhythmically in her quest for safety. The little scalawags screamed in a mix of glee and terror, cheering as they went, erratically opening passages between rooms as María darted in desperate strides, slowly yet surely gaining distance. And soon, also adults joined in the cheers and shouts.

She'd covered so much terrain and could not shake off the old coffin-dodger. Just how far could this cyclops run? They'd zigzagged through kitchens and dorms. 'Round the fountain twice and thrice. Out of breath and filled with panic María made a dash for the massive iron gate and began to climb among the woman's gasps and roars. Soon María realized she had won the race. Signora Porta could not follow. Could she?

But the day was young, and María recognized she'd successfully trapped herself. Her challenger did not show intent to walk away. Instead, she sat at the base of the gate, waiting while catching her breath.

A long time passed, each minute reviving an urge María had feared earlier on. 'The darned oranges' she'd thought to herself. She needed to get down and into a water closet, but the warden below would not budge. María silently pled with her guardian angel, mistakenly allowing her thoughts to get tangled and away from her as the hidden need overwhelmed her senses. She wiggled to delay the inevitable, then crossed her legs and pulled her bottom tight, but nothing could stop the bladder pressure from building. Her control was overpowered, and to her mortification she began effortlessly urinating on herself, the lacey petticoat Mama had carefully and lovingly sewn, the intricate gate, and over the matriarch who patiently waited below, now fast asleep.

María's accomplices, now spread throughout the courtyard, cheered loudly yet again while warm, golden drips rained over the gate warden below, inundating the woman's senses and bringing her back from her short-lived slumber. Shrieks of fury and disgust saturated the air, and a threatening discourse of insults put an end to the quarrel as she retreated to her rooms.

All in sight followed quietly. María's escape was finally clear. She'd played the ultimate prank to rid herself of the fearsome threat awaiting below. Relieved in more ways than one, and hiding her embarrassment, she allowed her posse to think her their heroine, waving her arms in a delectable bow to her adoring audience.

Shortly after, the Portas left the commune.

CHAPTER 3

The Marriage Contract
(Based on the Porta and Moreno-Leno Archives)

María Ascención Moreno Leno & Carlos Alberto Porta.
Marriage solemnized Saturday the 27th of December, 1924.
San Miguel de Tucumán. Argentina.

María grows into a charming young lady.

Nearly sixteen now, she was still small in stature, yet clever and hardworking. And so talented at knitting and crocheting that managed a steady small income without ever attempting it.

Her siblings loved her dearly -she always knew how to help when they got into trouble. It could be said she was the Subject Matter Expert.

Her sister América Argentina—the first female child born to the family on South American soil—was a witty, mouthy little rascal. Just as brother Juan and lil sis Emiliana. But her youngest brother Pedro suffered as a young boy, and María was known to always pray for him: "May the Good Lord protect his sweet soul and bless his innocent, weak heart." He was not only quite small, pale and sickly -all of which she had herself been as a young child- but often also the center of ridicule. María adored him and was well known for coming to his aid at the slightest threatening hint of cruelty.

Pedro was sweet, quite a darling soul, and the smartest child she knew, but he was frail and had, many-a-time while being tucked into bed at night, asked her never to go away from home without him. And she'd promised him so.

A love pact soon to be made known to their parents.

**

María and her family have lived at the conventillo for about five years. She has cherished her time in these surroundings, made many friends, and also lost many to the harsh waves of disease that hit the town and boroughs relentlessly—bouts brought by ill immigrants sadly meeting their demise soon after ending their arduous journey.

But her now often-boring life has been shattered by a revelation. Mama and Papa have advised her that she has been promised in marriage to a neighbor. Since her childhood years, no less. How could this be? Back then no one could have wanted a liaison with a hellion, right?

María has no idea who the fellow may be, although her inquiries haven't stopped since she learned of the agreement. "Todo en su propio tiempo, María. Todo en su propio tiempo" (all in its time), Mama had said. Then María hears that all parents would like to formalize the arrangement with a prompt wedding. Lost in desperation, she surprises them by swearing she won't go without Pedro. "I shan't," she asserts, "unless the groom will also agree to take my brother." Then, she'd warned: "I'm yet to meet the kind man who won't poke fun at Pedro." At this comment, her parents stared at her, baffled. But not truly, they'd known for long of their special bond.

Within days María also overheard her parents estimated that her marriage may greatly help the family financially. And María became livid. 'A welcomed relief at my expense.' 'The mere convenience of it!' But a deep sense of guilt had also flooded her senses. Was she victimizing herself? And truly selfish enough to deny her parents a financial reprieve after all they'd sacrificed for the family?

She's been promised to a strapping lad. "The baker's youngest son," Papa had said.

She could bet her parents had gone mad. From what she knew, his family arrived in town shortly after her own. They were widely known for their wealth, yet no less for their attitude…and for being one of the few families around to reside in a free standing, opulent home.

María assumed long ago that all but the old man would eventually drown in the rain—the snobs always had their noses high up in the air. Then she thought -no, she actually *knew*- the day she married into that family, they'd ensure she was cut off at once from her own impoverished acquaintances. How could Mama and Papa do this to her? She was irate, and facing herself in the black spotted old mirror she swore never to allow it.

Papa was a sweet man, but in all the splendor of his angelical patience, she'd learned long ago not to cross him. Many-a-time she'd encountered his thick leather belt behind her knees and across her tender bum. Too many times to count really, thankfully most as a small and troublesome child. Was that phase of her life truly over? It seemed it wasn't. She'd no doubt her current age would not deter him from disciplining her as he saw fit.

Yet defiance, though grim, was her only option.

***

The young man would be arriving in short. Mama made such a fuss and insisted on preparing an extravagant meal they couldn't really afford. Every inch of the apartment has been scrubbed and reorganized. And María donned a new dress purchased by father, which she could swear would bankrupt them overnight. She is no exotic beauty, rather small in height, but well endowed -or so the dress endeavored to reveal. "Beautiful grey eyes" Papa had said, smiling in reassurance. "The color of rainy skies," María countered with an attitude. She'd HAD it!

Following, a knock at the door tightens the noose María has felt around her throat all day. She hurries into the small living room to find her siblings standing in drill formation. Pedro breaks away, runs over and grabs her hand, holding on to her for dear life, tears streaming down his cheeks. And suddenly she remembers what her granny used to tell her en el país viejo: *"en la boca de los niños está la verdad"* (from the mouth of babes). And she is fearful Pedro's intuition might be justified.

Mama opens the door to reveal a magnificently well-suited young man sporting a rather forced smile. He says nothing, and is invited to come in. In silence, María notices his glances around the room, his eyes often fixed on Pedro's hands holding her own. Her brother's knuckles have gone whiter than usual, and María pats them reassuringly. And finally comes a head-to-toe assessment of her appearance, and he seems pleased enough. So do her parents. And María's heart plummets.

Sitting across from each other at the dinner table, María makes many unsuccessful attempts to engage their guest in conversation. He remains silent, observing the family's dynamics. 'He surely knows nothing about self-reliance,' she thinks. 'His dinner service always brought in by a servant'. On the other hand, he is quite easy on the eyes, although rather sporting a hint of condescension.

He repeatedly looks over at Pedro as if the child is a two-headed being, and finally her mind goes on overdrive: 'Pompous prick—THE NERVE.' Then suddenly he asks a question barely making himself understood. And María's jaw drops. No-one had mentioned this man was from Catalunya. Heaven help'er should she be punished with a husband whom she could not understand; even worse with a whole family of snobs behind him, none of whom would fully comprehend her word choice should she be hard-pressed to offer them a piece of her mind.

Opportunity of a lifetime taken, she fires back, using it to her full advantage to prove her point, asking him incessant questions he understands yet is unable to articulate quick answers for. Recognizing her intent, her parents veer the conversation over and again to easy subjects like the weather and current local events, unsuccessfully attempting to keep him engaged.

Exhausted by the exchange, he hurries to devour every crumb on his plate, then excuses himself and rushes out, promising

to call again soon. At least that's what she could make out of his mumbling.

And not two paces after his feet last met their threshold, Joan Segundo heard Sr. and Sra. Moreno reprimanding María on her rudeness and the wasted opportunity to get to know the young fellow.

María had a painful knot in her throat. She could not, *would not,* marry the youngest De la Torre. She'd sooner die. He was terribly rude to Pedro, and she couldn't imagine herself ever linked to such a man.

Deeply hurt, she ran to her room, slamming the door, and setting the rusty *pasador* (safety bar) in place. The door would remain locked for nearly four days, although Papa had proven once that no child of his could prevent him from entering any of the rooms under his roof. Luckily, as Gregorio had gone to work to help with finances, her parents were able to rent additional rooms -all connected, no less. Such luxury. The younger children shared space with her parents, while Gregorio had opted to sleep in the dining area over the flat-topped ram-shackled trunk housing all their clothing, which also served as sitting during the day, on one side of the sad looking but roomy table Papa had cleverly built out of wood left behind by the neighboring men. That left the smallest space (a cellar of sort at the end of the row) for María's use. But this was apparently to be short lived until they rid of her, which, should she allow it, would be happening very, very soon.

She could not but cry, and soon learned her tear storage was fast depleting. They'd perhaps dried out -fine time they'd picked for it! No tempting food smell could be alluring enough to bring her out of what had quickly become an intoxicating lack of privacy and space. And the collection of carved wooden Saints Mama had graciously nailed to the wall above María's barely-big-enough cot (as if to scare off the devil) now stared wide-eyed at her, challenging her to grow into the young lady she ought to have become by now.

She'd heard Pedro spend hours crouched against her wall, waiting patiently for her to emerge. He'd also spent two nights sleeping next to the cold door, his barely audible voice begging for her to accept him in. Oh, she loved him, so, so dearly. But she couldn't be a softy now. Not just yet.

In the middle of the third night, now starving and parched, and tired of staring at the large humidity stain in the old ceiling, she'd dared open the door to find him once more cocooned on the floor and shivering. Lifting his limp body and placing him on her bed, she hid him completely under the warm covers. Then she'd entered the narrow dining hall (Gregorio's empty room while he worked overnight) in desperate search of something to satiate her empty stomach—her last meal having burned within her long earlier.

She'd found bread, which did nothing but remind her of her promised husband. Her stomach churned and she could not swallow. And there it was again…another lump in her throat. *Absurdo, Cristo Jesús, Absurdo!* She'd grabbed a glass, filled it with water, and gobbled it down. This would have to do for now. She headed back to her room to find Pedro fully stretched, thoroughly enjoying the warmth now enveloping his frail bones. She moved him aside and managed to lay down next to him in the tight-fitting space. And for the first time in days, María slept. Deeply.

The morning found her well and ready to face the day, and her parents. But first things first, she needed nourishment. And surrounded by familiar scents and sounds, her young spirit couldn't but begin to feel hopeful.

Mama had prepared fried sweet cakes that lacked sugar. And watery tea. Portions were not generous, just barely satisfying, in truth. But they were welcomed regardless.

Mama was busy today, Papa leaving soon for work, and the children were already enroute to school. Her breakfast finished, María stood facing them, and managed in one breath to tell them she'd thought long and hard about her prospect, and her decision stood: she would *not* marry into the snobbish family down the street. And for emphasis she'd added: "*Pues hombre...* not for all the gold in Castilla."

Papa, now aggrieved, told her that in such case he owed much money to the old man baker, who had already paid in advance a portion for the upcoming nuptials. And it'd all been spent already in preparing her for the formal introduction. A lot of good it'd done!

María had been quick to reply she could find jobs as Mama had to help repay the high debt. But always quiet Papa could not conceal his upset before swiftly picking up his work jacket and hat, walking away, slamming shut the old—wobbly—door behind him. Rather stronger than he'd really intended.

Then Mama had stepped forward, a distraught look in her face, her blue eyes moist with sadness. She'd cupped María's face in her warm hands, and looking sweetly into her eyes, had kissed her forehead, and silently left, her frayed coat partly dragging on the humid ground as she busied herself to hide wiping tears.

María stayed behind, surrounded only by the devastating feeling that her loving parents may never recover from the agony and embarrassment she was about to cause them. Yet in all her deep reflections, she couldn't, not for all the saints up high, imagine why that darn family had chosen her to produce them heirs. Because she knew her Papa had not gone around offering her to strangers. The offer had come to him instead. While there had been plenty of girls around. Prettier even. 'Much prettier,' she thought. But in running a quick mind-picture of their families, a few did appear to carry some or another disturbing genetics. While hers…well…no one at home drooled. Yet.

***

A year passed. Mama and Papa never brought up the subject again. Until María's closest friend, Antonina Esposito, was found to be with-child and had been suddenly sent away to reside at a convent for the remainder of her confinement. As if that would stop the bun from baking!

This was María's turn to be shocked and speechless, which in all truth rarely happened. Immersed in thought she lost track of the conversation, to then come out of her stupor when she heard Papa say: "And Renzo's parents did not agree to the arrangement." And without rehearsing it this time, she'd gasped and stopped breathing for a moment. 'Think, María, think, fast! Renzo. Renzo. Renzo. Lo-Renzo Potolicchio? The horny deacon from Sunday mass?' María recalled him always eyeing them perversely during service, giving them disgustingly suggestive looks. The boy deserved a good beating. That's what he'd needed! But then, Nina had never mentioned they'd… they'd…the darn girl. They'd shared many secrets, and this… well…this was treason, plain-and-simple. And bound to cost all three of them dearly.

At the dinner table she'd caught Mama and Papa staring at her often and was quick to reiterate she knew nothing about her friend's rendezvous. And also, that they had nothing to worry about. Still, her parents decided it'd be best if María stayed indoors until the rumors had died down. As if they'd ever. María hated being judged by association but was perfectly aware such was the way in the conventillo. As the saying went: "dime con quién andas, y te diré quién eres" (Proverbs 13:20).

Such was the sentiment among every annoying migrant group she'd come to know.

'Life goes on,' she thought that evening as she muffled her cries under the covers, grieving the loss of a friend she'd likely never see again, and the partial loss of her own innocence. Also, mentally waving goodbye to her childhood. And as sleep and tiredness overwhelmed her, she prayed for her own troubled soul, but not before swearing *over every ancestor's grave in the faraway land of the Gods* (that would be non-other than Spain) that she'd bite Renzo's hand next time he held the ostia (holy sacrament) in front of her. "I'll show him the way to hell myself," was the last promise she'd mumbled as she'd dozed off.

***

María did not care for boys. She was happier spending time with her brothers and sisters. She truly was. She loved her home and her family and often, in her ideal world, dreamt with all things remaining the same forever.

Pedro was finally able to stand up for himself. He was strong and outspoken, loved school and learning, and she felt he'd grow up to do great things. Sad in a way, she felt him detaching from her. "Todo en su propio tiempo, María, todo en su propio tiempo" (Ecclesiastes 3:1-8), Mama had often told her. And she'd been right.

But now Mama and Papa had summoned her again. She assumed the intent was to question her once more on her knowledge of the relationship which had landed Nina in trouble, though she'd nothing more to disclose.

While at the dinner table, they'd began to explain how much they cared for her and that they would not want for her reputation to be compromised. 'Nothing new,' she thought as they spoke. And though they reminded her of the previous failed marriage agreement, María still felt relaxed and in control of the situation. But then Papa had taken on a severe look and proceeded to inform her that in view of the latest events, he had entered into a new marriage agreement on her behalf, for her own protection. A contract he hoped would suit her better.

For sure, she wouldn't be allowed to break his word a second time. And María knew better than to try and refuse again. She also knew her parents would always think of her first, so she dared only ask who the new and final prospect was, crossing her fingers they didn't intend to get her hitched to some vicious bloke like Vinni *'The Vulgar'* Barone. If he was the one, he'd also have it coming!

She was told he'd be calling on her in two days, when he returned into town.

***

The longest two days of her life were actually coming to an end. María wanted this day (and what she deemed to be her last supper) over.

Within the hour a knock at the door signaled the end of her wait (and of her freedom, as she knew it). And by now the family also knew their role in the hideously repetitious play.

So María waited for the door to open. This time her heart rate was normal, and her gown was simpler, but her long hair had been loosely braided by Mama, and América had carefully dressed it in tiny white flowers deliciously cascading towards her waist. She felt good about her appearance and also knew better what to expect in return. And this time Pedro did not cling to her skirts. All good signs, no?

Papa welcomed the young fellow in, and he murmured a greeting back. Tall, broad shoulders, hair only a bit darker than her own, wide jaw, and undoubtedly a plus: he appeared to have all his teeth. A good start, no doubt.

His suit wasn't the finest she'd ever seen, but it fit him well in all the right places. She was rather pleased, and said a prayer of thanks under her breath. Wonderfully thoughtful of papa, and clever too, he'd picked yet another good-looking man that would guarantee him some handsome grandchildren as long as she herself wasn't involved in their conception…well, that part was only wishful thinking. Anyway, María could hardly complain.

Once and again, she tried to place his familiar looks but could not. His skin was tanned by the sun and lustrous, the type of eye candy she and Antonina had always joked about. Dear, dear Nina. Was thinking about her sacrilegious?

He'd approached, smoothly grabbed her hand, and greeted her. His name was Carlos or Carlo, though the latter fit him best. She decided he'd be Carlo from there on. He smelled of outside air and cedar (or moth balls -she wasn't sure), but 'Lord of all mercies and the bright clouds up in heaven, did he have a devastating smile!' Taken by surprise she'd tingled all over, soon realizing this one had also spoken broken Spanish (but he was too smooth looking for her to honestly care).

He'd then moved aside, knelt on one knee, and started conversing with the children. A natural. He'd been dropped at her door by the angels themselves. Darn, she'd even noticed her little sisters where flirting with him. The brats!

He looked like a dark Greek god, but had the sort of lazy accent typical of the local IIs *(Inmigrantes Italianos)*. This did not bother her. She thought he sounded rather musical, noticing also that everyone in the room was drawn to him. Even Pedro now sat partly on his lap talking up a storm and showing him one of his homemade trinkets.

Carlo was undoubtedly a charmer, and this was not going well with her hope to remain un-affected by him. She liked him and tried to think of where she may have seen him before, silently crossing her fingers in hope he was not another perverted deacon. She looked at Mama and Papa and saw they appeared quite pleased. And a surprising warm relief washed over her.

After a successful (and rather loud) dinner, María learned with distress where his familiar looks found their origin. Carlo appeared related to... 'Please Glorious Lady of all Graces, don't let it be.' 'Oh please, Oh please, Oh please.' Was he one of the Portas she'd known as a child? This could not be. She liked him very much, and felt a rising surge of panic. She said yet another silent prayer, not in thanks anymore, but hoping the earth below would be inspired to suddenly open, swallow her whole, and digest her into the very flames of hell...which would be the case eventually anyway, so why couldn't God just wrap it up then-and-there and deliver her his final judgement before things went any further?

Her brain returned to focus and her ears caught Carlo telling stories about the poverty he'd known without a father at home from a very young age, and how the family's meals often evolved around *polenta con pacarito* (porridge with avian meat) after he and his siblings would go out and hunt for birds, slingshot in hand. And her soft-hearted papa had gained immediate respect for the young fella -this was a man he could trust his grandchildren to. Though the bird meat concept kept circling around María's mind...

And then when he'd announced his family had lived shortly in their commune some years earlier, María noticed with curiosity that he'd stared at her awaiting reaction, his sweet-honey-colored eyes full of mischief. And as a mode of confirmation of her most dreaded fears, all she'd managed to let escape from her lips was: "Do you come from a large family?" To which he'd responded, once more, a smile in his eyes: "Yes, but only my siblings are still around; both my parents are deceased."

And María had allowed herself to breathe again, though wondering his plan…his mother had gotten a taste of her potion, but he was apparently after more of it.

***

Carlo and María were married a short month later, among family and friends. Mama and Papa were overjoyed, but she wasn't quite sure whether *for* her, or because they were getting rid *of* her.

There'd been no financial gain to María's family this time around. Carlo was simply a young, hardworking man, in search of a wife that could face life's circumstances on her own two feet. And María's folks had foreseen in his kind and humble offer the perfect dual advantage: preserve her reputation, and secure her future.

The Morenos had all along been well-liked members of the conventillo. Through the years, waves of misery had ransacked many immediate dwellings. Folks from all walks of life had shared a common dream and purpose on arrival, but several had also suffered through peaks of desolation.

Many families had lost one or both parents to the harshness of life, illness, or to depression brought about by poverty or the distance from loved ones left behind. Circumstances had often brought folks together. And the Morenos had been a part of it all. The good and the bad. All, any, and many, had been adopted family members, no matter their origin. In the absence of blood relatives, the conventillo had played the role of home away from home, embracing all.

And this day, as done for each matrimonial festivity, the tall iron gates (María had peed over some years earlier) swung open in anticipation of good wishers joining-in to meet and celebrate with the latest couple forging paths together.

CHAPTER 4

A Humble Beginning

Grandpa. C.A. Porta
Birthdate: Tuesday the 4th of November, 1902.
Photo circa 1920.

The Argentinian railroads were constructed during the second half of the nineteenth century. They were fundamental in the development of the sugar cane trade, the dominant engine in Tucumán's economy.

Carlo worked as a traveling blacksmith for the railroad; he was often away. The funds he earned were decent, but they only stretched so far, therefore during leave time he complimented his income via employment at a local iron factory which produced an array of furnishings for the home and garden, some of which were now part of María's new home. He labored hard and while in town, he enjoyed having family and friends over. But he felt lonely at times, fully knowing he wanted a large family. He was accustomed to being surrounded by people, having been the youngest of about two dozen children.

Per María, below is the story that surrounded his family during their communal living. I must remark that insufficient records are available to substantiate the anecdote -and those accessible somewhat challenge it.

Carlo's mother, Carlo himself, plus twenty or so of his older siblings had embarked on a ship headed to South America when he was only six months old. His father and the eldest children had worked tirelessly to gather funds so most family members could travel at once. And so, the brunt of the Portas had departed Naples, leaving behind Carlo's father and two eldest sons. Don Angelo and brothers GiannAngelo and Ambrossio had remained behind to further procure and earn their own passages. Sadly, Don Angelo and eldest son Gianni perished of pneumonia within the year. Ambrossio, now all alone, married soon after and chose to never leave his native land.

Carlo didn't know in detail the exact events that took place during their own trip down, though he recognized the end-effects on his mother's life. His oldest surviving sister, Prisca, had told him at a very young age that fourteen of their siblings had perished of bubonic plague (the black death) during the crossing, and that their bodies could only be thrown overboard.

He then understood why his dear mother had cried herself to sleep each night since her massive loss at sea. And why for all the years to come until death was kind enough to find her door, she'd never been the same person Prisca had known her to be. She'd been overcome by a sadness, bitterness, and regret that ate at her very soul. And once news of her husband and eldest son had reached them, her once witty and happy self was only a distant memory never to reside within her again. Grief had consumed her 'til the end.

***

Carlo and María were pleased with their union. And approaching their first wedding anniversary, baby Ángel arrived on a windy October night. This was the start of a very fruitful life for the couple, who, over a fifty-year marriage were blessed with seven sons, four daughters, thirty-nine grandchildren, over seventy-five great-grandchildren and many more hard-to-keep-track-of descendants.

Their first child was born at María's tender age of eighteen, and their eleventh near her forty-sixth birthday. Her last labor was the only which put María's life truly at risk, and the only for which *maternidades* (birth wards) were available. The first nine children were birthed at home without issue. More to come on number ten.

Three of their sons followed Carlo's footsteps and went to work for -and ultimately retired from- the railroad, and their seventh son, Ernesto, became one of President Peron's godsons.

María and Carlo's children, grandchildren, and great grandchildren married into families from Argentina, of course, but also from Spain, Poland, North America, and Indonesia. And to Middle Eastern, Spanish, Italian, German, Welsh, Dutch, English, Peruvian, and Chinese descendants. Several of them left their native lands to reside permanently abroad, and one served military assignments, stations, and deployments in Japan and the Philippines, Bermuda and Hawaii, and intermittently in the Middle East, and Western and Northern Europe, as an officer in the United States Marine Corps.

Many held successful careers as tailors and seamstresses, master carpenters and blacksmiths, microbiologists and CSI agents, politicians and accountants, insurance salesmen and financial advisors, engineers and IT experts, environmentalists, pharmacists and estheticians, teachers and school principals, police and military enlistees, archaeologists and museum guides, psychologists and attorneys, counselors and entrepreneurs, writers and translators, gym and yoga teachers and dancers, musicians and singers, chefs, bakers, caterers and butchers, bus and taxi drivers, professional and amateur soccer players, bouncers, gangsters and pranksters.

There were no Catholic clergy, but several evangelical souls, and even some Mormon missionaries. And regrettably, not everyone down the bloodline remained a law-abiding citizen.

Among Carlo's happiest moments were the famous Porta Sunday dinners, with very well populated tables flanking the humble yet enormous patio walls. In a world overwhelmingly dominated by immigrants, more often than not, the space was shared with folks from faraway lands. All were greeted cheerfully no matter their origin, language skills, or belief—a trait his children and grandchildren absorbed and practiced throughout their lives. Nothing could swell his chest with deeper pride.

Carlo was the voice of order at home and wherever life found him. No child of his dared contradict him, nor say profanities in his presence. He was thoroughly loved and respected by all who came to know him.

He retired from the railroad after fifty years of labor, and sadly spent the last days of his life bedridden by diabetes and age-related ailments, his large bronze bed surrounded by visitors, some of whom his sons would have rather thrown out. Carlo would never acknowledge that, at least not out aloud. He was always too concerned about hurting people's feelings.

He was the known leader of the family, a humble household of many modest yet welcoming rooms lined up on one side of the property, conventillo style -clotheslines and all. A home that through the years became a haven to many. Carlo often wondered how folks found him, and checked frequently with acquaintances and the nearby train station whether his domicile was advertised as a form of shelter. He was always assured such was not the case, yet a never-ending chain of arrivals streamed to and through the Porta's modest entry gate regardless the time of day.

And anyone inquiring had been aided without judgement, as budget and space allowed, and many had even ended up working for the railroad, whether they'd planned it or not.

At his viewing, folks lined the nearby sidewalks to pay respect to the family who had supported his kindness through many sacrifices. And at the very end of his journey, as the hearse carrying him to his final resting place drove over the bridge housing below the main rail throughway in and out of town, traffic was held in place for sixty seconds while all locomotives parked in the rail yard below blew their whistles in salute.

A humble yet successful life indeed.

***

María also lived a long and happy life. Always very proud of her youngest brother Pedro, who went on to become a successful businessman, and whose youngest son graduated in the first class of nuclear engineers in Argentina.

She was candid to admit the fact that in two opportunities she was…ahem…arrested for clandestine gambling at a nearby club while Don Carlo—as she called Grandpa—was still alive (but away for work, thank goodness). Close calls, both. Also, both times after being loaded on the horse drawn police wagon, she was quick to offer the officers a go at her little whiskey flask. And when that hadn't worked, she'd faked a heart attack when they refused to take her word about her having "*just* stopped by the club to use the restroom (at 3 am no less), without knowledge of what took place two doors down the hall." She was then released and (quite literally) got away with it. Twice.

María spent a lot of time alone while Carlo traveled. As the children aged, married, and went on to start their own lives, Carlo often encouraged her to schedule extended visits with them during his absences, clever man that he was. And she did as instructed. Thankfully.

She loved cooking and baking, knitting and crocheting. But she was above all a narrator and an established drama queen.

Because of her size of not-quite five feet in height and less than a 100 pounds steady, she was referred to as *abuela chiquita* (particularly by my long-legged Polish first cousins). And she loved it. But to her own children she'd always been known as *L'mamma*—how Grandpa referred to *her*.

At large gatherings, María and sisters Emiliana and América were not timid to stage a dance number, carelessly lifting their long skirts to show their footwork, while their hands skillfully played *castañuelas* (castanets). Each would pin a flower to their hair and show off their skill in the form of swift jumps and pirouettes in *jota aragonesa* style, normally danced to the tune of guitars, drums, and even bagpipes. They encouraged the audience to throw money at their feet, a well-known money-making opportunity by Spaniards.

Grandpa always said that at parties the gypsy in her woke-up.

María was sassy, contagiously happy, deeply loved, and unquestionably proud of her children baring resemblance to their father—even if in nothing other than principles and mannerisms. She was a clever little character, fact reflected on her own fervent prayer blending our family's ancestry: "Our Father, who art in heaven, hallowed be Thy name; Thy kingdom come; Thy will be done on earth as it is in Spain...Give us this day our daily focaccia..."

Honestly, it is no wonder she was kicked out of catholic school.

María was a strong believer in a woman's superpowers, and swore that a mother's harsh look could burn a hole through a bully's cranium; and that a mother's spittle could remove rust off metal. And Heaven help us, she probably used both approaches at one point or another.

She'd mastered the crocheting and knitting arts early on, was 100% self-taught, and both the speed and quality of her work have remained unmatched through the ages. She had a steady clientele that proved loyal through various generations. Mothers could not get enough of her handmade goods, neither did their children, and grandchildren after them. Families during that time were ample, and even larger than the Portas themselves. And this had kept María in full employment throughout her long and cheerful life.

During my childhood years, Grandma María spent a great deal of her time at Parque 9 de Julio, where she'd set-up shop early mornings each weekend during the winter months, particularly on winter break around Independence Day (09 July) when herds of tourists flooded Tucumán to visit the House of Independence, and attend the numerous *gaucho* (Argentinian cowboy) parades, and the *peñas* held downtown (local food and live music). All activities culminated with time at the park, where she'd sell far beyond what her little hands could really produce in any reasonable amount of time. She'd sell out her extensive inventory (always kept two armoires-full of finished items before the season started) and returned home with numerous requests for more to be worked on and delivered over the next several weeks and months. And folks would flock from far away to retrieve her work.

Grandma was a great saleswoman, easy to like, and even easier to adore. But her biggest pride and joy were, undeniably, her vast and more-precious-than-diamonds progeny.

After Grandpa's passing, her little head of hair turned silver in no time, but she continued to live life to the fullest for another twenty years.

CHAPTER 5
Eleven Blessings

Mom. T. H. Porta.
Photo circa 1955.

Pasaje Irigoyen 1136.

Hilda, my mother, was the fourth child and second daughter born to Carlo and María. She was smart as a whip. To her disappointment though, she was held back from school from the age of nine to help around the house with meals, laundry, and general chores. She was the only of eleven children not given a formal education, yet the one who craved it most as a child.

She enjoyed reading atop the mulberry tree -lived for those moments- and always recalled observing in awe the day her papa and coworkers had labored hard to save the young specimen from a ravishing storm that had unleashed its fury the previous sunset. As they'd worked and battled with relentless wind, she'd admired its enormous roots—they held the promise of an amiable giant.

She'd climb and sit on a limb above the center of their patio with a handful of old books to read over and again—the latter not due to lacking understanding of the contents, but rather out of necessity. What she lacked were funds to purchase new publications at the old trading shop 'round the corner. But the exquisite sensation in the fresh air rushing through the tree's branches in early spring was delightful. And the rattle and tickle of the drying leaves made her shiver as the fall awakened. Then, the savory ripe fruit (which her mamma always complained-about for staining the patio floors) added an unmatched treat as her mind wondered and reveled at the mysteries held within the worn pages of her now fast unbinding manuscripts.

First things first, the dishes were washed, and after placing the younger children for a nap, she'd gingerly leave the dark sleeping rooms and climb over the lower branches with a couple of fresh lemons sliced in halves and sprinkled with salt...her most favorite and stimulating treat. Her papa always said she had a peculiarly Italian palate.

He kept a variety of citrus trees, apricots, figs, and last but not least, the colossal of the backyard: *la palta* (the avocado tree). The children loved their large garden. Their home was unmistakably tight for the bulk of them, but the yard delivered boisterously on sweet indulgence.

They'd moved into this home shortly after Hilda's fourth birthday.

At the time, her parents had been appointed caretakers of an orchard in exchange for generous living quarters for their growing family. But the old landlord had passed away suddenly, and his daughter—now manifestly in charge—appeared to have set her cap on Carlo who was young, strong, and as handsome as they came. This hadn't sat well with María -she'd have *none* of it. She'd noticed the hussy's skirts swirling around her very own husband as he went about his tasks, and she'd started packing their belongings. She had the family out of the wretched property within two days.

They'd crammed tight into her parents' place while Carlo fulfilled his next railroad assignment, and with five children in tow and one in-dah belly, María had been quick to find a home of many rooms not so generous in size, and a large patio which ran along the right side of the property, front to back.

The home was a typical build of the era: *una casa cho-rizo*—a resemblance of the old conventillos sprinkled around town. Its address: Pasaje Irigoyen 1136. Not an official street, I must add, but a *Pasaje* (an alley breaking plots of land, typically situated between main avenues, and mainly created for pedestrian use rather than vehicular traffic). Pot Hole Ct. would have fit it best. But it would have to do.

She gathered all the funds she'd put away for years before and after her wedding, together with the little dowry her papa had (barely) afforded her on her lovely wedding day. It all had added to a considerable savings, good enough for a rushed down payment. She'd also committed to a few monthly install-ments, mixture of her own expected earnings from crocheting and knitting, as well as part of Carlo's salary. The disheveled dwelling needed lots of help. But once again, it would have to do. No one was taking her babies' papa away. NO ONE!

She considered exchanging her mama's little pearl necklace for some much-needed repair or furniture for her new home, but ultimately decided to keep it for a rainy day. Surely with such fast-growing family it'd come in handy at some point later on.

Upon his return into town Carlo was humbly yet pleasantly surprised at his wife's astuteness, and happy to confirm he'd count with many willing—yet tiny and sticky—helping hands.

Together they'd cleaned the yard of debris and discovered an entire back fence made of bamboo and live sugar cane. The children were thrilled!

Then they painted the rudimentary kitchen and learned the difficulties of keeping little hands from whitewash.

They reroofed the open dining area in the patio, built a new door for the rustic bathroom and small storage room, and the Portas now had a superiorly happy home, all their own…where projects abounded, and so did love.

And in best Mediterranean tradition, María had proceeded to expel the premises of *Malocchio* (evil eye). After filling a large bowl with lukewarm water, she'd done the sign of the cross over it and offered a silent prayer, then dripped three consecutive drops of olive oil into it (using her right pinky finger, mind you) and repeated the ritual several times while the children watched…frightened.

And then there had been all the superstitious practices of avoiding walking under a ladder; doing the sign of the cross anytime a black cat crossed your path; avoiding breaking mir-rors as well as opening umbrellas indoors. And so forth and so on. Eventually Carlo and the children got used to all her cultural (more like delusional) restrictions, but they often wondered when things went wrong where they'd messed-up by ignoring her warnings...because days weren't always smooth as silk.

Hilda eventually had ten siblings, every last one of which she adored. And all of whom had been properly taught by Grandpa that class was a consequence of behavior, not of pockets full of money. Concept which she reinforced as she cared for them.

1. Ángel Rafael (1925)

Ángel was the first born. A man of short stature, but a big and caring heart. He exuded unending patience and good intentions. He looked and conducted himself very much like Grandma María's brother Juan.

Formally trained as an English teacher, Ángel was an avid reader, with particular interest in all things mechanical. He eventually went to work for, and retired from, the railroad.

He'd been allowed a deferred compulsory military service which in the day could be postponed from the age of eighteen until twenty-six, specifically for schooling purposes or work commitment. He'd requested delayed entry due to both circumstances.

He'd also at this point dated for a couple of years a gorgeous girl of his own age. She was also first-generation Argentinian; her parents having migrated from the then Russian Federation, today's eastern Europe. It was said she was a beauty of dewy olive skin, waist-length chestnut hair, and the purest of green eyes.

Things looked promising, hence without hesitation he'd proposed marriage before heading out for his two-year commitment, wedding plans placed on hold until his return. Sadly though, a few months ahead of his return, his affianced Anja fell suddenly ill, and died of complications from peritonitis. News having reached him too late to return to see her during the wake, and devastated as he was, he chose to remain away and finish his service.

Ángel returned home at the age of twenty-eight, having completed two years with an Army company. Though not the first of the Portas returning from military service, the family was thrilled to embrace him back into its womb, and nurture his understandable grief.

Simultaneous to his return into town, Grandma María's sister América visited from a neighboring province, her daughter Norma in tow. Norma, only seventeen, was a charming brunette, curvaceous and high maintenance – quite like a stellar mountain road.

It must be mentioned that, although first cousins, this was the first time Ángel and Norma had met. A fruitful visit, all in all, as three short weeks later, when Norma and her mother's parting was imminent, Ángel -against his parents' adamantly opposing wishes- proposed marriage to Norma the eve of their departure, which coincided with her eighteenth birthday celebration. They were married promptly, and for over sixty years.

The happy couple forever dealt with weird looks from those who learned with surprise about their close blood ties. And were also showered with never-ending jokes by their respective siblings. Yet they had a long and joyful life together. They shared five children, three of which much older than I.

And although the couple went down in history as defying the wisdom of Grandma María, they were very much loved, understood, and welcomed by the family. Even when out of desperation at their sudden wedding announcement, Grandma had told them that should they go ahead and marry, they'd be "damned to eternal punishment, manifested through the birth of intellectually limited children. Because there is no God under which such union would be deemed acceptable."

Grandma had a typically Catholic fear of the Lord All Mighty (she had excessive reason to fear, given all her transgressions and offenses to the Absolute Power). But I wouldn't have dared contradict her pronouncement -just in case. In the end I must happily report that, though feared, the slow-minded children never arrived, with sincere thanks to the divine intervention that lent a helping hand in the process. I should add that their children turned out anything but slow.

Their second child is my dear cousin Chabella (María Isabela), who married a tough Spaniard ten years her elder—a character of a man of whom it can truly be said that he broke the mold, had there ever been one made to fit him.

I cannot omit to mention their third child, Rosa Ana, who helped me sneak into the movie theater to see newly released Grease one rainy evening when I'd forgotten my ID and the entrance police would not allow me in. Ahhh, the 70's.

2. María Ángela (1927)

Aunt María, Grandma and Grandpa's second child, was my mother's confidant. Another high-maintenance beauty, she was pretty, somewhat smart, and very business-like. She'd been accepted for employment at a local bank in Tucumán, and later-on at several retailers -one of them, Calzados Real, where she was in charge of the children's section. The store was one of uncle Pedro's various businesses. Yes, uncle Pedro, Grandma María's youngest brother.

Aunt María did exceedingly well in the job market during a time when at least locally, few women dared officially seek non-domestic work. And even fewer were given an opportunity to enter a world then overrun by the male species.

Aunt María could have had any man she wanted, and turned down many proposals. And just as everyone thought she may remain in eternal spinsterhood, she met, somewhat tamed, and married a younger man from Buenos Aires. Miguel Ángel Barrionuevo came forth, at first look, as promising. He held quite a profitable government job, and adored my aunt through the rest of his short and miserable life, plagued by ailments caused by the drink he never managed to put down.

Aunt María was forty on her wedding day, and never had children of her own. However, she seemed perfectly content with the freedom this granted to dedicate countless hours of her time to care for her China doll skin and beautiful chestnut hair. She was always well poised, a pretty little thing, and also perfectly oblivious to the circus of younger siblings around her.

She and Mom had played chaperone for each other for many years before Mom married. It can be said aunt María spoiled Mom a bit thanks to her good income, and in spite of Mom's consistent gift rejections. And though Mom never expected much from her family in recognition for her sacrifices, she did on occasion welcome her sister's appreciation (not to mention her exquisite taste in all-things-apparel).

And so, many stories were told about their youthful adventures. Like the time when during Carnival season (1952) they attended a grand ball at one of the newly emerged clubs in town.

They'd spent hours fixing themselves up for the occasion and had been overtaken by excitement as they approached the venue's front façade and welcoming gate. Everything shone and glittered, a waltz playing loudly on the speakers inside, all signaling the start of a dreamy evening.

All had gone without a glitch until the last melody of the evening was about to play. Mom thought it a real nuisance that their special night-out was coming to an end. They had had a splendid time, danced to every popular tune, and met numerous eligible bachelors. Such event and opportunities were hard to come by in their neck of the woods.

All the ladies lined up against the walls, lively and tall like calla lilies prime for harvesting (one or another little weed among them, though), all hoping to win one last suitor for the evening.

Mom glanced around and spotted a couple of scoundrels from the lower boroughs advancing towards them. The rough kind of folk, y'know? And she'd wondered which of the bird brains at the entrance had allowed them in. They were dressed in the height of fashion but boy-oh-boy, they reeked of alcohol and sweat. Quite like spoiled onions.

As they approached, Mom's stomach churned and almost flipped over in disgust, the few fancy hors d'oeuvres she'd snacked-on at the entrance now threatening to rise back to her throat.

She'd had a running with their kind a few years earlier while caring for her own younger siblings. They were the type you did not associate with unless you didn't care about your reputation.

Mom recognized one as the troublemaker helping on-and-off at the general store on Avenida Mitre. A so-and-so Musumeci whose presence alone always seemed to *portare iella* (bring bad luck). The others looked familiar, but she could not place them. One thing was for sure: their appearance at the local social scene could only signal trouble.

The eldest of the two approached dainty and always proper aunt María. As she very politely tried to rid of him, he became insistent; menacing.

Mom, used to dealing with a herd of males at home, stepped in and kindly asked him to go away and allow her sister to enjoy the short remainder of the evening. Then the youngest of the two approached and lifted his hand. Only then Mom noticed he held a large mug of beer. He readied for a sip, yet in what appeared an afterthought, he looked at María in the eyes and managed to slur *"classe troppo bassa per té?"* (am I too low class for ya?) while lifting the goblet over her head and drenching her in the foul, frothy liquid. Aunt María froze. Several of the young men around jumped-in to confront the morons, only to be shocked at Mom's prompt reaction. She stole the metal cup and smashed it hard over the idiot's head, then seeing the older one reapproaching, she hurried and gave him an unrehearsed knee and toe encouragement right in his "safety deposit box," as she called it.

Never had her painful and pointy stilettos felt more like a good investment. The creep could not rise from the floor. The surrounding men cheered her on, all offered to dance with them the last song, and a whole gang of them accompanied them back home to ensure the fools from the dance did not chase after them during their journey.

Still, my aunt had cried all the way home in her ruined outfit. And Mom swore she'd kill the clowns with her bare hands if ever again they'd dare come within 100 feet. Though I bet you she didn't quite know how far that really is. But Italians are that way. They excel at threatening their victims, even if they don't really intend to do much about it. Perhaps it's a matter of principle. Or a matter of frightening people away.

After that episode, aunt María lost enthusiasm for events of the kind, while Mom's popularity grew as *l'italiana infuocato* (the fiery Italian).

Eventually, Mom and aunt María had dared attend a carnival dance on rival soil—Club Asociación Mitre. It was actually aunt María's idea because she'd "just happened to purchase a new dress and it would have been criminal to leave it hanging in her armoire." So, Mom had agreed to it, or she'd never hear the end of it.

The moment they'd entered the hall, there'd been a chap at the end of the dance floor who started checking out Mom. She did not appreciate the impertinent way in which he looked at her, so when all couples headed to the dance floor and Mom saw him head over to ask her to dance, she tried to ask aunt María (politely, mind you) to accompany her to the bathroom (to hide), but her sister acted cluelessly as usual, and even worse, seemed to purposely ignore her. And Mom had then grabbed her by the neck and the back of her fancy belt, and dragged her into the bathroom in a loud rustle of petticoats and screeching high heels. Luckily the room was empty and had a couple of comfortable loungers in it.

Well before leaving the house, aunt María had known that should anything turn out wrong this evening, she'd be blamed for it, so she'd gone along with Mom's little farce for as long as she could. But all the best songs were being played and aunt María refused to wait any longer, handing Mom an ultimatum while freshening-up her lipstick. "So," she'd said, smacking her lips a couple of times. "What's the worst that can happen? You dance, or tell him off. Big deal. You tell men off at home every day. If it's a matter of experience you're concerned about, I don't think you're lacking."

And so, after nearly sixty long, lost minutes in the restroom, they'd walked out thinking *the guy* would have definitely given up by then. But only two steps back into the dance area, he'd resurfaced and approached, and Mom had felt she'd no option but to agree to dance.

Much later in life, the guy (by then my Dad), told me he'd "been waiting near the bathroom entrance all along."

He'd worn his not-too-new, yet not-too-shabby grey suit and red scarf. And the chap had turned out to be quite the chatterbox. Aunt María had observed with curiosity how Mom no longer tried to hide from him, but had rather ended-up dancing with him the entire evening. When Aunt María had come near them, she'd been surprised to hear them actively engaged in conversation about Mom's large family, a strange thing, as she and Mom always remarked that anytime they mentioned their family (particularly the number of brothers they shared), guys always found an excuse to disappear.

But this gent had stayed and even enjoyed the tale. And at the end of the evening, he'd asked if he could "see them home." And Mom had politely responded that "it couldn't hurt," while Aunt María rolled her eyes.

And upon exiting the venue, he'd asked to be excused for a moment to retrieve his *wheels* from the parking area, which left Mom salivating and rubbing her hands at the prospect of being driven home…much like a fly having landed on a sugar cube. But he'd returned pushing a bicycle (uh huh! not enough wheels for the lot of them). And he'd said to them, somewhat apologetically, that he hoped they didn't mind. He hadn't had a vehicle for the evening.

And things being what they were, Mom couldn't turn him away at that point.

They'd walked along, talking all the way. And that had been the start of Mom and Dad's courtship. And some years down the road, he would become her loving husband, and one of the Portas' most favorite in-laws.

Before wedding bells though, Dad, who enjoyed savoring all sort of gatherings "even at the enemies' gates" as he so eloquently put it, convinced Mom and Aunt María to once more attend a carnival dance at Associación Mitre. He reminded them that clubs other than their own neighborhood one also held nice seasonal parties. Jokingly telling Mom that this time around she would not have to worry about hiding from him. And he'd finally succeeded in persuading the two hardheaded women to go along.

The party was nice indeed, and the music to die for. They had had great fun dancing the night away, and aunt María was ecstatic with the friend Dad had brought along as her blind date. She'd told me once that Dad's friend was quite pleasing to look at, but she'd initially thought she'd been played a joke because his glasses were so thick, on first look she thought the man would need a cane to get around. But he'd turned out to be most gentle and attentive, and the most fun and enthusiastic of dance partners, and his company had turned the evening into a total blast.

The problem with carnival dances was (still is today) that venues often allow groups to engage in water balloon fights and the sort, and once in their cups, some attendees tended to become creative. And rather belligerent. This is how "some idiot," as Mom always recalled, recognized her from a basketball game she'd played (and won, against his team), and came straight to her, and dumped a whole one-kilogram bag of flour over her head. Mom was shocked, but quickly overcame it. The guy and his chums had had their laugh, and the main offender had received a hard punch in the gut from Dad. Yes, from my sweet Dad who would never harm a fly. Luckily, Aunt María's blind date had swiftly pulled Dad away before he got punched back and dropped like falling timber.

Dad offered to take Mom home immediately, but instead she'd asked to be escorted to the restroom to "rinse her eyes and compose herself." Dad agreed, and Aunt María had knowingly signaled to him (like a good Marine would have) to keep both eyes on her, while she and his friend stepped on the dance floor one last time.

Had I been in Mom's shoes, I would have asked to be escorted off the premises and out of sight immediately, to avoid the spectacle. Mom being Mom, was p-od. She'd been left fuming, with a strong urge for revenge. As the Spaniards put it: *con la sangre en el ojo*. And as one of Grandpa's friends often said: "Letta me tell you samma-thin, ya donta pissa-an Italian, anda walka awaya."

My sweet Dad guided her towards the restroom, a hand at the small of her back, as she uselessly attempted to neutralize the stinging white substance from her tearing eyes. Once passing the main restroom door, her *better* eye fixated on a nearly empty beer bottle left at the room's entrance. Mom grabbed the bottle and reached for the first open stall. It had been a long night full of fun and drinks, and her bladder was full.

Shortly after, Mom reappeared at the restroom door, hands at her back, noticing Dad was engaged in graceful conversation with an acquaintance. Which served her purpose to perfection.

It did not take much wandering for Mom to locate the fool sitting at a table, a smoke in his lips, and a hand still rubbing his stomach right where Dad's fist had crashed earlier. Mom approached from behind, and though there was no possible way to camouflage her ruined hair and outfit, she moved swiftly, and stood behind him just long enough for all his friends and him to realize she was there. Following the gang's line of sight he'd turned, saw the bottle in her hand, and promptly figured what she was about to do. Realizing he'd no time but to welcome the shower she was about to baptize him with, he looked up and opened his mouth widely to welcome yet another cool beer…only realizing his mistake when the warm liquid started gushing over him.

The bottle had been filled with Mom's warm pee, and he'd swallowed some before reality hit. He stood, convulsing and spitting, while she emptied the rest of the bottle's contents on him. She'd now had the last laugh…and ran like she'd dogs at her heels towards where Dad -oblivious- still waited for her by the restroom. Poor soul. She pulled him by the hand and begged him to get her the hell out of there.

Aunt María had heard the commotion in the distance and knew -*simply knew*- her sister would have likely had something to do with it. Feeling which was confirmed when she saw a head covered in flour swiftly retreating from the scene of the crime.

And Mom's fame as l'italiana infuocato continued its trail down in history. Or so I'm told.

By now you must wonder the cause of Mom's family's obsession with drenching people in pee. And I can only respond that I-don't-know! And that I'm glad I have not been found at the giving nor receiving end of such recourse.

3. Carlos Guido (1929)

Uncle Carlos was Mom's immediately older sibling. Carlos was a sweet man, his size and looks a replica of Grandma María's brother Gregorio. He also worked for the railroad. He married many years before Mom, to a wonderful lady by the name of Juana Rosa Ferreira.

Juana and Mom became the greatest of friends; hence Mom became their first child's godmother, and eventually Carlos and Juana became my godparents. They were always wonderful to me, and made me feel so special, always!

I clearly remember Uncle Carlos' funeral in February of 1984, and Grandma's sadness at burying one of her own children. I could not attend Aunt Juana's services. I had already been away from Argentina for several years by then.

Carlos and Juana shared five children, two older than I. The first, María Rosa, was the eldest grandchild born to Grandma & Grandpa Porta. She recently turned seventy years old.

4. Tomasa Hilda (1931)

Mom was a diehard fan of the Harlem Globetrotters all her youth. In 1951, as the country readied for their arrival into Argentina to perform precisely on Mom's 20th birthday, she was thrilled about a chance to see them live. But reality set in early-on. They were playing at the Luna Park Stadium in Bs.As. She'd need to travel in advance with a chaperone. And the entrance cost alone was well above the Porta's budget. It would take several of her brothers and a good half-year before they could gather sufficient funds to secure her attendance.

But she'd dreamed regardless, meanwhile continuing to train with her brothers, who'd sneak her in at the neighborhood club each time management didn't supervise the practices. She loved the game and was good at it. Still, the Porta brothers had been unsuccessful at convincing *the guys* that Mom could fill-in when they were away from town on railroad business.

As a woman, she'd stood behind, yielding space and voice to the men while they discussed her ability right in front of her. Not her brothers though. They relied solely on her to do their cooking, laundry, and mending, and knew better than to bad-mouth her. They also knew that pins and needles can render painful when found in your undergarments.

She'd finally had enough of their useless talk, so she'd stepped forward and asked for an opportunity to demonstrate that she could do as well as ANY male, not just the Porta boys. So, one of her brothers had told the rest of the troop that they *better let her.* And the guys had waved her off and agreed to *let her,* assured to prove the contrary and get a good laugh in the process.

Such is how the following time the team faced an opponent but the points didn't count… Let's stop there for a bit. I honestly am not sure there was even a league for this meet. More than likely, it was just a group of guys that got together to play, which happens often at basketball clubs. I dare guess that professionals, they were not.

Anyway, so the points didn't really count because (according to Mom) they weren't really that great a team. So, Mom was substituted in -as a teaser of sort. And among the male booing coming from the bleachers, she'd remained steadfast and had scored "most of the miserable points the team had attained." Her own words.

Grandma María, and all three of Mom's sisters (one still in nappies) had screamed their heads off in the stands, and angrily argued with grown men, and even swung their bags at them until the end of the *nail-biting* game. The four had loudly booed and danced to the demise of the opposing team. And to their delight, Mom won the game for her "team of turds" (again, her own words), and to the surprise of those who had doubted her skill -attitude which hadn't been taken lightly by the Porta brood. They always meant business.

That was Mom. Who in her twenties was barely eighty-five lbs. and no taller than 5' 1". But the reader should know that even at that height, she was taller than her own mother—and that oughta count for something. Mom was as fisty and relentless as her mother though. They could have been better described as two peas in a pod.

Now, much has been said already on her behalf. But there is plenty more coming soon.

Chapters worth.

5. Ricardo Agustín, aka Mocho (1933)

Uncle Mocho and Uncle Juan (#6, next in order of appearance) were Mom's favorite brothers. The trio planned and did everything together—they were inseparable well into old age.

Mocho (slang for tight curly hair), was two years younger than Mom, quite clever, and the family's comedian. He was tall and greatly resembled Grandpa, both in built and coloring. A bookworm and a perfectionist (and OCD-ish like me), he was always a joy to be around. His home was always kept in perfect order and coordination. And when not, I understand the heavens might as well be falling over us. I must add that I never witnessed the extreme perfectionist side of him.

He'd married a beautiful girl, Sofía Chimielowiec (aka Rosa or Sho-Sha, as her mother called her). Her siblings and widowed Polish mother Katarzyna (known to us as Doña Catalina) frequently joined the Porta's Christmas celebrations while I was a young child.

As soon as married, Mocho accepted a promising job in the province of Salta, where he and his young family resided for a few years. He built engines, loved his job, and was a wiz at it. This eventually took him to work for larger companies and ultimately at the Swedish Scania plant in Tucumán, from which employment he ultimately retired.

Mom spent a few months with them in Salta when single, at which time Sofía dealt with health issues during her first pregnancy.

Rosa was a heavy smoker, and died of lung cancer in the mid-2000s. Her mother preceded her in death, but not by long. She was of great help to the family during aunt Rosa's illness and various deriving ailments. The children knew not how to live without their Polish grandmother.

Doña Catalina was the tallest woman I ever met. She was pale, with large hands, narrow shoulders, wide hips and fore-head, and ankles always swollen under exceptionally long skirts. She also wore the largest ribbon-tied short boots mimicking that of Russian soldiers.

Her paper-like, see-through skin was so pure that thin blue veins were visible at close distance. Soft long silver strands of hair were always held back in a tight bun, under a plain linen scarf. She had small, kind eyes, and never had a mean or loud word for anyone, even when my rascal cousins tried her patience. She doted on my uncle, and in return he believed her an angel personified.

Mocho and Rosa had four children, three older than I. But the oldest, well… we'll come back to him. Mom loved Mocho deeply, and often told a story about him as a toddler, and how Grandma and Grandpa almost lost him on such occasion…

Grandpa was always looking for ways to make extra money to support his little growing tribe. He did beekeeping as a side job, and for such purpose he'd sealed off an enclosure near the end of the long and narrow property, by the back fence line, where the thick and tall sugar cane met and sheltered the surrounding lots -many still unoccupied. Just as his fruit trees, the apiary was closed to access by the children to avoid any mischief. His eldest was the exception.

Ángel, by then almost eleven years old, got a thrill at following his dad around and helping anytime Grandpa was on break from his railroad shifts. Grandpa enjoyed doing stuff around the house and never failed to locate something that needed looked after. And he took great pride in Ángel always volunteering to learn and assist.

They'd spent the cooler hours of the morning checking the boxes for the darn wax moth that the previous year they'd fought hard to rid of, and now they sat at the shade of the mulberry tree, some frosty lemonade at hand while the sun glared with enough fury to make the blazes of hell jealous. Next morning was maintenance day at the boxes they kept at a neighboring property.

But Grandpa had a commitment later this day—the bocce tournament was in full swing and he was eager to meet up and challenge his old comrades once again. Counting his blessings for a quiet house while all the younger children napped, he prepared to take leave but was suddenly stopped by Ángel who apologetically asked to return to the enclosure where he'd forgotten the smoker they'd need promptly in the morning. To Ángel's surprise, Grandpa told him he could go and get it while he readied himself for the evening, emphasizing to ensure the gates were properly locked upon his exit.

Grandpa headed to shower and Ángel marched proudly through the trellised pathway leading to the padlocked gates. Papa trusted him, and he was thrilled.

The afternoon was steaming hot. Ángel decided to rush-in and back out, then he'd still have time for a couple of marble games with the youngest from the family just moved next door. And rush he did, without locking the gate behind him upon entering. And even worse, without noticing that two-year-old Mocho had tip-toed at his tail, sporting nothing more than his latest infatuation with nakedness. As Ángel turned left at one corner to retrieve the tool from the shelves, little Mocho had continued forward, silently chasing after the bees moving around the entry. Having reached the end of the enclosure, Mocho fully approached the hives, fanning his chubby little hands to brush away the pesky fliers.

Oblivious about his brother's presence further inside, Ángel rushed to leave, re-locking the gates behind him. But only steps later he felt his heart rise to his throat at the sound of his brother's screams. He ran back and tried to unlock the gates, but his hands trembled so hard he dropped the key twice. Finally getting a hold of himself, he managed to open the heavy door and push himself forward.

His legs appeared to give-in at the sight. All seemed to happen in slow motion. Mocho laid immobile, covered in insects, not fighting. He'd even stopped screaming, though he hadn't stopped trying to scream. No sound came out now—all he could manage were loud gasps for air.

Ángel tried to shoo the bees off Mocho, but couldn't. They were enraged and now started swarming around him as he struggled to lift his baby brother. Mocho had passed out, no longer able to help Ángel in his attempts for rescue. Ángel started shouting for his parents, but the bees entered his mouth. He could feel the stings on his throat and on the roof of his mouth. He tried spitting them out, but choked and vomited instead. His eyelids shut off under the beastly force of the pain - the agony of it was overwhelming. And he knew the bees had already killed his brother. Surely, the little cherub could not resist such torment.

Grandpa heard him, and ran to the entrance of the enclosure with nothing on but a wet towel around his waist. He'd grabbed the garden hose as he approached the gate. Before starting to pass out, Ángel heard him give a full turn at the rusty, squeaky spigot. The bees headed towards Grandpa when the full force of chilled water first hit them. Grandpa aimed the hose right at Ángel's back, and Ángel, in deadly pain and still holding tight to his brother, fell to his knees. He never felt them hit the ground though. All had gone dark.

Uncles Ángel and Mocho suffered stings over 90% of their small bodies. There was hardly any skin surface which hadn't received the malefic retort of the angry cluster. Both brothers turned out to be allergic to bee stings and suffered greatly for weeks in the aftermath of the event. Ángel recouped a bit sooner than Mocho, and in seeing his brother so gravely hurt, he'd cried his eyes out night after night as they waited for Mocho's return to the living.

It was months before the toddler could breathe correctly again or sleep by himself without waking up screaming. He also never dared approach the backyard again until some years later.

It is said that Grandpa did not return to work, nor slept for weeks, while looking personally after his boys. He was devastated for not having gone himself after the smoker. He fiercely adored his children and was particularly furious at himself for the pain his little ones had suffered, and for nearly losing them both.

The day after the episode, Grandpa transferred all the boxes to a landowner in the southside of the city.

6. Juan Enrique, aka Cabrito (1937)

Juan was born four years after Mocho. He was tall and bronzed as Grandpa, but slender as the Moreno brothers. A sweet yet not-so-soft-spoken man of broad shoulders, he'd eventually joined the Porta troop working for the railroad. He was a conductor, often out of town, and loved it.

He acted as witness to Mom and Dad's courthouse wedding. And the favor was soon-after returned by Mom when Juan married his sweetheart -a girl he'd met during his stops at the station in the neighboring province of Santiago del Estero.

Aunt Dolores Hilda Serrano passed while I was a teen, having been affected by rheumatoid arthritis since her youth. She was bedridden for several years.

They had two sweet children, one older than I.

7. José Alberto (1940)
8. Josefa Asunción, aka Pepa (1942)
9. Pedro Miguel, aka Colibrí (1944)

Uncle José (named so after Grandpa's grandfather Giuseppe Achille) was nine years younger than Mom, and aunt Pepa (named Josefa after Grandpa's mother) about eleven years Mom's junior.

At the time they were both born, Grandpa had once again taken a second job during his breaks from the railroad, working as foreman at an orchard near the family home. The owners, an older couple from Spain, had married too late in life to birth children of their own, and seeing Grandma and Grandpa were quite fertile and somewhat struggling to provide for all the needs of such a large family, had offered to take José and Josefa for as long as the children or the parents welcomed the help. They were enchanted with the tots and ready to give their love and their dedication to them.

Grandma and Grandpa weren't thrilled with the idea, but they recognized a bit of help could be a welcomed relief. Plus, their children would be only a couple of blocks away. And so, it was, though young Pepa didn't enjoy being away from all the excitement of a large family, and within months asked to be returned to her parents.

José on the other hand, was more of a lone wolf and felt relieved at the chance to be on his own. He thrived in his new home and although he often visited his biological brothers and sisters and always took part in all family celebrations, he grew a bit apart from them in upbringing and expectations from and for life. His foster parents worshipped the grounds he walked on, and he'd the best of everything and an excess of confidence in himself and his future. His new parents had no extended family to speak of, at least not in Argentina, and never mentioned longing for anyone left behind in Spain.

José was never adopted officially, however most everyone had assumed him the couple's own child. At the age of eighteen, he headed to start his military service, shortly after his foster mother's sudden passing. Sad as he felt to leave his rapidly aging father alone, he couldn't wait to get his compulsory commitment over with and return to start his life dream of owning a business, to care for the dear old man who had given him so much, and to repay him for all the comforts and advantages he and his wife had doted on him.

José made his way out of town, feeling somewhat excited yet uneasy; and unaware that life would be so cruel as to return him to an empty home a couple of years later. Empty in all sense of the word, his father having passed after ravished by a rare disease about a half-year before Jose's return. Also unbeknown to him, the sad event had brought forth unheard-of relatives to the late couple, who without delay had appeared in town and filed a petition with the local authorities for complete control over all possessions.

Resigned to the developments yet somewhat hesitantly, upon his return José marched to the Porta's household, asking

-unnecessarily, I must add- for shelter. The family was thrilled to have him back.

Through Grandpa's acquaintances he quickly established a relationship and employment with a local iron shop owner. He then met the love of his life: Antonia Vicenta Cabrita (aka Pirucha), and settled down. Without delay José went on to materialize his dream of owning a business, using skills gained during his time in the military, and the business principles his foster parents had taught him. His company, a high-end furniture and kitchen cabinetry manufacturer, specialized in exotic woods and ornamental ironworks also producing doors, fences, stairwells, etc. He did well for himself, and employed his younger brother Pedro, a superb master carpenter nicknamed *Colibrí* (hummingbird) for his colorful personality and cheery attitude. Today, the company José and Pedro built together still exists and thrives, run by José's son, Pablo.

José and Pirucha had three children. The oldest, my gorgeous cousin Marisa, just a couple of months older than I.

Pedro on the other hand, married young to a local girl (Inés Ferreira). He died of lymph node cancer almost at retirement age, in 2003. They shared five beautiful children, all younger than I.

Aunt Pepa married young to Carlos Aparicio, a promising residential painter who worked for the local municipality throughout his entire career. They had three children, just one older than I.

10. Ernesto René (1949)
Ernesto was one of my favorite uncles though I loved them all. A sweetheart of a man, softspoken, good looking, and a great dancer to boot.

Having been the family's seventh son, upon his birth the family took advantage of a decree which entitled him (parents allowing) to become one of the President's godsons. He then became one of President Perón's godchildren. This status provided privileges such as skipping the (then compulsory) two-year military service, as well as access to a fully paid education until the age of 21, housing assistance, and a myriad of other choices -most of it, only if and when wanted and requested.

This decree was also in a way meant as a government incentive to help increase the country's population. But as the reader might appreciate by now, the Portas had no need for such motivation. Ernesto came because, well, because back then people had children 'til they could no-mo.

At the time, the military service was obligatory unless a young fellow had exceptional circumstances at home, such as being an only child and the only financial support to his parents; being one in a multiple birth (though I have no clue how the unlucky one was chosen under said circumstances); having some sort of disability; or already being married and having a wife or a child -or both- to support.

I know what you're thinking. How did this compulsory measure work? During December all names and/or ID numbers were put through a drawing by district, and published ahead of the New Year in the local newspapers. Our paper was the good old: *La Gaceta de Tucumán*. A whole section was dedicated—page after single page—to listing names and numbers. Each young man about to turn eighteen in the upcoming twelve months would locate himself by name and ID number, and thus was instructed in which branch of the military he would serve, and when and where to appear, ahead of being taken away for a twenty-four-month boot camp. That was the real-men-maker era.

When Uncle Ernesto was about to turn eighteen, he was automatically exempted from serving because of his distinguished godfather. He'd always been quite humble, so to no one's surprise, since they wouldn't take him, he opted to enlist. He was granted station at a base in the Province of Entre Ríos. Although his status as big man P's godson got him a posh job before arrival, I still recall Mom's tears each time we received post from him. He was her baby brother after all. One she had herself raised from birth. He was the light of her eyes. And although he was a fully grown man by the time he drove into town some years later, she never stopped seeing him as the baby in wraps she had been handed by her father the day Ernesto had first joined the family. This was a day filled with worry as their mother suffered at the hands of a new midwife. My Mom was about eighteen years old, and Grandma María around forty-two.

In early 1973, we all prepared for Ernesto's wedding. Both, bride and groom came from large families, and the upcoming event promised to be one to remember. Ernesto married a wonderful girl (Yolanda Benita Herrera) a few years older than he, and they shared four children, all younger than I. He retired as a rep for Coca Cola and died at age seventy-three of prostate cancer.

Anecdote: During one of my last visits to Argentina prior to his passing, he'd called me aside and confided in me that he'd always been secretly in love with "Ahhh, Cindy, capisci?" He'd meant Cindy Crawford, and had asked that should she ever cross my path, I should make sure to "'and 'er 'is numba." The man was a Casanova.

11. Alicia del Valle (1952)
Alicia knocked at the Porta's door unplanned (in the beginning) and unannounced (in the end), just over three years later (twenty-eight years after G&G's arranged nuptials). Grandma was by then nearly forty-six, and Grandpa was fifty.

Concerned for Grandma's welfare after Ernesto's birth, Grandpa held family assemblies early-on, but only to communicate how things would be handled this time around. Because everyone already knew that his decision was *THE LAW*. He'd arranged for his eleventh child to be born at the hospital; an option not available for the previous ten children.

Aunt Alicia pressed for an early arrival as Grandpa had returned home late from a very tiring trip out of town. So, Grandpa got a hold of Ángel, Carlos, Mocho, and Juan, and sent them -on their bikes- to do the rounds and gather the troops from home and work and bocce commitments, and from wherever else life found the family scattered about at that precise moment. And together with Grandma, their ten children, a couple of daughters-in-law, and an undisclosed number of unborn grand-children in tow in their respective wombs, the entire tribe made their way to the maternity house. They loudly demanded care and immediate attention, filling the entire waiting area of the new -yet small and primitive- town birthing center.

Aunt Alicia was born prematurely, tiny as she remains to this day, and the cutest little mouse ever to grace this earth. She became instantly the most doted on and terribly spoiled child to ever exist. Just one little baby girl and so many brothers at her beck and call. She was my hero, representing nothing but the purest of Girl Power.

But Grandma had a hard go of it. First birth outside their home, and first tremendous infection which almost took her life and chased after her health for the remainder of her years.

She never stopped painstakingly reminding Aunt Alicia of her sacrifice to bring her into this wonderful world of ours, each time my sweet aunt tried getting away with something. And she tried often. And also, often succeeded.

Being the last of the Portas, in her very early youth Aunt Alicia inherited the one spare (and only oversized) bedroom at Grandma's house. The property had undergone many architectural changes in a futile attempt to accommodate the ever-growing family which had finally broken down as each sibling married and left the beloved familial home.

Her bed resembled Grandpa's. It was brass, large, with elaborate finials atop strong columns for legs, its feet resembling a beast's claws. I don't know what emperor had been fleeced in an effort to acquire this art piece, but such was the Italian way, and as the Sicilian saying goes… don't ask, don't tell or you could find yourself sleeping with the fishes.

Her room was a true testament to the 60's. Dark and somewhat psychedelic, with a multicolor strobe light in a dark corner next to the hall leading to the patio; a colossal picture of the Archangel Michael defeating Satan hung just above the massive bed frame, Satan's bright-red popping eyes large enough to scare anyone shoeless. Gotcha!

High up on another wall, pictures of highly worshipped musical performers of the era -in all their masculine splendor- were on vivid display for all to see, framed by an oversized rosary with pearls large enough to shoot out of a cannon. Of course, this all but confirmed the girl's priorities were well in order. All of it thrown together was just about sufficient to intimidate any humble soul out of their wits.

I'd always close my eyes as I walked through her room, arms raised and hands ahead to hopefully stop me from running into something, and hurrying my step while crossing my fingers and promising Jesus I'd be better if he'd help me endure the passage. There was simply too much exposed and exaggerated masculinity for my (still very childish) taste. Though not much has changed by now, folks.

Aunt Alicia wore high boots, skimpy skirts, and sexy ribbed shirts that her brothers always told her to cover up. And she often played "Chain of Fools" out loud on her little *tocadiscos* (turn table). I don't think I would have been surprised to find someone smoking some funny weed in one of the corners of her room. I also often wondered what she kept in all her locked drawers, although knowing her and her free spirit, I'm certain she would have openly told me and even shared it with me accordingly, had I asked. In her liberal mind, the girl had nothing to hide.

Alicia was an architecture student. Shortly after turning twenty-one (also in 1973), she married Alberto López, a young army corporal tall as a redwood, whose family resided near the Portas. They'd met at a bus stop, and after a couple of years of courting rushed to tie the knot as Grandpa's health commenced to noticeably deteriorate.

Grandpa wanted to see all his children settled before his departure and had discreetly, yet encouragingly, pressed the gullible young man -in a Sicilian sort of way, I'm told- to formalize his intentions in short, or move out of the way and allow some other poor and unsuspecting fellow to fall into the inevitable trap. Yup, Grandpa did not appreciate others wasting his time. And now those who know me can tell where I got *that* gene.

Aunt Alicia and Uncle Alberto's military wedding at the small San Juan de la Cruz chapel - location which had set the stage for most of the Porta siblings walking down the altar, was simply lovely. The ceremony and large reception were held on Christmas Eve, 1973. It was a ridiculously hot and humid day; all the children having labored hard setting up tables and sitting arrangements for the crowds expected to turn in. And turn-in they did.

Grandpa, no longer feeling his best, asked to be assisted in readying himself, and demanded to be brought over to the church to join in the giving away of his youngest child. He sat happily in the front pew and observed with pride.

There was nothing done in short scale by the Portas, and pure evidence of it manifested in plain view as all seven Porta brothers walked through the small church portico, the eldest holding the bride's hand in the crook of his arm, the other six flanking the teensy-weensy-little bride on each side and behind her. And my poor soon-to-be uncle knew that he better be serious in this life-long commitment, or he'd face severe punishment and possibly end up himself swimming with the fishes.

Tears streaming down Grandpa's face the entire length of the ceremony; he could not be prouder of his brood. After church, a crowd descended into the Porta's large patio now sporting all the glamour an Italian affair of very modest means could afford. Food, wine, and merriment abounded. Grandma and Grandpa were proud as peacocks. The party went on flawlessly 'til the wee hours of the morning, ending with the bride and groom's departure as daylight peeked out. A long and noisy round of fireworks was lit and showered on us, literally matched by a sudden summer thunderstorm. The pouring rain soaked and ruined all remains of the event, and sent folks running for shelter, and ultimately for a ride home.

Both Ernesto and Alicia had at least one child each before Grandpa passed away. He was happy to see them all successfully married—their young, promising lives, thriving.

***

Although it had been an arranged marriage, Grandma grew to love and respect Grandpa quite early on. In truth, he was easy to love.

She always referred to him as "Don Carlo," which after eleven children we thought sweet, yet funny. She'd always known without a doubt the tremendous influence he had had over their ample offspring. The boys would have been unmanageable had it not been for Grandpa's fierce ruling and standards. And the girls… well, Mom and her youngest sister Alicia had been a real handful throughout their respective childhoods and youths.

But they'd all respected him highly and loved him uncon-
ditionally. He was a paragon of discipline, the voice of reason,
and the kind word and gentle touch they each needed as they
discovered all the advantages of adulthood, and the compro-
mising difficulties of marriage and parenthood.

Our dear patriarch bound us together, and many years after
his passing we still managed to gather as before. And every New
Year's Eve, many glossy eyes and teary cheeks surrounded the
old dining table still set in Grandma's patio, reminiscing of his
wisdom and generosity.

But his chair was never again occupied. None of the boys,
men by then, felt they could ever fill the tremendous void Grandpa's persona had left in our lives.

There is a song that will always remind me of him sitting
easy on his rocking chair after dinner, listening to RAI Italiana
broadcast, a fernet in his hand, a smoking pipe in the other,
and my Dad and uncles hanging around, singing in choir the
advertisements, often making him laugh.

Glivingston73. 2009, May 23. *Jimmy Fontana Il Mondo.* [Video].
Format [Video file]. YouTube. https://youtu.be/HFyCfFJC-
0no?si=PF9dcg4o-ihOxidl

A more modern version (my favorite): Il Volo Official. 2012,
February 27. *Il Mondo (From PBS Performance 'Il Volo...Takes
Flight').* [Video]. Format [Video file]. YouTube.
https://youtu.be/b06_ffOYE4U?si=bHtub4wMqdiAPU5p

I recall once when Grandpa was asked what he liked so
much about this romantic song. The inquiring party had perhaps
thought he'd incriminate himself saying it reminded him of a
lost love. But he'd replied that it'd been written for *Italia.*

María Ángela Porta.
Photo circa 1950.

Ricardo Agustín Porta & Sofía Chimieloviec's Wedding. 1958.

Juan Enrique Porta & Hilda Serrano's Wedding. 1960.

Josefa Asunción Porta & Carlos Aparicio's Wedding. 1962.

José Alberto Porta & Antonia Vicenta Cabrita's Wedding. 1963.

María Ángela Porta & Miguel Ángel Barrionuevo's Wedding.
1965.

Ernesto René Porta & Yolanda Benita Herrera's Wedding. 1973.
Also shown: Dad (upper left), Mom (upper right),
Norma (lower left), me (center), and Alicia (far right).

CHAPTER 6

H&R

(Based on the Ocampo and Porta's Archives)

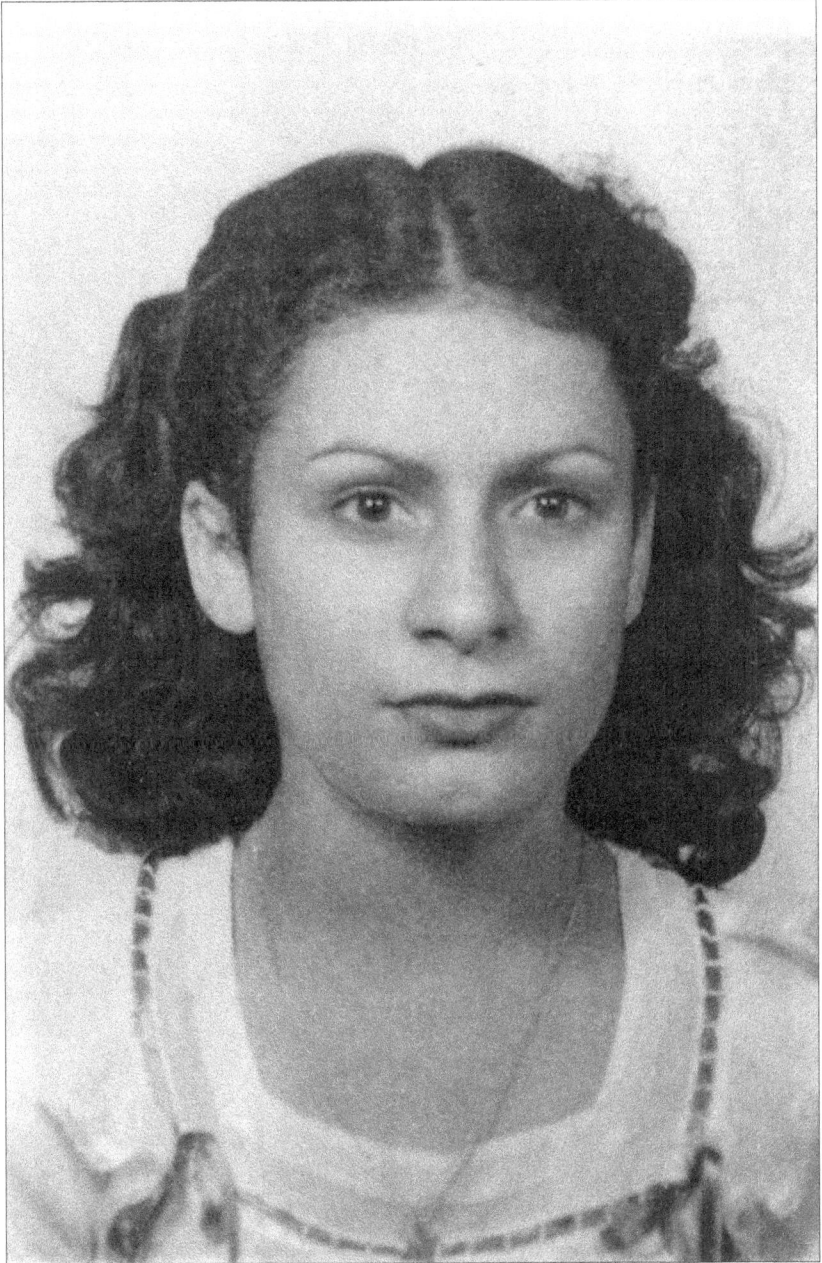

Tomasa Hilda Porta.
Birthdate: Thursday the 21st of May, 1931.
Photo circa 1950.

Roberto Ocampo.
Birthdate: Saturday the 30th of August, 1930.
Photo circa 1950.

Mom and Dad's Courthouse Wedding.
Friday the 11th of September, 1959. Midday.
Pictured with witnesses Juan E. Porta (Mom's brother)
and Irma Reynoso (Mom's best friend).
S. M. de Tucumán.
Argentina.

Mom and Dad's Church Wedding.
Saturday the 12th of September, 1959.
Iglesia San Juan de la Cruz.
S.M. de Tucumán.
Argentina.

Hilda was an excellent housekeeper. She looked fiercely after her siblings, and in turn they looked after her. This would become the theme throughout their lives. Hilda's youngest brother Ernesto, and sister Alicia, were born during her transition from youth to adulthood. They often thought of her as their own mother.

She hadn't dated much, when at the (then considered) ripe age of twenty-four, she met a handsome young man and found herself quickly engaged to him. Nesto Padovani was a young yet established banker, who sadly enjoyed his drink in excess. Mom's brothers did not like him very much when up in his cups...and with the toothpaste out of the tube, the engagement came to an abrupt end a lot faster than it'd began.

Not long after, she met a timid, humble man who worked as foreman at a government facility in a desolate town further south, overlooking repair of vehicles used in the municipality. He also owned his own car repair shop a bit in the opposite side of town from Hilda's parental home.

Roberto was an accomplished entrepreneur having worked to support a family since a very tender age. It is said that his father, of whom he always spoke fondly, was of Peruvian descent and had died of heart disease during his mid-forties shortly after Roberto's twelfth birthday; an event which literally marked the end of Roberto's childhood.

Back in the early 40's, as the oldest boy at home and on the day set to return to school after laying his father to rest, Roberto's mother had marched him to the school principal's office where to his bewilderment she announced that he would not be returning. She'd arranged for him to labor as an autobody worker at a major shop a couple of miles from the family's dwelling.

But Roberto had had no knowledge of such plan. And his father would have never agreed to it. He'd known his eldest son's hopes and dreams of studies and travel.

But he'd left this world suddenly. And now mother was in charge.

Sadness and desperation descended over him. But he'd never dare consider -nor ask for- alternatives. As with all his life challenges as he aged, he faced disappointments head-on, looking to turn his new trial into opportunities. He had to -he was now the man of the house.

Then, on a positive note, his father's resting place laid halfway between the house and his new daily destination. As he walked in either direction, regardless the hour, he'd briefly visit the grave every morning and evening. As usual, it hadn't taken him long to find something to look forward to. I must add that my Dad always managed to find a positive outlook on life's trials and tribulations. And often met challenges with a smile, no matter how difficult a time he was going through.

Life went on. His father had been a praised gardener who'd worked tirelessly to provide for his wife and five living children. Finances had been fair and often quite good, facilitating the purchase of two large properties, one of which during the last century hosted one of the largest domestic tree species in the city and province. Until a delusional cousin of mine chose to cut it down and no one could do anything about it, though Dad was deeply saddened yet again by this loss. The humble house nestled behind its giant roots (his childhood home) was a place Roberto cherished and visited regularly through his last days.

Dad's parents, Jesús and Isabel, lost two children to disease shortly after their birth. Following, Dad's mother became quite overprotective around her offspring, which led Dad's three sisters to leave the home as soon as they came of age. They sought refuge in a borough in the outskirts of town, where females on their own were seen as lose women, a real tragic situation at the time. But aching as it did, the mere thought of acquiring such reputation was still better than a life at home with such overpowering mother.

Later-on, when the two eldest sisters married, the youngest of them left the province with one of their younger brothers in tow. They took residence in metropolitan Buenos Aires, where they resided the rest of their lives, never looking back nor regretting any decisions put to action in their youth.

A few years passed before Dad's mother married a long-lost acquaintance and even widowed again, but not before birthing Dad's only half-brother Carlos René, the one sibling Dad came to adore. My uncle René was nearly twenty years Dad's junior. At his birth, Dad felt alone caring for their home, their spare property (which his mother would never agree to sell) as well as his now aging mother with a newborn.

He was lonely and needed a distraction. Quite desperately. He was fond of music and in his own words "artistically clueless but mechanically capable AND quite ingenious." He was a simple man with many friends, and always admired for his ability to make things work.

Through his employment he was fortunate to meet some very good lads planning to start a band. He loved the idea and asked to be taken in as their set-up technician.

And so, it was. The group traveled to nearby cities, joining in carnivals and getting gigs at private parties and clandestine local clubs. Dad found joy in this and gained many great friendships that lasted a lifetime. They became his *cumpas* (trusted and tried friends). Main among them were Signore Venturi and Signore Gianetti, both of which my sisters and I thought were the purest of (old) eye candy. We couldn't be too far from the truth though, because anytime the gents would visit Dad at home (particularly Gianetti), a continuous parade of women trailed our sidewalk for no reason at all.

Not your typical tall, dark, and handsome Italians, both were rather on the shorter side, and strawberry blond with blue eyes. Venturi worked at *Casa de Gobierno* (the seat of government, equivalent to our Capitol Buildings in the U.S.), while Giannetti owned jewelry stores. The latter was his own biggest marketing tool, always in tune with the latest trend in Italian shoes, tailored trousers, silk scarves, and jersey shirts which he wore unbuttoned low, his blond chest hair a thick fur patch. And jewelry...did the man wear jewelry. The flashiest, largest and brightest, and gold, lots of it -thick, heavy chains that could pull a vehicle off an embankment in any given storm.

Meanwhile, Roberto continued to work for the government while supporting his mother and young brother. As a young lad himself, and with views of a family of his own, he purchased a building lot about six kilometers northwest of the town's center, just ahead of the sugar cane plantations. It was a beautiful yet humble patch of land within a citrus orchard where he eventually built a humble home and spent the rest of his living days.

The land had belonged to a former mayor, Don Zenón Santillán.

In 1901, Santillán sold part of it to the city for them to build a park within its boundaries. But the idea never took root. City planning chose to build a park closer to downtown and such is how Parque 9 de Julio was born. This was the park where my Grandpa Jesús had worked.

Then in 1907, before proceeding with the sale of the unused land purchased from Santillán, the city donated a portion to the military for the purposes of building a base.

At the time of Santillan's passing in 1910, his plot was still 600 hectares strong (approximately 1,500 acres) on which, over ten-thousand long and narrow ridges had been planted with sugar cane. The groves ran adjacent to the lot Roberto bought.

***

Hilda and Roberto dated for three years. Their wedding date was postponed twice over their prolonged courtship, due to the untimely death of Mom's Uncle Gregorio, and her grandmother Cipriana (Grandma María's brother and mother, both who had migrated with her from Spain).

Finally, Grandpa had asked them to go ahead and wed without further delay.

He had a point: there were too many family members, and no one knew when the string of bereavements would end.

So, midday on September 11th, 1959, after a simple ceremony at the courthouse, Dad drove the wedding party (Mom and their witnesses: Mom's brother Juan and Mom's best friend, Irma Reynoso) around the main city green spaces -*Plaza Independencia* and *Parque 9 de Julio*- honking the horn of a brand new *Estanciera* (Willys Jeep Station Wagon), loaned to him for the occasion by one of his bandmember friends. After, they'd enjoyed a quick lunch at the Portas where the entire family was in party mood and prep mode.

Next day had been exhausting, yet exciting. Dad partly worked, and partly helped running errands for the evening event, then had returned to his ancestral home to prepare himself for the church ceremony and the family's humble celebration held later that evening. But his mother had eyed him in protest all along.

And a few hours later, Dad was dropped off at the church front steps by his good friend (the car's owner), who'd been sent back out to retrieve the bride, her parents, and her two little siblings, namely, uncle Ernesto and aunt Alicia.

The ceremony was perfect. Mom looked radiant, and Dad was elated. This union entailed such emotion: the start of a new life, and his link to a family of his dreams. He'd married a wife and a large and loud family of immigrants, and the prospect of it excited him beyond words.

After the ceremony, the bride and groom made once more the rounds in the streets of the city, honking the car's horn for all to know of their joy, and laughing out loud while they allowed sufficient time for the family and guests to make their way from the church (Iglesia San Juan de la Cruz), to the Porta's patio, where a modest celebration awaited in the increasing chill of a wintery crisp night.

Dad, spur of the moment, decided to bring his bride over to his mother's home (*the lion's den*, as Mom called it), so Grandma Ocampo could see how lovely Mom looked.

But his mother refused to receive them. Mom was upset to the point she almost barged-in and offered the ogre a good portion of her fed-up mind. Dad stopped her -thank goodness. Before Mom got a chance to show her new mother-in-law what her Italian and Spanish bloodline was really all about.

Regrettably, Dad's mother only saw the marriage as her one loyal and financially supportive son being stolen away. She never cared much for Hilda nor the children they'd shared; me among them.

Regardless of her opposition, the social event at the Portas was well received and well enjoyed. The band played all of Dad's favorites to the delight of the audiences, and late that evening already bordering on morning, Mom and Dad retired to their new home. The unassuming little house Dad built for her, and thanks to the Portas, for an almost guaranteed extensive brood... he'd hoped.

***

Dad was picked up by a vanpool truck at around four am each weekday, and dropped off at the house's front door at six pm. He labored hard at his place of work, and once home, put some additional hours at his own shop before wrapping the day with a shower, dinner, and quick sleep. He never tired and never took a day off. And never complained about it, either. He was the most 24/7 person I have ever known. And the happiest and most grateful.

In the early days of marriage, Mom spent a lot of time by herself, so she'd called on her brothers to bring her two youngest siblings, Ernesto and Alicia, to keep her company. Days were then not so long and lonely.

After my sisters and I arrived, Mom's life was always busy and happy. Although I should mention that by the time Mom married, she'd pretty much felt done looking after "snotty children." Her own words. She had wanted just one child. But five years after my oldest sister was born, I came along, unplanned, and so did my sister Norma (very) shortly after. And I never heard the end of it, making me terribly hesitant to dare show-up unannounced and unwanted anywhere (else).

As we grew up, Mom embraced the opportunity to train at a machine-knitting academy near downtown, and also with a newly arrived neighbor, a skilled tailor from Italy. Developing this talent benefitted us for life. Mom made all our clothes and school uniforms, doing the same for many of our neighbors' children. Eventually Mom also made my wedding dress.

She spoiled us with perfectly fitted clothing. To the extent that, when I left the country and needed to update my wardrobe (particularly after my body had gone through childbearing), I found it impossible to find clothes that fit at all -at least not as I was used to be fitted. I'd never known my size to start with, accustomed to tailor made clothing, right down to the panties. Which would never be the case again.

Mom was good at it, made a steady little income without trying, and adding to her savvy in all things domestic, she was an expert at budgeting. The woman could beat any economist at stretching a dollar. Well, pardon my English…I meant, she was good at stretching a *peso.*

She'd been so good at it, quite like her mother before her, she'd been able to put away enough to purchase a nice building lot in the outskirts of town, without Dad even noticing. This became her *rainy day.*

I remember when Dad found out. He was happy for her, curious, and wanted to see it. And we all -including Grandma- had piled into Dad's Renault Gordini and made our way there. It was desolate, what can I say. Very few folks dared yet to make the pilgrimage to that far end of town and beyond. Far enough indeed that with time it became its own district.

But Dad was impressed. He'd asked her what plans she had for it. And she'd had none. To her it was nothing more than a "it'll eventually grow in value" type of entrepreneurship.

From then on, she'd asked Dad to take her to look around every so often to see how the neighboring lands developed. So, they were the first to meet the folks that started to build immediately next door. And they'd liked each other very much.

Eventually life got in the way and Mom and Dad had not visited for a while. And Mom had met with said neighbors during an errand downtown, and they'd commented how sad they were to learn she sold the property. Mom was speechless, until she'd snapped out of it and told them she hadn't. And they advised her that she then needed to make her way over immediately because someone had started to build a home on it.

Mom rushed home and we'd all piled into the car again to make our trek over. And the neighbors hadn't been kidding. Someone had indeed settled in the space and the building was approaching completion. In the next couple of weeks Mom made several trips to the city offices, only to find that there were many land owners going through the same predicament. An attorney client of Dad's was retained, and all things considered, he'd made quick work out of her case and of the many others that came his way as a result. Mom got her money back. And then some.

***

At the beginning of Mom and Dad's life together, the only neighbors around were an army military base about a mile away, a church across the street, a little farm down the road, and further behind, and into the thick orchards lived an eccentric character who mostly kept to himself and never socialized with the neighbors though was known to throw peculiarly wild parties on occasion -for his own acquaintances. Every once in a while, he'd parade himself on his vespa-like wheels, his face and hair powdered in the exact manner Regency men had sported. We never heard his voice. Not once. He wore Boho-like, wispy clothing and long wrap-around sashes that trailed behind him as he drove passed us.

These folks would go on to become our neighbors for life.

Later-on, a bakery opened further along our street, in a corner lot on the same side as our home. The owners were from Catalunya. They had a son at least ten years older than I, who eventually went on to become a PE teacher. Mother and son were quite blonde and blue eyed and stood out in the crowd -in *our* crowd. I found myself waiting in line at their shop one day when an animated argument broke between mother and gorgeous son Jordi. I quickly understood why my granny had turned down her initial Catalonian suitor. Even with an ear accustomed to foreign tongues, I couldn't discern a single syllable.

***

The little farm was owned by an old Spanish couple, Filomena and Francisco. They raised animals and had one or another planting, trees, and bees. However, they didn't have what they wanted most: children (a lot of couples we knew married late in life; though such was not the norm, it happened frequently).

They shared with us their goat milk and cheese, and large duck eggs. We loved the yummy cheese. And Mom often used the milk and eggs for pastries for our *meriendas* (teatime). We seldom saw her husband, but she always visited us, and used our phone. She was half deaf so her conversations could be heard clear from across the road, and beyond. Far, far beyond.

Filomena was thin and pale; a shy and sweet character of warm eyes and an even warmer heart. A lot like village characters in British period movies. And just as in those movies, I could hardly understand her squeaky lingo to save my life. I also remember her clothing and skin smelled quite like burning coal.

Before I was born, I hear she'd offered to take Alicia, to look after her and spoil her for a few hours each day when Mom needed or wanted to run somewhere for an errand.

Also, well before Norma and I were born, Filomena gifted my sister Alicia a Billy goat. It was named Billy the Kid. The cutest thing, I hear. And with literally no one else around, Mom and Dad chose to let the goat roam free on the property. In Mom and Dad's lack of knowledge in the animal-raising field, Billy grew large and strong, much faster than expected. Faster also -from what I understand- in both, speed and attitude. And quite the meany he turned out to be. And one day, amid Alicia's screams, Billy-the-Bully-the-Kid was found pinning her against the house wall, event after which he was immediately turned into a fanciful roast. He hadn't known l'italiana infuocato was house-bound that day.

And such is how Tucumán's own Billy the Kid became noteworthy and earned a mentioning in the family's annals of history.

***

The church across the street was built by order of a Spanish Chaplain, the Reverend Joaquín Cucala-Boix, a Colonel in the Argentine Army, 19th Infantry Regiment, and later on the *V Brigada de Infantería de Montaña*. At first, he always came across as a frightening—large and stern—man. Many feared him. He however became one of Mom and Dad's lifetime friends.

Padre Cucala had been assigned to Tucumán to teach Greek at the seminary among the chain of mountains that neighbor the foot of the Andes. He also spent part of his time ministering at the military base. Meanwhile, he purchased part of an orchard on Viamonte Avenue, opposite to the lot Dad eventually acquired, and built a small -humble- chapel which he named Montserrat after his own Lady of Catalunya. Then patiently sat back and waited for the orchard to thin out and new families with children to flock to his humble house of worship.

When he and Dad initially met, he'd shown Dad around and said: "If you build it, they'll come," (Genesis 6-7, Hebrews 11:7). Then he'd winked an eye and bumped Dad's elbow with his own, saying: "The same goes for you, my friend."

Later, when Dad started to build across from the chapel (years before marrying) Padre Cucala approached him again. He was ecstatic his first faithful soul had finally arrived. Dad told him he'd for sure attend services, but that in looking ahead, someday he'd marry, have children… And before he could ever finish talking, Padre Cucala had lifted his right hand and jumped in, telling him not to go looking elsewhere, because he was about to start building a school and he'd make sure that by the time Dad's children were of age, the school would be established and flourishing.

My oldest sister was born almost a year after Mom and Dad were married, and was named Alicia after Mom's youngest sister.

She was baptized at the chapel across the street -Montserrat. And as promised by Padre Cucala, by the time Alicia was of school age, Colegio Montserrat was thriving. And by then so was our family.

Alicia and I attended Montserrat for twelve years each. She was in the ninth class to graduate, and I was in the thirteenth. Norma, however, chose to attend a public-school downtown to finish her high schooling.

***

About the origins of our Monserrat community. The Mont-Serrat summit in Catalunya, holds the abbey of La Moreneta de Mont Serrat (the dark-skinned virgin). Its story goes more or less like this: The image of the virgin (also known as 'la Virgen Morena de la Sierra', her hands and face tarnished by smoke from wax candles and incense) was discovered on the mountain in the year 880, after two consecutive Saturdays when a column of light had fallen from the heavens into the mouth of a cavern up in the mountains. The village shepherds, accompanied by the local priest, had followed the light up into the sierras and came upon the virgin's image. But its size and weight did not allow its removal and transport to the village, hence a sanctuary was built around the image in the 1500's. Then it was completely rebuilt after the civil war of 1811, and it required further work after damage done during the Napoleonic wars.

Her image and history were brought from Catalunya to the Americas by priests from the Benedictine Order, who were sent to proselyte around the world, Padre Cucala among them. Such is how she arrived in Tucumán, and one of its very few churches and schools around the globe became my very own childhood backdrop. And though I hear that in present times

Montserrat is not as well respected an institution as it was in the day, it still serves the community well.

Though we had some very religious relatives, my sisters and I were the only ones in the cousin pool to attend catholic school. And Grandma María was of course proud of it. Our school was a very celebrated and well-respected institution in Barcelona. And this brought it closer to her heart.

Sadly, because of Padre Cucala's association with the military, his name was stained and linked to the crimes against humanity which tainted the country during my upbringing.

***

Before Norma and I were old enough to attend school, I recall Mom locking us two in our cozy home on dark and cold—early—winter mornings, just the couple of minutes it took for her to walk Alicia across the street just before formation call, as the flag hymn—the *Aurora* (Dawn)—played on loudspeakers. Locking us why, I'll never know. There was no one around really, except for wild animals (and there, perhaps, resides my answer). It was relatively safe otherwise. Wonder aside, the awareness of being left behind, added to the melancholic hymn notes, always made me very emotional, before I ever knew or understood the lyrics that matched the nostalgic sounds.

Since early childhood the song has been my undoing each time I've heard it. Then as I grew up, I found it difficult not to choke through its words. And even today the tears inevitably fall at the images they evoke...I see myself standing on our couch, attempting to look out through our large living room window, which overlooked our yard but blocked sight of the school. And my tears flowed. I wanted to go along with Mom, but she always thought Norma and I slept through it. I'd tippy toe my way to the window as she and Alicia walked away. And even faster back to bed when I'd hear the key turning in the keyhole, upon Mom's return.

The piece had been commissioned to an Italo-Argentino composer, Héctor Panizza. If the reader enjoys tenors' works, this performance should be a feast for their senses.

T T M K. 2015, April 04. *José Cura "Alta pel cielo" Aurora.* [Video]. Format [Video file]. YouTube. https://youtu.be/45iDYpx-ijz0?si=TLNltwfW4SHW5WgM

***

By the time my own schooling days began (1971), Montserrat had been godfathered by the Army base near our home. Well ahead of patriotic holidays, our teachers trained us on plays reenacting the upcoming historic date, and when the school gates opened for parents and neighbors to partake of the occasion, the Army band, also in attendance, graced us all with beautiful renditions of military and classic marches as our theatrical sessions opened and closed.

Tears streamed down my face each time, to the amusement of my classmates. It appeared I was the only one moved by their notes and words. I loved school though. This school, and these very schoolmates, no matter how silly, many of whom I attended with for the full twelve years. The surrounding orchards no longer so, the neighborhood had grown enough that each schoolroom was full and even overflowing at times. We were children of all walks of life, many immigrants in the mix, just as our own parents and grandparents before us.

CHAPTER 7

A Simple Way of Life

I remember illness in my early childhood, losing a lot of weight and most of my hair to disgusting parasites. I also clearly recall Mom laying me flat on the thick brick pony wall that surrounded the patio, forcing a revoltingly grainy, mustardy-colored medicine down my throat to rid of the bugs crawling in my intestines. Such nastiness…all of it.

I also recall when one Saturday afternoon Mom was so fond of the matching dresses she'd made for the three of us sisters. She'd helped us bathe, combed our hair shiny and tight on high ponytails, and had us all dolled up in no time. Mom was a pro at readying children for an outing, processing us in assembly-line style.

Alicia and Norma sat in our swing, quietly waiting until our parents were ready. We were going out. This normally entailed a stop at Confitería Champaquí for scrumptious triple layered chicken sandwiches (dainty yet delicious), then on to Parque 9 de Julio for *helados* (creamy gelato), and a quick turn in the little choo-choo that went around the park Grandpa Jesús had worked tirelessly to maintain. The original park design had been commissioned to French architect Charles Thays and was, in its beginnings, four times its current size, much of which was repurposed to build government and private facilities, after the military dictatorship of the seventies altered the original design.

During our trips into the park, we always took time to admire the *palo borracho's* bellies covered in thorns (silk floss trees). How Dad loved those peculiar trees!

On the way home, we always made a prolonged stop by Grandpa and Grandma's. And finally, we treated ourselves to the local delicacy from the kiosk on the crossing of Calle Suipacha and Avenida Sarmiento: *Especial de Milanesa* (fresh veal schnitzel served sandwich-style with the works – my mouth not big enough yet [or ever, really] to gather the big-honking-pile of yummy ingredients into reasonable bites). We were very fortunate our parents could do all this for us.

So, back at home, as we anxiously awaited our departure, I, and my never-ending need to keep my hands working on something, had dug out a magazine with many colorful pictures. In no time I found Mom's fancy and super sharp scissors (which she'd told me never to use for paper), and had started working on the makings of a collage.

Sometime later, when everyone was ready and we got up to leave, we discovered that the lap on my dress had become entwined in my cutting action, and now I sported almost a complete lack of front skirting. Mom was rather upset, but as she switched my outfit, I noticed her unsuccessful attempt to look stern. And I went down in history as the girl without a lap, because it happened to me more than once…or even more than twice.

***

As the years passed, I somehow became infatuated with architecture or any hard surface that replicated life through curves and soft edges. Dad always said this was engrained in my veins and that I couldn't deny my genes.

I loved when Mom had to run downtown for an errand and would agree to bring us along. Downtown was where (I thought, and I was right to an extent) *the ancient homes* had been built by the first wealthy dwellers who had traveled long and often to and from Spain, Italy, and the Eastern European and Middle Eastern territories. The homes resembled the pictures I so treasured when reading about the old world, the land of my not-so-ancient-yet ancestors.

A recently-built bank took almost a whole square block and displayed such splendor on its marble balustrade. The purely white stucco House of Independence and its gardens were beautiful and meticulously cared for. The government palace stood proudly across the town square, resembling an old and lively chateau. The cathedral and other religious buildings were stunning and peaceful. All of it represented quite a different atmosphere than our real day-to-day existence in the humility of the *barrios* (the lower burbs).

When Mom was in a rush for time and could not bring us along on her errands downtown, she made sure to bring back *Bocaditos Cabsha* from *Bonafide* (chocolate covered wafer sandwiches with dulce de leche filling*),* or *Longaniza* from *Mercado del Norte* (spicy Calabrese brick from the northern market). Both, the purest of indulgence.

***

But we were poor. Dirt-poor by first world standards, one could say. Drink-water-from-the-hose poor. Clean-your-toosh-with-thin-apple-wrappers poor. Who-gives-a-bleep-bleep-about-thread-count poor. Though we did not pay acknowledgement to it—the mere thought never affected our lives. We didn't know, nor would have minded, the fact we were poor - unless or until someone made an issue of it, that is. Poor compared to what? We didn't know any better, and chances are we wouldn't have been better off if our ancestors had not migrated to South America. Perhaps we would have had it even worse, given the wars, and the destruction left behind. Plus, we only noticed differences if we wondered far, far, beyond the hinterlands.

Truth being, we held steady in a distinct middle-class category, and quite above the poverty level. But we were still third-world citizens, though only those of us that eventually experienced the first world would be able to recognize this fact.

Then, and still today, most everyone down there measured wealth in terms of food basics. I recall how the conversation went when the adults spoke about a well-to-do family: "They eat well, uh huh." Such was always the final comment which determined someone was *above* us. And I'd always ask myself: 'we don't?'

We were happy regardless. What we allegedly lacked did not depress us. We were rich in principles. And in having THE ABSOLUTE BEST family under the Lord's heavens.

Realistically though, our resources were overall limited. And such is why as an adult fortunate to reside in a first world country, I marvel at people who romanticize and even brag about *roughing it* for a week somewhere. They entirely miss the fact that a voluntary stint planned in advance, where resources are brought along (or even a phone call away), does not come close to 'roughing it'. It is both a bit silly and offensive to those who have truly lived (often an entire life span) through real rough conditions. Unintentionally. And without options.

***

Christmas and New Years were holidays to remember, usually also extremely hot and humid. Mom's family would gather at our grandparents' home. All eleven siblings married already, only one without children.

I had many cousins. Too many, really. The oldest about 15 years older than I. The youngest born when I was a teen myself. Age wise, I pretty much sat in the middle of the ever-growing cohort. The cousin pool mostly broke into clicks by age. We also got in trouble by age. I remember how we were referred to when the adults discovered what we'd been up to: "Hmm I bet the ten-year-olds did this. Get them over here!" Or: "I don't think the four-year-olds could have done that, could they?" Yup, they had us figured out by age. Or size. Or both. The exact same theory that had allowed Grandma to get away with stuff as a smaller than normal child.

I also remember many of us, of all ages, would gather at Grandma and Grandpa's back yard and build huge houses out of bamboo and sugar cane with enough space inside for us to play and hide even during long summer storms. I also remember slicing my hands with the sharp leaves in the building process. But after the walls were up, we'd sit inside and chew on sweet sugar cane for hours, which gave me chills. And made us all pee a lot.

Also, many of us of varying ages had once dared go into the abandoned house next to Grandma and Grandpa's own. It was a large Victorian dwelling of many rooms, high ceilings, tall and skinny doors and windows, elaborate gas lighting, and a huge wrap around porch with intricate cornice brackets, and a tin roof crest by then rotted by rust. It had belonged to one of the well-to-do colonist families, long gone by our time on this earth. It was always dark and imposing at night, but I think vagrants used it as shelter, as on occasion we saw the flicker of a candle inside. It used to scare me shitless (apologies for the honesty). And any time we visited G&G at night, I'd avoid looking in or even walking on its sidewalk unless an adult came along. Our uncles always said the spirits of the family members who died at the house had never left, and that their profiles could be seen clear as day on dark nights, dancing around the rooms and peeking out the front window curtains. So, it seemed not only the wind whistled its way around the deserted front garden. But truth be known, my uncles were as good as Grandma at spinning a story and used their skill to keep us away, and out of trouble.

One of my boy cousins had sneaked into it and found all sorts of treasures, the last family having left many belongings behind. And he told tales which most of us did not believe. So tired of the old *lies*, we'd all made our parade out of G&G's house, trying to appear as casual as possible so as not to be found out. Then, cousins Caíto (seven years older than I), Carlitos P. (four years older than I), and Carlitos A. (two years older than I) helped us girls get through an unwelded corner of the huge iron gate, passed the overgrown large front yard, and onto the stairs leading to the vast porch. After unsuccessful attempts to pull the tick trefoils and hedge parsley from our clothes, we'd finally reached the entrance, covered in the thickest of spider webs.

The boys kept acting like they'd done it a million times, so we followed along, and someone finally managed to open one of the doors just enough for the whole tribe of little devils to creep through. And as soon as we had, though we'd tried to be quiet, all our excitement about whatever may be lurking around in the magnificent space turned into the purest of fears when always-wondering-cousin Pablo P. broke away from our little clan of crooks and entered a huge room. He shone a *linterna* (flashlight) at the tall ceiling to reveal hundreds of bats hanging upside down, then made his monkey-crying impersonation, wakening them at once from their lethargy. They began to screech and fly around looking for a way out, and our legs weren't fast enough to get us the hell out of there.

I remember uncle Ernesto and aunt Alicia's faces as we rushed back through Grandma's front gate. They'd known we were up to something when they'd seen us sneak out, and they were laughing hard. We knew they'd never tell on us though. They were awesome and themselves quite the rule breakers so we counted them among our allies.

***

Everyone gathered after noon on December twenty-fourth to start preparations. And remained at my grandparents' home until late on January first. Food prep for so many folks and such a prolonged period engaged the entire adult and younger tier of relatives. And then some -this was no small affair. Just the married siblings plus the grandparents added to twenty-four, then came the thirty-nine grandchildren, all the extended families, and all the friends that chose to join in.

We set up shop in a long, long, long table under the patio roof at Grandma's house. Grandpa at the head, and my uncles lined up on each side, with me and my cousins between the tall guys. We each were given a job which we took very seriously (but only as long as Grandpa remained at the table). We were young, yet old enough to know not to mess around when Grandpa gave us an assignment. Here also, we worked assembly-line style.

The uncles purchased several kilograms of soft *pan de miga* (large size sandwich bread). It measured about 12"x12" and was sliced less than ¼" thick, the typical size and thickness for party events to this day in Argentina. Grandpa, at the head of the table, would signal the start of what felt like a race, asking to see our hands to make sure everyone had washed and prepped accordingly. Total silence reigned. Then he'd suddenly and ceremoniously announce: "Get ready...set...go!" And the cheers were vicious. He piled about four inches of bread and set to work. He'd trim the little bit of crust on all four sides with a superbly sharp knife—splendidly done, if you asked me. He passed it to the first uncle in line to spread the Mayonnaise. The bread had to move along swiftly because the piles kept coming. Next, one of the kids added the super fine shredded lettuce. Next one, the thinly sliced tomatoes. Then came a bit of salt and pepper, and then the expertly pulled apart rotisserie chicken or roast beef; green olives, pepperoncini, and tiny dots of mustard. Finally came the bread cap, already Mayoed. Another uncle with his sharp knife would slice it into six or even nine small sandwiches, and pack them carefully into large fridge trays wrapped on the interior with dampen tablecloths which kept the bread from drying. Those trays were surrounded by giant ice blocks until serving time.

We made thousands, calculating ten to twenty per guest, per night. I figure each pack of bread made about 250 *copetín* sandwiches (hors d'oeuvres size). On the opposite side of the table, they made cheese and salami sandwiches. Thousands of them. And what a blast we all had while at it.

Mom's brothers were a most entertaining bunch though they tended to rush and compete only for speed and quantity. In the end, when the tables were set, someone inevitably ended up with a simple serving of Mayoed bread with one skimpy shred of lettuce and a pinch of pepper, while a little dog someone had brought over ate all the floor spoils and caught a terrible stomach ache.

The uncles also tended to get creative when we started to run out of ingredients. And as much as Grandpa did not encourage their mischief, he couldn't help himself, especially when his boys showed such strong resemblance to his own mannerisms. The *mano a borsa* modism ("ma che stai dicendo?" or best known as *pinched fingers*) was alive and well in all arguments and discussions.

Grandma and the adult women made no less than 1000 *empanadas* (hand held, baked or fried meat pies); Russian salad (similar to potato salad, with the addition of peas and carrots); *clericó* (fruit salad that my uncles would spike later on); *kipes* (Arabic meatballs); seasoned twenty or so whole chickens which they took to a deli to cook in large rotisserie ovens; baked about twenty-five kilograms of *panettone* (Italian Stollen); and numerous kilograms of *facturas* (Argentinian pastries). Homemade pizza was a staple, and so were different types of olives, nuts, and candied fruits. Something else always present at the tables was *budín inglés* (fruit cake); *mantecol* (a solid type of peanut butter that broke off in buttery layers, the flakes melting in your mouth—simply de-li-cious); *cannoli* (cream-filled puff cannons); flans; profiteroles and *millefoglia con crema pasticcera* (puff pastry with Chantilly cream); *pastafrola* (quince tart), and cakes (never dry but rather drenched in syrups and a bit of espresso or liquor, in Italian tiramisu style).

I was lucky in the fact that, because Christmas is in the middle of summer and we were far from fresh-fish offerings, the family, though abiding by many Italian customs, did not follow the *Vigilia* with the *Festa dei Sette Pesci* (feast of the seven fishes). We swayed more towards the Argentinian custom of alternate proteins.

But the group still labored hard in the hot and crowded kitchen. It was really amazing the volume and quality of food the women produced in such limited space. And they did not mess around. No culinary sins were allowed, particularly on dishes from the homeland (G&G's homeland, that is). I think mishaps were considered felonies. And such is how our *Ñoquis, Raviolis, Cannelonis, Milanesas Napolitanas* (breaded veal, fried, then smothered in marinara and topped in mozzarella, then baked), *Tallarines* (Fettucine), *Capellettini* (Venus' belly button), and Ossobuco were the best in town. Hands down. Because all the cooking was done with *Amore*.

Grandma's Spanish specialty was *Arroz Amarillo con pollo* (saffron rice with chicken -a version of Paella without the seafood- as there was no fresh seafood to be had…once again, luckily for me). There was no equal for it in the entire world then, nor is there today.

We were an oversized family and so were our tables. If people today saw the wealth and happiness then, even in our not so affluent family, they wouldn't believe we were talking about the same family, nor the same Argentina of today. We didn't have more then, but the circumstances and self-worth were fundamentally different. Every aunt and uncle were young, gainfully employed, and happy. The siblings shared literally everything, from furniture to kids' clothes, to money when someone was in need. I couldn't be more grateful for having grown-up then and there. It was a time of sincere joy and quite simply a very cherished, unforgettable period of my life.

Some attended midnight mass, which did not interrupt the flow of the gathering, nor the meal. Folks ate before heading out, and upon their return, all the same. We ate, danced, and cheerfully shared a firework display until the wee hours of the morning for as many nights as the excessively inflated pyro-technic supply lasted. We rested a few hours in makeshift beds scattered among the various rooms, then showered…in ONE bathroom! The shower shifts literally took all day, nonstop. Then the party started over.

Parents left for work from Grandma's house and returned by day's end throughout the entire week. We never had to ask who was attending, nor for how long. The understanding was that every family member came. Always. And stayed. Always.

But one early morning while still dark, Mom's brother Carlos left for work -he walked to and from the main train station each night. He was due to start work at four in the morning. After a long day of preparation and then celebrating Christmas Eve, he'd readied a backpack with a number of treats for himself and his friends at work, and left happily, headed for a new day of labor -he had no bad day. And about ten minutes later someone ran up to Grandma's entry gate, urging for folks to come out. Uncle Carlos had been mugged, beaten down to a pulp, his backpack and wallet stolen. An ambulance had been called but hadn't shown yet. He'd be taken to *El Policlínico*, the railroad worker's hospital not far from the Portas' home.

Dad and my uncles (the whole lot of them) literally piled into a large car Dad had driven this day to transport all the last-minute necessities for the start of the party. Uncle José had taken Mom, Grandma, and Carlos' wife Juana, in his truck -they'd follow the ambulance.

When everyone arrived and saw Uncle Carlos' truly sad shape, Grandma had fainted. And after she'd been aided and he'd been placed on the ambulance, *the boys* split into groups and went out to the various homes of people celebrating in neighborhoods near the station, asking if they saw who did this to him.

With some solid clues, they had rushed back home, and acting as good roman soldiers not allowing time nor room for cowardness, they readied to go out after the thugs, until Grandpa had stopped them. He'd told them there were too many of them, the adrenaline was high, and for sure they'd be thrown in jail if they acted upon their anger. He'd also said he could not have a son in the hospital and the other six in the slammer. Then he'd asked them to chill and have the police come and take the information. My uncles were *very* upset, but still did exactly as he'd ordered.

Then, Grandpa had entered the still-steaming kitchen and himself prepared a box of warm and savory food for Carlos' team, and sent it with uncles Juan and Ángel to the station to advise what had happened, and to volunteer to cover his shift and then some, so Carlos' coworkers could go home at least for a bit to be with family on Christmas Day.

***

I had boy cousins who were famous for getting their pudgy fingers blown off by firecrackers, particularly uncle Pedro's kids. I guess the year was at least long enough for them to forget the previous year's mishap and pain, so they'd commit the same stupid mistake again, among the moms yelling at the dads for facilitating the darn *armamento* to their innocent offspring.

In our defense, we were not as clueless as we looked, but inevitably among so many, a few of us hadn't turned out quite the brightest crayons in the box of life. And we quickly learned that the old saying "you can always tell a Dutchman, but you can't tell him much," applied to all bloodlines. Indeed, as much as they like to claim it for themselves, the Dutch do not have monopoly on bullheadedness.

***

Most wonderful of all was the dancing around tables surrounded by happy faces, decadent yet simple foods, and *tarantella*-filled melodies. Grandpa Carlo was thrilled to have everyone join in. Friends, extended families, and immigrants of all origins and walks of life were never turned away but instead welcomed and celebrated.

And once you danced a *tarantella*, there was no way you were given a chance to sit down. The moment the uncles and male cousins saw that *"eri leggero e veloce in piedi"* (you were quick on your feet) you danced the night away, simply because there were too many of them and they would rather insist on keeping you on the dance floor, unless you got right-down-nasty at them. Only then they knew you meant business.

There was a bit of music for every taste, like some Pérez Prado sounds which were quite popular at weddings at the time. Most of the music was danced in the style of conga lines, or in big circles, holding hands. It was loud and cheerful.

After a couple of rounds though, the lines got moving at fast speed, and sweaty hands did not hold as well as they should, so occasionally a line would break and the last person would inevitably be swung around and go flying against a wall, or even worse. It happened to my dear godmother one time. She'd shown-up one evening in a gorgeous, tight and sophisticated silky confection of her own making, which didn't do much to protect her from losing her balance. So, instead of being splattered against a wall like some annoying insect, she'd bounced off-of-it like a bat out of hell and fell, booty first, into a military size pot of spiked fruit salad that sat innocently brining in a corner, chockfull, and loosely covered. Its lid and my sweet godmother's rear entered the pot with such force that her upper legs to her knees, and torso up to her armpits were stuck and submerged in the salad. Only her arms, calves, feet, and her head -thank goodness- were free from the mean trap. The juicy contents had spilled all over the floors when fruit and sweet brining liquids rose between her legs and out of the flattering low cut of her dress, front and back.

And it'd taken twenty minutes and three grown men to free her completely. Two holding-on to her flailing arms and legs, and another poor soul pulling the pot off her rump, which had been considerably wider than the pot - at least at the time of her unplanned entry. She was literally booby and booty trapped, and yelling for help from her husband, uncle Carlos, who sat on the floor, smartly away from her reach, laughing hard, until Grandpa slapped his fool head and told him that he had to replace the lid she'd ruined. Then he'd walked away to hide his amusement. He was no fool, my gramps.

Then my godmother had threatened my poor uncle not to dare call an ambulance or she'd die of embarrassment. He'd said that in that case he'd need to use squeaky wheel grease to get her out unless she wanted to walk into the emergency room with the pot stuck to her assets.

That was the Christmas I'd planned on finally sneaking a taste of the famously delicious fruit salad my uncles always spiked. And though my dear uncle had not cared that his wife's rear-end spent nearly half an hour submerged in the cocktail and drank it regardless, I passed on it.

***

Dad hadn't grown up surrounded by such love and exaggerated merriment. The Portas instantly offered him a one-time (giant) dosage of affection he couldn't possibly turn down. He thoroughly enjoyed their company and could not tear himself away from it. Each year he looked forward to the festivities, helped in its planning when October rolled in, and took part in any silliness the Porta siblings engaged in.

From planning stages through execution, it was a fantastic, memorable time. Being one of the very few who owned vehicles in our extensive family, he was in high demand on the days previous to the start of any event, picking up and transporting all the necessities for the upcoming grand celebrations: large utensils, army size cooking pots, giant blocks of ice, massive amounts of ingredients, and even larger amounts of fireworks. His friendship with Rev. Cucala-Boix facilitated the borrowing of large utensils and kitchen tools from the military base to accommodate the needs of our own troops.

Dad loved *milongas*, a faster style of tango danced in a playful way. This was the preferred music of the *barrios* where he'd grown up. The more solemn tango pieces were danced in the bigger cities or *finer* parties.

One tune he danced over and again was *La Milonga de Buenos Aires*. He played it out loud at his shop, and occasionally as it played, he'd come into the house holding his right hand to his heart and the left one up high, all the while performing his fancy footwork and dancing around Mom.

Searching for it, I located a video which brought tears to my eyes. I had seen Dad dance to it all through my growing years. And the dancer in the video I located has such a remarkable resemblance to him both in looks, stance, and dress style, I forgot for a minute that the man on the video was not him in his younger years. I hope you will find time to view it.

Tangogaga. 2014, July 15. *Christian Marquez et Virginia Gomez (Los Totis), "La Milonga De Buenos Aires", (4de4).* [Video]. Format [Video file]. YouTube. https://www.youtube.com/watch?v=M-35NJPNaQ8

Dad looked forward to dancing at familial parties, first with Mom, and in the late evenings when her feet would start to hurt, he pulled my aunts to the dance floor. He was something to see on his feet—people moved aside to watch him. He only stopped when parched. And after a series of milongas he danced back-to-back, he called everyone to attention: "Damas y Caballeros, su atención por favorrrr…" Having captured everyone's notice, he'd tease and ask people to keep off the dance floor for a few minutes so it could cool down after his brilliant footwork. He was such fun to watch. And when the dancing was done over wood floors, he said his feet were so fast, his shoes had shaved an inch off the old slats.

Truth being, Dad was a complete introvert. But when near Grandpa and the Porta clan, he transformed. He felt emboldened to do things he never did around his own family. His mother hadn't exuded love and understanding. And so, Dad had felt more like himself when around Mom's family.

And seeing how much he enjoyed music; Mom had gifted him a radio one Father's Day when I was still quite little. He celebrated this for hours, listening and dancing along like a child.

The first National Radio in Argentina had been around since the mid to late 30's. But the large equipment was so expensive, only high end restaurants, cafés, and billiard rooms had them.

As I grew up, RAI Italiana was as well-known as the two local stations. I think that (but could be wrong) the one-hour blocks were recorded by the National station in Bs.As. and then transmitted *en diferido* to the inner provinces. Later on, I believe RAI became available 24-7. And this is what the Portas and many folks we knew listened to (except for our Middle Eastern neighbors, next to -and down the road from- our house).

Dad's radio set was the cause of much joy, and also of much playful argument whenever he played it loudly on Sunday afternoons as the old soccer rivals Atlético and San Martín, or Boca Juniors and River Plate, faced each other on the lush greens. Mom was a dire fan of local Club Atlético Tucumán, and Boca Juniors in the pro-league. Dad, of their rivals. And although - only jokingly, thank goodness - this generated much controversy, many meals were promised to be withheld from Dad should he root for, or celebrate, a win by one of his favored teams. Nothing had deterred him though, to our continued amusement.

That very radio went with Dad wherever life found him. He listened to it religiously at his shop day in and day out, and carried it along whenever his space was full and he rented additional plots of land to cope with the ever-growing demand for his skill. As well, when we spent hours on end at Grandma's house preparing food and setting tables for an upcoming event. And even when he took us to the riverside (Río Loro) for a barbeque. He always brought it into the house at *mate* (tea) time for us all to listen to, together. Likewise at dinner time.

I believe it required four or so, very large batteries. The box was so heavy I could not hold in my then very small hands. He listened to this very radio for over forty years. It always kept him company almost until the very moment he was rushed to the hospital and passed away right after his eighty-first birthday.

***

The only thing that ever bothered and brought down my uncles and Grandpa were migraines, just as much as they bothered Mom. Up until the time Mom came down with them as she aged beyond thirty, only men in her family suffered from them, and in the same great manner. It was said that Grandpa's father Angelo - and Grandfather Giuseppe before him – also carried the ailment. Giuseppe to the point of being committed to an institution after turning a recluse due to their intensity and regularity. His family thought he was losing his mind, which is quite possible when there was no way -then- to mitigate the aggressive toll on his body.

I recall quite well Dad's concern with Mom's and her brothers' bouts. It would take them days to come out of each debilitating episode. I suffer from them myself also since my thirties, and the degree with which they assault our bodies can lead to significant weakness and disabling misery. Sadly, I have come to understand too well what all of them felt and went through.

***

As we grew up, Dad became quite successful in his entrepreneurship, and kept a very tight schedule managing his home ventures, added to his regular out-of-town job.

In his private shop he did quite a bit of business with an ethnic group that roved through the provinces. Its elders were born in Spain, though they spoke a dialect I'd never heard then, and even today. They were well-known for their savvy pickpocketing skills, and owned large vehicles, semi-trucks included, which Dad was paid handsomely to repair and maintain. Though most feared them on approach, they had known Dad since he was a young lad working at someone else's shop. And they'd developed a especial kind of affection for him. They had nicknamed him *Cacique Toro Sentado* (Chief Sitting Bull, who'd become widely known by our male population -they delighted in his depiction in old westerns).

I'd say each group that rolled-in was fifty to a hundred strong, or at least so appeared to me then, and even now. They moved into large empty plots of land; their extended stay, referred to as *asentamientos* (settlements). They parked their campers and trucks around the perimeter and set up circus-sized tents using the truck beds and trailers as stakes. They lived openly under these makeshift tents and sadly but honestly speaking, they were not welcomed with open arms because their presence was often regarded as trouble.

They normally departed as suddenly as they'd arrived, leaving behind an aftermath of waste, and not uncommonly, carrying, without permission, one or other item belonging to members of the community.

The women roamed the streets stopping passers-by and knocking on doors asking for anything folks could spare. They dressed in long -soiled- voluminous skirts which dragged unnoticed over the dusty sidewalks. Their skin was leather-like, darkened and dried by extreme sun exposure. Their long, matted hair, was braided top to bottom, and their often-gorgeous green eyes and blondish lashes flashed at the male population, as did their swinging hips. They walked around in groups, normally accompanied by several children. On occasion, some even sported a babe hanging from a bare breast.

Everyone made it a point to start locking doors as they approached. Afraid. Particularly of one older matron, who's high age had been harsh and had robbed her of all her tender beauty. Her hair and eyes were dark as night, and her breath foul like rancid pickle juice (Dad's own words).

***

Dad was crafty and spent hours on end at his shop, long after his aids would leave for the day. He worked hard figuring out how to make vehicle parts which were too difficult and costly to purchase from manufacturers abroad. Most vehicles entering the market at the time did so from France, Italy, and the USA.

He became well known in our town, and soon customers rained in from adjacent provinces, asking for him to provide chassis parts at any price. He was highly in demand, but he was often a softy when it came to collecting a fair value for his work. Mom feared he'd end up losing everything he'd poured into his business.

His clients were demanding indeed, but also cheap, and he was always too ready to please. He did not make parts for money as much as he did for the pure satisfaction of seeing his work succeed. To him it was more of a hobby than a job. I imagine he would have been a great artist had he been given a much dreamed-of education. There would have been no limit to his potential. What he lacked as far as formal instruction went, he made-up for with imagination, charity, and a sincere heart which knew no end. And this, dear reader, is not a matter of romanticizing his soul now that he has departed. What I tell you about my dear Dad is the whole and purest truth and can be confirmed by anyone who came to know him. My Dad knew no evil.

His business soon took off. And he took in young lads that dropped out of school, and trained them in *everything* he knew, and switched them around between mechanics, auto body, tune ups, tire rotations, and electrical work, to ensure they became well rounded and trained in all aspects of the business. He felt more as a teacher and father figure than he did as their employer. And he paid them for a full day's work far beyond what he needed to. Mom could never stop him from doing so (no matter how much she tried). She always feared he'd go bankrupt. But *nothing* he did was done for money or recognition, but rather for personal enjoyment. He was never as satisfied with his work as when he was able to give of himself. And nothing made him happier than to gradually see each of those boys grow into family men, running their own businesses with identical principles as those he'd instilled in them.

Among the "boys" there was Michele Lorcatto, a tall blondish boy of Italian lineage who never finished high school. Dad took him in and taught him how to work. He was such a great kid. Mom and Grandma loved him, because he could be trusted with *any* chore and he never tired of helping.

He always had a smile on his face, and almost permanently too. One evening when he was late getting home, he'd started running as he left the shop, at such speed that he didn't notice Mom had just finished picking up clothes from the wire clothesline (conventillo style), which still hung lower than normal. By the time Michele noticed, he'd run into it, slicing back half inch of flesh on each corner of his mouth. The *pobre hombre* was unable to talk for about a month, and Mom and Grandma took the role of translators. They had their work cut out for them.

***

Dad did so well in fact, that before I started elementary school, we'd traveled by train to the Province of Córdoba to pick up a brand-new vehicle he'd purchased. A Renault Gordini, manufactured at the Willys-Overland Motors & Kaiser Argentina plant.

Back then, most European designed models were strictly manufactured in Europe, forcing a long transatlantic trip southwest. Shipping was not cheap. Once accepted by Argentinian customs, they were sold primarily in Bs.As. to wealthier big city dwellers. Very few made it inland, as not many could afford brand new European cars at the time.

Willys was the second largest producer of automobiles in the U.S. after Ford Motors. In its attempts to start selling in the southern Americas similar units to the well-known and craved European models, Willys entered into a joint venture with a Brazilian manufacturer, and later on with Industrias Kaiser Argentina (IKA). The latter had set-up a factory in 1955 in the Province of Córdoba, on land donated by the Nores Martínez family of Estancia Santa Isabel. Today, the very site is home to Renault Argentina, manufacturing some known models like Nissan Frontier and Nissan Alaskan, in addition to many others designed specifically for the local market.

Brazil manufactured Jeeps and made them popular in Chile. To enter the Argentinian market, Willys had chosen a version of the Renault Dauphine made for racing, and had come up with a family version: the Gordini.

Dad was an auto aficionado and self-taught-expert at all-things-automobile and had fallen head-over-heels for it as soon as its picture was posted either at a new dealership down-town, or on a highway board (sorry, I was very young and do not recall this part clearly). He wanted it, no matter the cost, silver blue, exactly as shown in the advertisement. Then one day after an errand he came home delirious and openly told us he'd "fallen in love all over." Thank goodness he'd planned ahead, and proposed, before Mom snapped out of it and smacked him: "A brief getaway *for all of us* to accept the car hot from the press."

Mom wasn't fooled though. This trip was the realization of his dream to see a car manufacturer at work, first-hand. And confirming this, his face had lit-up like a Christmas tree when we entered the factory's floor, which an old friend of his from the shop out of town had arranged for us (for Dad, really). His friend had recently been hired, and knew that Dad would jump at the chance to visit. And with this, I honestly think Dad's bucket list was complete.

We were experienced at traveling short distances by train. Though in this opportunity we had travelled all night, and upon arrival into what appeared the closest town to the factory, we stayed at a guest house for a couple of nights. The house was large, with thick plastered walls painted in white, built in a square shape surrounding a courtyard to which all rooms opened grandly. The open patio floors were beautiful, bright-red lacquered brick, laid in intricate patterns. The air was fragrant from the delicate vines hanging off the pergola; lavender bells and dark berries scattered all over the ground.

We were exhausted, but excited to see the main city, much larger, greener, and alive than our own. Both evenings we'd walked around downtown and grabbed a quick bite and an ice cream cone. Then the third day we'd gone on our fieldtrip, retrieved the car, and headed home on the evening train after the vehicle had been successfully loaded on to one of the rail wagons.

Dad kept and loved this car for the rest of his days, having at one point restored it for Alicia to drive, and eventually altered it into a convertible version, which he rented for weddings and the like.

Following, is a line-up of vehicles manufactured at the Córdoba Santa Isabel plant (today's Renault), from its opening in the mid 50's, and through 2020. In retrospect, I am sad that I was so young when Dad took us to tour the facility. I was unable to truly appreciate how ecstatic he would have felt. I wish we had a recording of his face when we entered the floor. He was a softy too -he'd probably teared up. He told me once that his love affair with the brand begun on his wedding day (September 11th, 1959), as he drove his friend's brand new Estanciera around downtown, with Mom sitting next to him. That vehicle is shown below as the 1957 model.

Dad's brand-new Gordini that we picked-up in 1970 is the 1960 model.

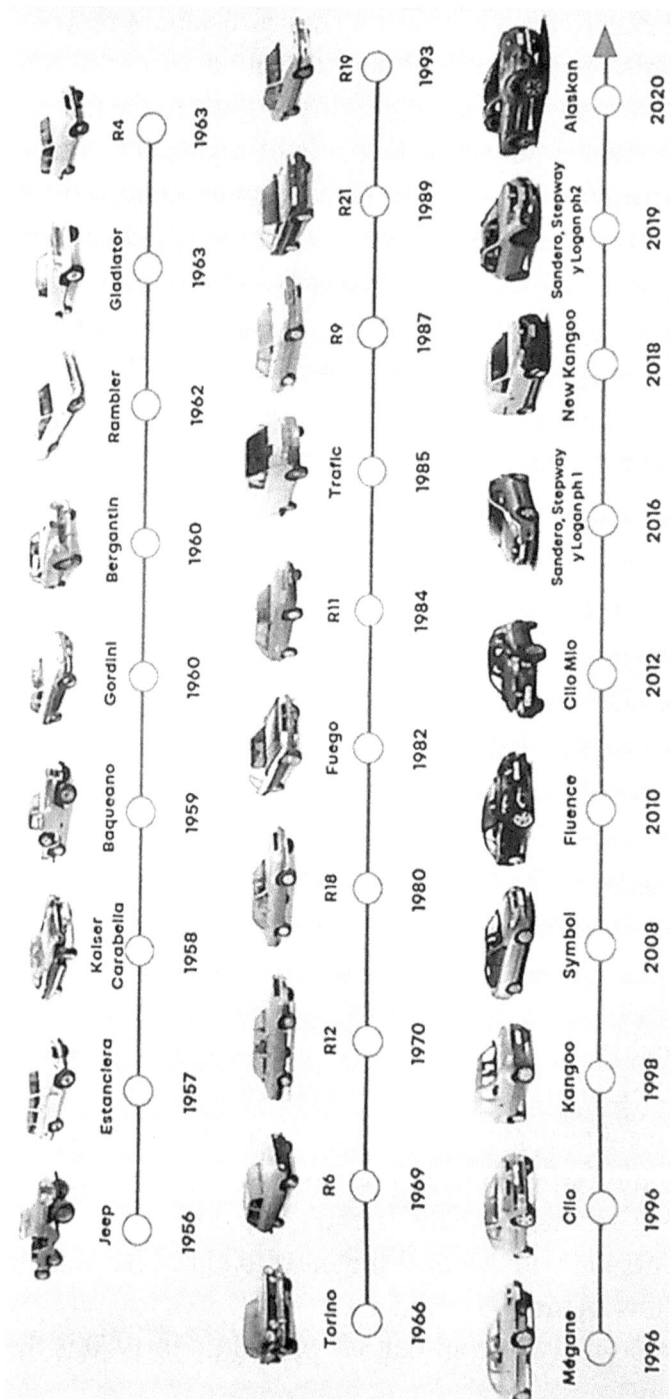

IKA/Renault Manufacturing Line – Photograph use authorized by Ms. Lucía Ploper;
SUSTAINABILITY MANAGER RENAULT ARGENTINA
COMMUNICATIONS MANAGER/AD INTERIM/RENAULT ARGENTINA
EXECUTIVE DIRECTOR RENAULT FOUNDATION

In the mid 70's he negotiated with a customer that ultimately let him have his Torino (1966 model). He loved that car and kept it for a few years, until he had an opportunity to trade it in for a Rambler (1962 model). The tune changed then, and he would not stop talking about *it*.

Then, when the 80's approached, a customer talked him into accepting an R12 (1970 model) in payment for a large job. And I think he fell in love again. This model was popular and a good looking one. It didn't take long before he had three of them parked in our driveway -they'd quickly become a bargaining chip for larger commissioned jobs. He could never turn one down!

Along the years, there had been also a Carabella and a Bergantin which he restored and kept for show and advertising. And for *fancy parties*, as he called them.

***

Another memory brings me to a wedding we attended quite far from home. It'd taken us a while to get there. The groom was one of Dad's second cousins. There was a live band playing, and they were quite good! The band leader was the groom's brother, and the band's name was … Venus (?). My Dad was enjoying himself so much, but we had to leave early because I came down with a huge case of indigestion and got quite ill. I feel bad for causing Dad to miss part of it. He loved sitting in front of a band. As much as I do.

In the 70's and 80's, Dad was a huge fan of Olivia Newton John and Sheena Easton, and enjoyed watching The Great Valley, Perry Mason, Bonanza, The Great Hulk, The Untouchables… he enjoyed all American shows available. And they were all mostly offered as part of the evening programing. I did not mind them, so we spent that time together chatting and laughing. Then Sundays were for Formula 1, soccer, and Grandes

Valores del Tango (a primitive version of today's AGT, paired with professional Tango singers and dancers). I have many fond memories of times spent with him watching these. I know Dad would have enjoyed having a son to share things with.

***

I recall one Sunday Dad brought us to Río Loro, which Mom very much disliked. In truth, Mom only enjoyed attending family gatherings. Elsewhere she saw danger at every turn. I always thought bowlegged cousin Caíto's malicious pranks were if not a worse threat, a far superior nuisance.

I was four or five years old, and it was not our first time visiting this location. The day was hot, and the river crowded. Though this stretch of water wasn't broad nor deep, the water level seemed high after a couple of large storms in the preceding days.

And against Mom's wishes, Dad had encouraged and even helped us get in at the very edge, where the willows dipped their low branches into the bubbling, chilled waters. It had felt good.

I had never known Dad knew how to swim. We girls didn't. Mom would not let us near the water until we learned to swim at school (which in the end I never did, for a number of reasons). Montserrat had a nice swimming pool, unlike most private institutions located in the downtown area where real estate is tight and expensive, so they (together with public schools) are served by public swimming pools.

This day Dad was giddy. The shops where he worked were nearby. He knew the area well and was always happy and eager to share it all with us.

Once in, some teens near us were playing water volleyball and got a bit rowdy. With them agitating the flow, and a fast wave that came along carrying some debris from up the mountain, I got scared and let go of the little shelter I was under in order to swiftly get back on the ground if so needed. Just a slight bump by one of the folks next to us, and suddenly I was rushing downstream, twirling around in a sitting position, now a part of the swoosh. I can only see Mom at intervals as I spin around. But I can hear her frantic screams alright.

One of the guys playing next to us tried to catch me, but my side of the current moved faster than his arms could reach me. And my overall size did not help. Dad ran away until I could see him no longer. I thought, *'Great time to disappear.'*

I was honestly scared senseless. I saw no way to stop. I didn't know the surroundings, nor how far the rollercoaster rafting would last. I fought tears but they blinded me still, and I could not see if I was about to bump into something, though in all the twirling around I did see there was a dip and a bend coming up, and as I started heading in that direction, I suddenly got pulled out of the water like a little leaf. And that's where Dad had gone. He'd run down the bend, hopped on a floating platform of sort, and jumped into the current to wait for me. He'd then been quick, and luckily not as affected by the rushing water. Only then I realized how very small I was, and how helpless I had been.

Dad said he and his friends had used that stand often, for good fun. And he had been my hero that day. I only got a few scratches and bruises to show for that adventure, thank goodness. But also got a good scare that lasted me a lifetime. Truth be known, if anything (else) happened to me that day, he would have been killed. By l'italiana infuocato. I'd seen her, as he caught me, pulling up her sleeves and readying for a fight. She'd been so upset all the way home; she hadn't said a word to either of us. Point taken.

***

Dad was a favorite uncle, on both sides of the family. The only exception being our cousin Ricardo (Ricardito as a child, and Caíto as the monster he grew into). Caíto had a legendary fall that almost costed him a leg, but he also had great doctors that decided to reconnect his shuttered bones with a metal rod. It was in the late 50's or very early 60's, which constituted back then -and back there- quite an advance, even though it was common practice here by then. That leg appeared longer as he grew-up. At least I thought it did. And the limp was noticeable, though he worked hard at disguising it.

Caíto, uncle Mocho's oldest, was the brattiest child. He towered over us all at over 2 meters in height as a preteen, with skin clear and pale, but the meanest eyes resembling the purest aqua sea glass, his Polish blood deeply rooted within him.

Whatever he did, he got away with because his mother held an infatuation of sort towards her first born. And she turned her head the other way. Over and again.

No matter how many times his dad, his sisters, or any of the aunts and uncles told him to leave the rest of us alone, he simply wouldn't. He got a kick out of scaring the bejesus out of the younger kids -us girls in particular. Too many times to count, he would hide and jump at us, and scare us beyond the next international border crossing.

Dad saw him watch us and plan. And he'd also seen me cry in terror of the cruel giant. So, one evening while Caíto waited for us behind the wall next to Aunt Alicia's room, knowing that his sister and I would close our eyes as we quickly walked through the space; wonderful Dad had silently followed us, and grabbed him by the back of the neck just as he'd emerged at our side. And he'd dragged him out towards the front of Grandma's house (and thus away from his adoring mother). And did not let him go while he informed him in detail what he'd do to him next time he caught him bothering us.

Then Caíto had been told to apologize for being a pest, which he'd refused with a mocking stare, though he hadn't dared do so twice after Dad grabbed him hard by the crotch and mumbled something only for Caíto to hear. And that had marked the end of an era of purest harassment by cousin Caíto, who even in his old age, is not but an unhappy soul. In truth, I often felt sorry for him. He carried a bitterness that would have been more appropriate for his ancestors.

Still, Dad was always a favorite. Particularly when someone got hurt. He was the absolute best at making people feel better, so we always made sure to have him handy when the vaccination vans were scheduled to roll-in near the school, loaded with nurses that dispersed throughout the neighborhood and knocked on doors offering to freely inoculate school-aged children, infants, and pregnant females.

There weren't *dispensarios* (neighborhood clinics) in our neck of the woods, so the Department of Public Health facilitated transportation of medical personnel throughout the subdivisions distanced from the capital. And as they went about their job, Dad told jokes and acted silly to divert attention for all of those who could benefit from the distraction as they got poked and prodded.

Such was also the case when one *King's Day* (a gift-giving celebration held down there each 06 January). Dad had dropped by Grandma and Grandpa's house bringing treats that Mom had prepared and sent over. Aunt Pepa also happened to be visiting her parents, bringing along her oldest, Carlitos A., about three to four years old by then.

Sweet Carlitos had received a gift from *The Kings* (aka The Three Wisemen) in the form of a Superman suit. My thought on it is, had the Kings in all their wisdom, foreseen how he'd act while wearing it, it would have been *wiser* not giving it to him. I mean, the child had been so hyperactive this day -not normal for Carlitos A., truly. But he'd worn the suit for hours, and the proof was in the pudding. Meaning, the pudding he'd splattered all over the front of it.

And he'd now disappeared. No one could find him, and he wasn't answering when called. My aunt was in a panic until my Dad went to the front yard calling out for him. Meaning business -he had to get back home soonest, afterall. And Carlitos finally responded. From the tall roof top. My Dad told him not to move while he came up to get him, but Carlitos immediately responded: "No need Tío Roberto! I can fly, watch me!" and without thinking twice (nor once, I believe) he'd stretched his little arms forward readying himself to soar and glide, launching himself down. But superpowers, he had not! And he'd split his head in half when his skull met the edge of Aunt María's favorite cement urn planter, which now sported a chip and no one would ever hear the end of it, regardless whether or not Carlitos survived his first flying adventure.

He had the wind knocked out of him, and my dear Dad, the godfather...I mean, not THE Godfather, but Carlitos' godfather, had to pick up half of his brains from the front garden and rush him to the hospital for a suture job truly out of this world. And you'd agree, had you seen it.

Dad had his hands full that afternoon attempting to comfort his little godson, and as he'd left the hospital that evening, he'd assured Aunt Pepa the child would be okay though it'd be a while yet 'til he felt better. And as he walked away, he'd said to her: "No doubt that child carries your blood." She looked at him, perplexed, then he'd added: "In my short acquaintance with your family I've come to learn that you're not really Italian unless you can make *yourself* truly miserable."

Sadly, years later when Carlitos grew up and showed huge promise in soccer, his dad took him to be tried for one of the very rare premier club openings, and though he had quite awesome skills, he was refused a chance because of his flying accident earlier in life. No club would sign him up in fear of a lawsuit should he get a head injury that completed the job he started as a young child.

Carlitos, like many boys in Argentina, had, at an early age, given up his infatuation with world justice and Marvel Heroes when he'd become besotted with Argentina's famed soccer stars, most of whom (then) began their careers when discovered by scouts in the streets of Argentina, bare foot naked, kicking a cloth ball around, in the unpaved streets of the poorest barrios. And though he grew up into a genuinely happy and successful man, stardom on the soccer field never became a part of his life story.

***

Dad loved flying kites, which he normally did with our male cousins. He built his own and made all of it look fun and easy. He enjoyed himself tremendously helping little guys set one to sail.

Pasaje Yrigoyen, where Grandma's house was and still is located (although the street has changed names by now), did not get much traffic. Hardly any at all for that matter. Back in the day the street was unpaved and driving on the packed dirt wasn't too bad except while - or after - it rained. The huge ruts got the most experienced driver in trouble. So, the long stretches between those who dared grace us with their short-lived presence served us kids perfectly—we could play for hours on end without worries. We had become quite skilled at gliding through the uneven terrain, even behind a kite.

***

Dad was great at giving advice, and often reminded us: "Hay que pagar las cuentas" (pay off favors quickly to avoid being held hostage to them). But what he did best was tell stories -quite like Grandma. He also liked telling jokes, but he laughed easily and couldn't ever finish his tales.

As far as storytelling and anecdotes went though, he had a staple, and it was no joke - quite literally. It was an old Argentinian legend told in the *haciendas y ranchos* away from the city. A version of what was known as La Leyenda del Perro Familiar. It told the story of a pact that sugar cane planters had made long ago with the devil, to surrender one employee in exchange for each successful harvest...

Plantations employed large amounts of people who were brought in by the truckload from other *pueblos* (villages). They worked long days that began and ended at dark. And seemed that, regardless how watchful an eye was kept on them; one employee would always go missing during *La Zafra* (the sugar cane harvest). When the absence was noticed and people were questioned, they'd always bare witness of a meek dog having appeared in the dark and lonely roads to several of them. It was said that folks would run and hide from it, because it initially portrayed itself as very sweet, insisting on walking behind or along pedestrians, or next to a slow-moving car. As the fable went, once the travelers got accustomed to its company, the beast would suddenly grow long black hair and huge teeth, and it would swiftly take over their souls.

Yes, my friends, enough to scare the crap out of anyone given the perfect circumstances. And Dad picked this tale for dark, windy nights, when the power went out and we all gathered 'round the dining room table staring at the lonely candle that would eventually burn out and leave us in the dark. Gullible and terrified. If Grandma was around, needless to say she loved it. Was even the first to scream in terror (not really in fear, but masterfully getting *us* scared).

Dad always started the tale in a different way so we didn't expect the repeat, but also always managed to turn the story around and give it the same end as all others.

Mom would get furious and warn him, waving a finger at him: "Roberto, terminala por favor! Ya basta de pelotudeses," (Please stop it already. That's enough non-sense). Though her actual words were a bit...let's say...stronger.

* * *

Then there had been some snafus by Dad when he was running too late to stop by the barbers' den after Mom had pled with him to get his hair trimmed before one of the multiple family events we were due to attend. But in winter Dad would avoid it with myriads of excuses and in the end would be running too late to comply with her request.

One time he'd ultimately gone into the shower hiding a small salad bowl and trimmer, and had done his best at making himself presentable. And had come out of the bathroom sporting the most peculiar mushroom trim. There had been no time to fix it before we had to be at Aunt Alicia's house, *pronto.* Not that a fix would have been possible by any stretch of the imagination.

No sheer (or shear) perfection expected, and none achieved. Dad and my uncles had laughed about it all evening, driven to tears.

CHAPTER 8

The Day Things Began to Change

We'd noticed Dad's once perky personality was somehow fading. There was a screen of concern shielding him from us. It was work-related, he'd said as much, though he never agreed to talk about it any further.

I recall Mom's brothers visiting us while Dad was away at work, and Mom confirming to them what we were noticing. No one could break through to him to find out what was wrong. His brother (Tío René) now a newlywed young lad, had come to work along with him temporarily at the auto-body installation out of town. Dad's overseeing tasks had increased over the last year and my uncle's always willing and positive attitude had been a welcomed relief. He'd jumped at the chance to secure employment and stability for his new family.

He and Dad worked long hours and both seemed quite content with it, except for a growing number of low-toned conversations between them, which consistently came to an abrupt halt whenever someone approached.

Tío René had also become a regular at the Porta's gatherings, as were a couple of Dad's older sisters and their families. It felt great to have both families embrace each other this way, although Dad's mother still refused to take part in our celebrations, particularly so if Mom's family was involved. Dad's mother never cared for my mother, nor ever asked to see her. Yet Mom would have given anything to please her, if not for her own sake, for everyone else's.

Normally if Abuela Ocampo asked to see us, Dad would in turn ask Mom's permission to take us over, and we'd be prepped in our best attire and behavior. But I could never shake the feeling I'd get clear into my bones as we entered her home. I resembled my mother quite so, and often felt like an insect being peered-at behind a magnifying glass.

Quite the contrasting feel we received when we visited the Porta home, for which we needed no appointment, permission, nor formality. We marched straight into the patio where Grandpa sat imperiously in his massive rocking chair. He never failed to be surrounded by friends, family, or co-workers. But upon our arrival, his smile always lit-up.

Mom was a favorite of Grandpa's. He knew and let all know that much of the family success had relied on her willingness to sacrifice her own wishes to help her parents raise the family. Parents and siblings alike had depended on her for child raising, tutoring, meal prep, laundry and house chores as they'd all gone about their own jobs, schooling, and wants, away from the family home. All of them also fully counted on her endorsement of a mate when they started to seriously consider marriage. Everyone loved Mom and would have sacrificed anything for her in repayment of her own forfeited dreams.

***

Mostly what I recall from first grade was the fact I had the prettiest teacher in the school, and in all of Tucumán. Srta. Maggy was a gorgeous young girl of (I believe) Italian and Andalucian ancestry. She had the purest blue eyes, and long, straight blonde hair like golden silk. And she'd just married a prominent attorney as beautiful as she.

But shortly after school had begun, there had been news of Grandpa's only living sister passing away. So, Mom and I had made the trip across town to attend the viewing. I'd never been over to this house for a visit, but Mom knew everyone, and they all knew her.

Grandpa's sister laid in wake in a large bed made larger by the fact that she was no taller than me. At least it so appeared, in great contrast to Grandpa's grandly projecting presence. I could see it myself at that very moment, as he stood in a corner near the front door, greeting folks as they entered. His sister was nearly 90 years old, with skin lustrous like porcelain, and sweet looking features. Her child-like body had been carefully groomed and was on candid display. Her family was manifestly proud of her.

Large candles flanked the humble bed frame and made for a rather calm atmosphere. A precarious heater blasted in a corner while outside the rain bounced on the tin roof, and a tree branch scratched the window glass. The weather was awful -gray, windy, and wet. An unbearable chill had begun setting-in.

The immediate relatives sat around the perimeter of the room, maintaining a steady flow of conversation. Visitors arrived and swiftly mingled before leaving the premises. The room was small and could only accommodate a small group of folks, but the stream of mourners was pronounced and relentless. She'd been around a long time and was evidently known to many.

And this, folks, is the extent of my memory of this occasion, other than the fact that this had marked my first time having to make use of an outhouse. And I must confide that it took away all desire to ever use one again.

The year went by swiftly, and on the last day of school, my class was to dance at the final play before we left for summer vacation. We had trained for a couple of weeks the steps to the "Carnavalito", a tune from the High Plains. Mom had made my *campesina* clothing—a little white blouse with intricate cotton lace around the neckline, shoulders, and on the little puffy sleeves. And a sweet little skirt with beautiful picot lace in rainbow colors around the seam. The outfit was completed with *alpargatas* (rough fabric flats with jute bottoms that scuffed your toes and heals raw) - the purest punishment in footwear.

We had performed to perfection and the parents had asked for an encore. And someone posing as a photographer took pictures but we never saw him again. I remember I was so excited to get my picture taken. First time (and last) I'd genuinely smiled for a camera and the guy never showed up with the prints.

Moral of the story: Don't bother to smile for pictures.

***

Second grade was a breeze. Nothing truly remarkable or of consequence took place, except when towards the end, in mid Spring, the local news announced a chartered plane carrying a rugby team from Uruguay to Chile had disappeared, having presumably crashed on the Argentinian side of the Andes. I recall all adults talked about the efforts going on to reach the area, which were often thwarted by the weather.

Again, time passed slowly (as it usually happens when you are a child). As the school year came to an end, my class was rewarded with a field trip to the Pepsi Cola bottling plant in the outskirts of the city. And after an amazing tour of the facility, the company had set up a long table on the shady green lawns at the entrance to the compound, with sandwiches and icy Pepsi. It was such a luxury for many of the kids in our class.

Then a couple of weeks later, a day or so before Christmas, survivors from the crash had been found, and in being questioned how they'd managed to remain alive for such extended period under extreme circumstances, it had been revealed they had resorted to eating flesh from the deceased. The horror of it had remained with them and with most that heard about it. Now, this was not (yet) a time of censorship, so what was out there, was out there for everyone. I remember it'd left such horrible impression on me. Paired with plain fear. I struggled with it -it'd lingered on my mind.

***

In the long and lazy soon-to-be summer days, finding things to stay occupied was a challenge. In the siesta hours I loved going next door. The Guiñez', our previous neighbors, had long since left. In the back of the property sat the remains of their home, now in active dispute due to a conflicting will. New owners -former vineyard dwellers from another town- were about to transform the brick ruins into their new homebased business. The man was a merchant from Syria. The much younger wife, a daughter of Syrian immigrants. There were talks of four children, all several years older than me.

The front entrance to the home was by then blocked by building materials, among which, a ten-foot-high pile of sand to be used for the mortar. After one intriguing visit, it had become my most fascinating spot to climb. Its surface warm from the morning sun, its center cooling as my hands and feet sank into it. I knew not of a more delightful feeling. As I sat on its crumbling and soon-after moist top with a well-worn book on my knees and my hands fanning the silky surface, I couldn't imagine a more decadent pastime.

The afternoon hours were endless and simmering hot. An occasional long tailed lizard or starving snake peeked out of the tall grass gone to seed. And I no longer delighted solely on picture stories. By now I could read anything and everything, so I devoured my little collection of stories by José Mauro de Vasconcelos, over and again. I'd found a screaming deal on a clearance table downtown one time Mom had taken me along during her errands. She'd let me buy the collection and I'd been thrilled with his style and tales, though I soon learned not all of it was PG material, yet again, *don't ask don't tell.*

But I'd been warned never to leave the house without making sure Mom or Alicia knew where I was. I treasured these moments and refused to jeopardize my chances, so I'd ask Mom whether I could leave the house for a couple of hours as she'd finish the dishes and headed to the cool shelter of her dark bedroom to lie down and rest her head. Mom's ailment was eventually diagnosed as "suicide" migraines. They grieved her most of her adult life, and eventually contributed to its end.

She never refused my requests for reading time, a smirk on her face. She knew what this bit of freedom meant to me. It reminded her of her own younger years. However, with local news becoming worrisome, one day at lunch time Mom told us we could no longer be outside alone, and that our trips to see Grandma and Grandpa, as well as family gatherings of any sort—even public festivities—would now likely need to start and end earlier in the day, preferably during daylight.

So, my young mind's radar started to shift. Or perhaps to awaken. Soon after, once the dark of night would set upon us, we'd hear explosions in the far distance, and choppers above. And when I dared peak out the window just above my bed, I could detect the flicker of lights on the mountains lining the horizon, far west, behind our school.

Scarier even, as we rode the bus to doctors' appointments and the like, and we approached the military base a mile away from our home, a wealth of activity throbbed in the previously quiet facilities. And as our bus route reached the main base corner of *Campo Norte* (North Field, in the corner of Avenidas Italia and Viamonte), I could not help but stare in that direction. The long open patios surrounding the offices of the base were now partly blocked by patched linen sheets, to shield the half-naked bodies of young men lining up to be examined upon reporting in, before being sent to patrol and guard the mountains, where rumor had it, the uprising extremists had their operations' hub.

Mom would always whisper in my ear to look the other way.

And I was beginning to understand how very little I really knew.

Family gatherings did not end abruptly, but diminished slowly as each time we ventured out, our vehicle, as all others, were stopped at various check points, and documents for both, driver and occupants were held while thoroughly checked. The control was often done by local police enforcements, but at times also by the military.

Los Montoneros—an Argentine Peronist guerrilla long in the brewing, and particularly active starting in the 60's—were causing serious distress. Graffiti covered every exposed surface, even the once magnificent seat of local government, and other historic buildings. Each time the scrawls surfaced somewhere, the military would cover it with whitewash, and declare the area no longer accessible to the rebels. In this manner little by little the entire city was being blocked off to *the opposition*.

***

Nineteen seventy-three rolled in. Then March brought showers, crisp mornings, and the start of 3rd grade. The days were shorter again, and time went by a bit faster.

Winters were cold. At dawn, the patches of grass here and there and the sidewalks alike were silvery and sleek. Early mornings, Mom would layer film after film of clothes under our pinafores before walking us across the street to school, pulling us by the hand as Norma and I struggled to keep up with her pace. We could barely move under the heap of garments she managed to pile on our bending shoulders, afraid we'd chill to the bone and catch our death walking the few steps to our classroom door, or during breaks when the teachers and nuns would force us out of the warm rooms and made us to remain outside no matter how nasty the weather. Then a bunch of us would pull close together to stay warm, and sheltered under a trellis or gather up at the virgins' grotto to play quick card games when the nuns weren't watching. After all, they'd tell us to play and run, but as girls we were only allowed to run so fast or become so rowdy...the nonsense of it! All while they gathered and cozied-up inside to chat and gossip.

By noon the sun shone brightly and erased all signs of the oppressing chill, bringing back a much-needed respite from the freezing air that sat heavily over the valley at dark. Then, we couldn't wait to return home and pull away all the sweaters and thermals that quickly became bothersome and steamy as the sunny siesta hours approached.

***

Mom and Dad received a lot of visitors. Their siblings, plus their spouses, as well as many relatives and acquaintances, and customers and friends of Dad. Too many friends of Dad's to count were always knocking and showing-up at all hours of day and evening. I can with overwhelming certainty state that our front door revolved more than the fancy ones at the bank downtown.

In the summer it was important to have some frosty Coke or Pepsi (though Mom disliked both) and tapas at the ready; and some cheese and crackers, pickled olives and salami - the staples at any home expecting (and welcoming) company.

In winter, the leading star was black coffee and liquor shots that kept folks warm, happy, and somewhat alert (depending of course on the varying volume of consumption).

Giving and receiving specialty liquors for birthdays and holidays was a welcomed custom. Mom and Dad, being favorite acquaintances to many-a-folk, became the faithful recipients of quite an arsenal. Mom's little midcentury modern sideboard was stocked chock full of booze of artisanal quality. The selection was ample and heavy, and arrivals were often treated to the shot(s) of their choice.

Our home didn't have heat -such was the rule, not the exception. Today it still doesn't. Ninety percent of homes down there don't. Even the homes down south in Patagonia don't. Nor do the ones bordering the Andes mountains. Some of those closest to frozen peaks and glaziers have an *hoguera* (a fireplace of sorts), but we weren't affluent enough to see -less own- such a contraption.

What we had was an *estufa a gas* (a propane gas heater) which, due to the high cost to operate and the obvious fear it may blow-up, was used only under extreme-cold temperatures. Adding insult to injury, those in charge of determining what qualified as such extreme, were tough-folk (Mom and Dad) hence the *estufa* was overwhelmingly deemed only a luxury and a decorative gadget rather than a practical -usable- appliance.

***

Mom spent a great deal of time in her dark bedroom during the brightest hours of the day to appease her migraines. During my childhood they became quite constant and menacing -no thanks to me, truly. She'd lay down with half-frozen moist hand towels covering her eyes and forehead, serving the purpose of mitigating the throbbing ache, cooling her head, and that of providing further seclusion from any hint of daylight. But she never allowed her ailment to interfere with her duties. Not having been given the opportunity to attend school, she used to tell us, "You're going to school even if it kills me." And she'd meant it quite literally, I think.

We never missed school due to her illness. No matter how lousy she felt, she woke us up and helped us get ready, and prepared us a snack to take along (usually a warm mortadella sandwich in a fresh warm bun she'd procure daily from *Panadería Viamonte*, two blocks down the street, while we got ready). Nothing but fresh bread out of the oven would do, and there was nothing stopping her. No illness and no weather.

She always had a fresh and yummy lunch ready for us when we returned home. It was not until we had finished our lunch and started to complete our homework that she finished the dishes and headed to the dark stillness of her room.

Noteworthy: Argentinian children do not eat meals at school. Instead, they go to school early enough so that they can be home in time for lunch, which is the meal folks normally cook. Also opposite to the North-American custom, supper always consists of lunch leftovers.

***

I did not enjoy sleeping siesta. Even today I don't, strange as it may sound for a Latino. Back in my childhood and youth, I preferred staying up with Grandma when she visited. And when she was not present, I read, practiced my cursive, or drew pictures. Silent activities were the norm if you were a non-siesta-rebel.

This one day, everyone had felt a bit ill and feverish. It was blistering cold, and Dad had gone out of town to help someone haul a totaled vehicle to his shop. My sisters had crawled into bed claiming a sore throat, and I'd stayed up, trying to draw an intricate map, at an attempt to keep entertained.

The afternoon had been cloudy. A sudden thunderstorm darkened the sky early on, and big drops of dirty rainwater were no longer a threat but a promise confirmed. The temperature had dropped so much, I wrapped myself in a thick wool blanket that smelled like cedar shavings, and sat immobile on a chair, attempting to ignore the fact that my fingers and toes were numb. I'd lost all sensation in my hands and I probably should no longer dream of becoming an acclaimed artist; my paparazzi-filled life quickly becoming too farfetched.

Mom would normally be up and about by five in the evening no matter how ill she felt, to ensure we got our customary *merienda* (tea with toast or pastry). But five had come around and gone. No one was up, and Dad hadn't returned either. I was starved. And cold to boot. So, I dared go ask Mom, after carefully pushing open her door left ajar, whether I could… "Mami, puedo tomar…?" But she hadn't let me finish, assuming I was asking for tea. So, she'd responded barely audibly, "Yes, please go ahead. I'm sorry I can't come and fetch it for you just yet."

I could tell from her voice that she felt quite ill this day. I left her room, closing the door behind me.

And having all along heard that *un licorcito* (a bit o'liqueur) could do wonders to warm up the bones, I went into Mom's *armario* (sideboard), looked around for something that didn't look too awful, and among the various cognacs and vermouths, and a myriad of concoctions, I found a devastatingly handsome glass bottle that contained a thick and creamy yellow drink. One that on first sniff had smelt *absolutamente delicioso*. The seal broken; I filled the cap and took a gulp. I knew it was a drink all adults liked. Heck, I'd seen my uncles sip at it many-a-time. But I was oblivious as to its contents.

Initially, I'd hesitantly tried it, finding with surprise that it tasted plain and simply divine. Well, it burned like heck going down, and I bet my eyes were crossed by the time it reached my stomach, but boy-oh-boy, did it do the job. My eyelids sprung open and my nails had curled backwards, but when all was said and done I *had* warmed up. And talk about adding a pep to my step.

The blanket thrown aside, a couple of hours went by before Mom was up and about, and Dad returned, and had his radio going. Mom had come into the kitchen after she heard me attempting to sing along to Tom Jones' 'She's a Lady,' blaring on Dad's radio. And I was dancing too. Yes, I was shaking it—shaking it well! She was looking at me like something was wrong, and asked me if I had sufficient *merienda*, as she peeked around, unable to locate dirty cups or dishes.

And I'd looked at her, all sweet smiles and sleepy eyes, and told her that I hadn't eaten anything yet. Then, pointing to the console with my chin and mimicking a flying pattern with my hands as I grooved to the music, I took the opportunity to ask her: "So Mom, when you drink some of the thick liquid in the armario, does it feel like you're hovering around?"

She looked at me, her eyes now thin slits, trying to figure out exactly what I meant. She then opened the sideboard and said: "Exactly what thick liquid in the armario are you referring to?"

I'd come over and pulled forward the bottle that now sat, once again in the back of the stash, exactly where I'd found it. But nearly empty. Yup, I was hammered and sugared-up out of my mind. Juiced-up on the high alcohol content of *Zabaione* (highly spiked Italian eggnog).

And though my uncles teased me relentlessly after this episode, I never grew hair on my chest as they'd warned me I would, thank goodness. Yet, I slept quite like a baby that evening, ladies and gentlemen. Quite like a baby. Had to burn off that booze somehow.

***

Further towards year end, my most favorite teacher ever, Ms. Bellanti, caught a deadly form of meningitis during her pregnancy, her life and her unborn baby's in peril. We swapped substitute teachers every couple of days, a boring prospect while we optimistically waited for Ms. Bellanti's return.

I'd asked Mom to take me to the hospital to see her, but the reception desk told Mom over the phone that they would not allow us through. She was in the infectious diseases ward with no visitors allowed. I hadn't realized quite how bad her condition was. We were allowed to leave a message through the phone service, for her and her husband. And a week later, Mr. Bellanti stopped by my parents' home while I was at school, and had left a little gift for me. They owned a toy store downtown. When his wife learned about our message, she'd had him bring over a beautiful tiny doll…one I treasured for the longest time. By the way, in the end Ms. Bellanti and her baby did survive the scare though she didn't return to teach that year.

Meanwhile, spring arrived, and we were only a couple of months from the end of the school year. The weather was fantastic, and we itched to spend time outside. During class break, I'd finished my *Galletitas Manon* and then we'd run around so much, we were exhausted. We'd played *pilladita* (tag), and other favorite games (*pisa-pisuela* and the *farolera* very common for younger children down there). We were tired. But before we were free for the day, we'd get to learn how to write with fountain pens.

Mom had let me handpick a pen at the school supply store, and I could hardly wait until I was finally allowed to use it. The morning hours had seemed interminable, but the time had finally arrived, and I could swear I heard a drumroll. Our latest sub showed us how to insert the cartridge without making a mess, and let us start playing around to get a feel for it. And believe you me, I had found a new passion.

I am so enthralled with this marvel, that the hour flies by. It is now near noon, the end of our school day, when our pleasant calm is awakened by a deafening blow far to our right. Far, far beyond the school. It is followed by high-pitched ringing, so loud my classmates and I look at each other and cover our ears, terrified.

The next few moments go fast. A scattering rattle marches horizontally, from the left, under the floor. As it approaches my spot -next to the north wall dividing our classroom from the open patio- a huge blast lifts and suspends the floor under my seat, including the adjacent wall and ceiling. I hear the windows way above my head instantly shatter. Then a violent shake throws my head back, then forward, and as the floor, wall, and ceiling collapse down hard, my upper body plunges over my desk, and I hit my face so hard on the wooden desk surface, tears stream down my cheeks.

I'm crying, but realize no voice comes out of my mouth. Then I cover my head when I feel glass rain over me. I jump out of my seat to reach the door to the hallway, then I think about my little sister in first grade, her classroom door around the corner from my own. I have to get to the open patio and run to her, but another realization hits me: I can't hear a thing.

I run regardless, struggling to open way in the chaos, and before I reach the door, the right side of my head explodes in sharp pain while I feel blood dripping down the back of my throat. I feel more rattling under my feet and hear screams and hollow thumps against the walls and roof. I can hear again, though I would rather not.

I finally reach the door, and it does not take long for my mind to recognize the source of the commotion. I look out and above, and my eyes follow a giant plume of thick smoke, both black and white, reaching the sky north of the school, where smaller yet loud explosions continue to burst, burn, and whistle. As my eyes start dropping to the ground, the sight is that of shattered glass and charred items scattered throughout the lawn and flower beds. The sky is dark, and falling off of it like snow are burning pieces of plastic, cardboard, and…stuff. Afraid, I hold my hands together behind my back and walk around slowly, terrified, trying to identify what I see. Then I come to a stop, startled, and stand next to a small nest resting on the ground, two tiny birds lying within, immobile.

Once again, I am deaf. This time my mind appears to block away all sounds as I turn around, staring, while everyone runs and bumps into me, but no one stops. All moves either too fast or in slow motion, and I must swivel my head to the left as some sort of projectile approaches rapidly from the north.

I can only see what is happening, while all my other senses appear muted. I feel heat rising within me while strong gas-like fumes burn my nostrils. Then an overwhelming scent of blood descends on me, and a hollow feeling takes over my stomach. I press my inky hands over my nose and mouth to avoid inhaling further, attempting to push away or quickly swallow the taste of bile inundating my senses. There are screams of panic all around me, then realize I can hear once again.

I see grief stricken neighboring parents, the priests, a nun, and congregation members arriving from all directions, all trying to corral and shelter us children. I feel frozen in place, but I hear my name called and recognize Mom's voice. I half turn to see her running towards me while pulling my younger sister in tow. My sister -the scene around us had distracted me. Now a warm relief washes over me. But Norma's pinafore is partly wet and bloody. I look at her face for clues and notice the aftermath of tears over dirt or soot. Her chubby hands are bloody and I stare at her, wondering for a moment whether she is hurt or simply filthy with whatever is all around us. The horror on my face makes Mom realize what I'm thinking. She tells me Norma is fine, then she grabs my hand, pressing hard, almost hurting, and starts to run towards the avenue, dragging us behind, as we try not to fall while she quickly attempts to get us across the school yard, the road, and on to home.

I don't know how much time has passed since the explosions, but getting across the road is no easy task -it is blocked by vehicles, both civilian, police, and military. Further down the road there are fires, and the air is thick with smoke, reaching us, and overwhelming us. The sight is that of pure chaos. There is yelling, and sirens, and crying. And though we are so close to our front door and can't wait to reach it, Mom tells us to allow the emergency vehicles to get through first. In my confusion as we wait by the curve, I look inside an ambulance through its open back door and see several individuals, their bodies charred from head to toe, one bleeding from his ear, his eyes staring at me without blinking. That image will remain forever engraved in my mind.

I purposely look further towards the base, and see traffic is blocked to buses and other automobiles whose occupants have witnessed the explosions as they approached. They are now being detoured. But getting through in any direction is impossible, and many people are abandoning their vehicles and running instead, towards us, and the explosion site.

Mom manages to get us across and to our sidewalk. Alicia is already there, waiting for us. Within minutes, three of my uncles show up to ensure we are safe. They've ridden their bikes at an unnatural speed from their job locations across town and against the current, upon hearing news that *the guerrillas* had detonated a bomb at the Pacífico fireworks factory just blocks from our home.

Mom is in hysterics when she learns about injured friends and acquaintances, and clings on to uncle Juan, while uncle Mocho checks Norma for signs of injury, and aunt Pepa's husband walks around our house checking for damage, making sure it is safe for us to return inside. Our home is solid brick and mortar – all exterior walls, twelve inches thick. It'd take a lot to bring it down. But the heavy iron-framed windows on the north side, namely our living room and kitchen, have slid off the wall supports and hang down from a corner. They were literally blown off by the impact, the glass shattered, as is the glass on our front door.

But we were all safe, together, and the uncles stayed with us until Dad finally made it home -from out of town- a while later. Then all the adults together with an engineer client of Dad's checked the surroundings again to ensure the house was not structurally compromised any further.

***

The factory employed hundreds of people regularly. It was an ongoing source of income for many families in the immediate surroundings. Anyone old enough to be employed was sure to find a job on site, and it wasn't uncommon for two or more family members to work side by side. And suddenly most, if not all, were feared dead. Including my schoolmates' parents, grandparents, and siblings.

The building and the massive wall surrounding the property crumbled -a crater replaced the old landmark. The homes surrounding the site were severely damaged, and so was the road running alongside it. Our road. Later that week, funeral services were held dawn to dusk for the fallen workers and neighbors who perished in the attack.

October was the peak time for the factory, merely two months before the New Year. They'd just hired extra workers to keep up with the season's demand. The owners, the Pacífico brothers from the L'Aquila region in Italy had migrated to Argentina and settled in the area in 1916. They'd run a single firework stand that over the years gathered so much demand, the poor migrants barely managed to secure enough funds to purchase land and build themselves a factory. A factory that over the years fed much of the lower boroughs. A factory that never opened again after this day.

They had arrived by ship, poor as church mice, with literally nothing but the clothes on their shoulders, an old and wholly jacket with newspapers handsewn inside to stop the cold, and little wool hats. They never imagined they'd create an empire for the poor. Nor that a lifetime of hard work could -or would- literally, come crumbling down within seconds.

To my knowledge, the guerrillas never claimed the atrocity. Guerrillas were -in many instances- blamed for mass loss of life when in fact, many of these attempts were orchestrated by the military and disguised as terrorist attacks, with the purpose of turning everyday folks against the *liberation militias.* Clarification: anyone who opposed the military regime was categorized as militia, guerrilla, or extremist, no matter whether actively operating in antigovernment activities or not.

***

Nineteen seventy-four had brought news from Spain about Peron's illness, later followed by his passing, in July. And with it all, there was an openly recognized revolution in the making. The restrictions felt closer and tighter, and folks all around us speculated on where things were headed.

I didn't understand the arguments, nor the reasons Mom tried giving us, as to why at the moment we couldn't visit Grandma and Grandpa as often as we'd like. Political groups rose in protest and rioted in the downtown area, near my grandparent's home. Free movement within the city was monitored and often blocked.

***

Alicia came up with a tooth infection towards the back of her mouth. She felt quite miserable for a couple of days and Mom was desperately attempting to get her in to see a dentist. At the time there weren't many of them in town, and when they briefly blessed us with a practice, the field appeared dominated by Russian and Jewish professionals. The former were not the most personable, the latter not very decisive nor outspoken.

Without many choices other than rushing her to the ER at the public hospital (not a favored environment back then), Mom was able to get her in, immediately, to see a Dr. Cherenkov. They rushed over to ensure she was taken care of right away. Back in the day in such instances, most of the time the only solution given was to extract the tooth, rather than to repair it. And as expected, the doctor had moved ahead with the extraction.

Alicia was sedated, operated on, and shortly after, sent home. Only to wake up in the middle of the night when the anesthetics had started to wear off, in even worse condition than before, her face swollen beyond recognition. Mom had then had no option but to rush her to the ER, where they discovered that the doctor had pulled the wrong tooth! So later that morning Alicia was sent home once again, now without a second tooth. Two for one is usually a good deal, but not in this case. The event did nothing for her future confidence in the medical profession.

***

Then Norma had gotten quite sick, and we learned she had contracted hepatitis. She was considerably small, but gave Mom such a hard time when she was due to take meds, always resorting to extremes to avoid the nasty preparation at any cost.

I recall one day she'd run outside and into Dad's shop, and crawled under Dad's beloved Gordini, thinking Mom would let her be. This girl had no clue who Mom was, nor did she recall that Mom had raised many-a-child before we graced this world with our presence. Or that Mom was astute and agile enough to chase after anyone just as any athlete could.

So, this is how it went down.

Mom was trying to keep us in separate rooms for an eternity and prepped special meals for Norma, hoping that my sister would cooperate. The whole situation was getting so ridiculous with Norma threatening that she'd smack her head against the wall if Mom came any closer with the medicine. Mom invited her to go ahead and see if that would make her feel better. To Norma's surprise, the wall turned out to be of solid brick, and brilliant lil sis got a huge bump on her forehead. Somehow, she'd expected the pain and punishment would go to Mom, and learned very soon, yet a tad late, that she'd been wrong in her assumption.

Then Norma had run out and managed to get under a car in Dad's shop, at which time Mom also crawled under it, pulled and dragged Norma out. The car was parked in *the one spot* of the shop which Dad had not floored yet, so the two of them came out from under it all covered in mud and car oil muck, and goodness only knows what else. If not for the size difference, no one would have been clever enough to differentiate one from the other. Mom grabbed her by one arm and drew her back into the house, Norma fighting back all along. Mom's patience was waning, so she gave her a literal kick in the caboodle. Norma tried getting on my Mom's case for it, but Mom seized her mean-spirited little neck and hauled her in, marching her straight into the bathroom and placing her sorry little ass under the freezing shower. Norma started to scream. Poor Mom had had it, so she pinched her jaw tightly, forcing her mouth open while she emptied the little glass bubble containing the foul liquid right into her mouth. Then left her to continue her high-pitched ranting. And gagging.

Norma was famous for throwing tantrums. Her temper was more like a couple of tempers. She'd go on about anything and everything…particularly when Dad would go somewhere and would not take her along. Or anytime she did not get her way, no matter how unreasonable.

Mom looked entirely exhausted and ready to cry. Once Norma's hysterics dwindled down, Mom walked back into the bathroom, patiently washed her, dried her, wrapped her in a warm robe, and tucked her in for a nap.

And just as she prepared for a well-deserved shower, the phone rang, and she received word that Grandpa was not well. She quickly readied herself to go see after her parents before night fell.

Mom was always the first to be called. She knew the family dynamics best and there was no one, NO-ONE else who acted more practically, nor as efficiently. She called Tío Juan and Tío Mocho on her way out, asking them to meet her at *la casa* (Grandma's house) in twenty minutes. She also asked Aunt Alicia to *make* the doctor meet with them all in exactly thirty minutes, also at Grandma's house.

Thankfully, Grandpa was not as sick as they all feared. The doctor adjusted his medicine and within a matter of hours he felt better and even enjoyed his dinner and fell asleep in brief. Mom made it home late that evening having caught the last bus returning from downtown to the station near our home. She'd sat at the table to eat her first bite of the day and had fallen asleep in the process. Dad found her in the middle of the night when he'd gotten up for work, and had quickly tucked her into their bed, and reset and brought the alarm clock into our bedroom to ensure Alicia and I did not sleep through it and missed school.

***

For Mom and Dad's 15th wedding anniversary on September 12th, the whole family was invited to spend the day at our home.

The weather turned out gorgeous and cooperative.

Dad had just renovated the shop and had cleared and decorated it entirely. It looked and smelled brand-spanking-new. He'd acquired a massive grill where he and my uncles prepared *asado* (Argentinian barbeque) for the masses. Chairs and tables were set all the way around the large shop floor. The men had arrived early to season the meats and begin the grilling.

Mom had made salads, and helped Grandma make empanadas and bake breads...they'd both labored all morning, sporting their matching kimono-like full-fronted aprons Mom had just sewn the previous week.

We had a cake and two million or so petit fours catered and brought in. Everyone showed with presents and different delectable dishes to share. The adults played folklore music, and we'd all danced until our feet hurt. The day had been one of fun and unity.

Everyone was happy and had a blast, yet some poor old and bored soul came up with a daring challenge and organized a foot race for all things male. My uncles stopped and deviated traffic at the busiest time of day, for three blocks no less, to accomplish the foolish competition. They'd told the bus drivers and others circulating our busy street that traffic was cut due to an ongoing investigation. And my uncles (who carried the storytelling gene) had been not only believed but even thanked for the warning...

And so the games began.

Some had been skeptical to participate, having eaten and drunk well beyond advisable. Some were too slow or too tired and sleepy (too old, really). Yet in the end they all ran, to the delight of the audiences (meaning, the whole neighborhood). Afterwards, Dad had brought out some large canvas bags and rope, and there they'd gone again in a three-legged race, the third legs well wrapped and tied to ensure no cheating, though there had been plenty of it regardless.

They'd all argued and fallen, and several even struggled to get up. The races having gone on until there were enough winners so that no one felt defeated or inadequate, though there had been plenty of both here as well. They were all given a fair chance, whether long-legged, short-legged, or bow-legged. Even the priests came out to watch once the loud cheers and laughter had drifted into their offices from the otherwise usually quiet road.

Mid-afternoon came and all lunch remains were cleaned from the tables which were reset for the attendees to share *mate*, tea, coffee, and one or another shot of strong liquor—the drink of their choice. All while the sweet dishes were set out, admired, and partaken of to everyone's delight. And this portion of the celebration had included the Montserrat priests, who had ultimately decided to join-in after the hard laughs at the races.

And Grandma, encouraged by her paisano clerics, had gathered a following of proportion as she expertly whispered more stories of the past, particularly her adventures at sea in her childhood days, though now imparted with the wisdom of a lifetime. And she'd been playfully teased by the vicars, but had also been herself tickled at her ability to quickly turn around all lines of questioning that may have sewn any doubt about her cleverly told escapades. The story had been long and intricate, both tangled and detangled at great lengths, and the spectators -priests included- had thoroughly enjoyed her wit, and clapped and whistled for a while at her ingenuity. And she'd once again, bowed down to her adoring audience.

And when the time came for everyone's departure, they'd all helped to set things right.

In the process of carrying numerous items back into the house, I lifted a heavy chair which I carried for a few feet before

Mom and Dad's dog, Toby, had been scared off by famous cousin Caíto setting off a firecracker.

The dog darted from his perch, quickly making his escape back into the house. I was in its path and in his hype and terror trying to pass me, the chubby mass solidly hit my legs just so that I was lifted in the air, chair and all, and dropped on the cement. My tailbone was the first part of my body to make contact with the hard ground. I was in such pain; I could not get up nor walk. Dad rushed to me and lifted me, bringing me in to lay down on my bed. No one thought the pain which lingered a bit would ever be the cause of issues, however, in my grown years, I came to suffer from it greatly during my pregnancies -I could not sit or walk for long, but only crawl around in unbearable pain. And embarrassment. Then, much later-on in life, I learned my tailbone had been fractured, causing ailments that affected my spine when I approached my senior years.

But no more painful had it been for me, than for good-ol' Toby when, at his mature age, while napping under a car, he was run over by one of Dad's customers as he backed out of Mom and Dad's driveway. The dog could barely move any longer due to age, and this had left him entirely crippled. The veterinarian on call—the only one around, really—wanted to charge an exuberant amount of money to "try" to fix him. An amount Mom and Dad did not have in reserve and truly could not afford. We were all so very sad thinking Toby met his fate.

Then Dad quickly decided what the dog needed and built a made-to-size wheelchair for the pup, a sort of quad-wheeled aid not in existence at the time. The dog fit it to perfection, and although at the start he hesitated about it and plainly refused to get up and try moving around, he eventually had gotten a handle on it and successfully overcame his fear. He wheeled himself around, even at faster speeds than he could on his own and in his younger years.

Toby eventually healed completely and was no longer dependent on it. The only thing he'd never been able to manage on wheels were turns. Once he picked up speed, he had a tough time making corners and would spin around in an attempt to conquer the maneuver. He also would quickly look back and bark loudly as this happened, thinking someone was pushing him from behind. Dad was a genius though.

Shortly after the gathering, Grandpa's health took quite a downturn. He was hospitalized, leaving Grandma home alone amid the city's turmoil. My uncles took turns accompanying Grandpa overnight the first few nights of his stay at the hospital. Mom then insisted she'd also spend the night by his side, while her sisters retrieved Grandma from the family home to ensure she was not left alone for long. They had quickly put together a schedule which would rotate her among the different households for as long as needed. Thank goodness for big families.

Grandpa was released from the hospital just two weeks before the holidays, and although the events went on without a hitch, and he was exceedingly happy to be home and enjoying the season's celebrations, we couldn't but notice that a dark cloud was slowly creeping over his usually lively character.

***

Christmas day I was to receive my first communion. Montserrat was hosting a massive First Communion Fete. I had finished my catechism classes, learned all my prayers and scriptures, passed the test, and was all ready for it. Wanted it over with, quite honestly.

Of course, the day was hot and humid. We had stayed at Grandma's place after the Christmas Eve grand celebration and slept no more than a couple of hours before Mom woke me along Dad, to take us back home for the ceremony. Doña Milagros, a neighbor, waited for me early to do my hair. She did it so beautifully, it looked shiny and gorgeous. Mom had made my dress and card purse, a beautiful confection of cotton lace fabric (white broderie anglaise). Absolutely darling. Mom had also bought me all white socks, shoes, gloves, undergarments, a rosary, and my very own prayer booklet. This was one of the very few times in my childhood when I did not get to wear any refitted hand-me-downs as part of the overall assemblage. And I'd felt quite special. Bruised tailbone and all.

When Argentine children receive their first communion, they carry (or at least they did during the last century), a stack of remembrance cards stating their names, and the date of their first communion. These were blessed by the priest during the ceremony, then later in the day, during their first communion gathering or while visiting acquaintances, the child gifted friends and relatives the cards, and in turn the recipient gave a small gift. My remembrance cards were so lovely, I had a hard time giving them away.

One thing I received early on during my catechism attendance, which I can say with all confidence not everyone gets out of the course, was head lice. And Mom was LIVID.

My catechism class was taught by Julia, a girl in our neighborhood. She was the youngest of many siblings, and the only girl in her family. Her dad and brothers sold coal from their side yard. Back then many folks used coal to cook, heat water, and for home heating. I remember each morning hearing the truck that delivered large loads of coal into their yard. As the truck drove away, the large black pile could be seen above the rooftops of the surrounding homes. It was often completely sold out and carried away by mid-afternoon.

I believe Julia lost her mother at an early age. She looked after the house, her dad, and brothers. She was beautiful and sweet, a fervent catholic, and a hard worker.

Along with several of my school classmates and some neighboring children, the class was also open to children from the village surrounding the train tracks, many of whom did not attend school regularly, hence could not read nor write. Nor could they shower nor change clothes often, as there was no power nor running water in the land their families had settled upon. No matter the season, their situation was dire.

From June to August, *catequismo* classes were held indoors. By then long gone were the days when our lessons would be taught sitting around the church's little raised planting beds, or under the shade of a tree. As winter weather settled in, the rain and freezing breeze forced us into the smaller school classrooms the priests unlocked exclusively for our use each Saturday.

We were taught by different means, allowing even those who could not read nor write to understand and retain the material. Once inside and away from the elements, we were asked to sit up in a circle and listen. Needless to say, I loved it. There were visual aids (large drawings Julia prepared and even handed out) and discussion of scriptures much of which was done in storytelling style which I welcomed - I was well accustomed to the scenario thanks to Grandma's tale-telling sessions.

In my class, there were a couple of girls who everyone always avoided. They attended in grimy, smelly clothing, their hair oily and clumped with unidentifiable matter. And when invited to come closer to the circle, they'd hesitated, fully aware of their predicament.

They'd looked around for someone to invite them in. Twice. And now, on their third try, fully knowing it would be their last, I could not imagine how much this was hurting their feelings, so, when they looked in my direction, I had half-smiled, and they'd both come around and sat one to each side of me. And they'd seemed so happy and had participated in every single game and prayer from that moment forward. Julia noticed this, and as the class ended, she'd asked me to stay behind, to tell me how much she had appreciated my reaction. She'd even noticed when the other kids had moved further away as the girls approached, and I had almost retched a couple of times, but as much as I wanted to, I could not have moved away from them and broken their hearts. And honestly, before I noticed, I was talking with them, and laughing, and singing along, and not understanding why others could or would not do the same. Then, I noticed how the youngest had the prettiest brown eyes and freckles, and her older sister carried herself with a warm calm most folks would not perceive unless they closely approached her.

So, after nearly half day sitting next to them, I went home happy, but scratching wildly.

Mom had pulled me aside to check what in the world was the cause of my behavior, and discovered that the girls had shared with me much more than I bargained for. Mom found half dozen lice happily going for a stroll among my locks, and I'd been banned from getting close to my sisters for a couple of weeks. I was told that I was lucky we were on winter vacation so I needn't be kept from school and from the mere embarrassment of it all.

I never heard the end of it. But little did Mom know that I already considered myself lucky. Because Ms. Julia said one day I'd get to see Jesus as reward for my good deed.

***

For Grandma and Grandpa's 50th wedding anniversary (December 27th, 1974) Mom arranged for the main priest then residing at Montserrat to travel to the Porta's home to preside over a celebration mass.

Grandpa felt ill, but was very alert and as full of expectation as he'd ever been on a grand family event. Halfway sitting, halfway lying on his bed, he managed to remain awake and cheerful, never minding nor sharing his pain and anxiety. He'd looked handsome in a light-colored plaid shirt and white bow tie, happily staring around at all the movement and preparation. And often paused to take a long look at each of the numerous little grandchildren brought to his side and taking turns to softly embrace him and shower him with butterfly kisses.

Grandma, donning her best dress and pearls, her mother's only worldly possession brought from Spain (which had lasted through many rainy days by now), sat next to Grandpa as Padre Vicente Zueco Vázquez de Zaragoza (a mouthful, I know, and another Spanish name longer than a prayer for the poor) officiated to the crowd of family, neighbors, and acquaintances spilling out of the rooms and on the patio and side yard. So much family, so much love, and so many arms ready to hug and love them both, brought many to tears that day. The priest stayed with the family throughout the celebration, glad he had agreed to Mom's request. Years after, Padre Vicente still remembered the day, anytime he returned for a visit at Montserrat and ran across the street to hug and chat with Mom and Dad.

The Padre (a beauty in disguise) was a favorite of the ladies. He looked quite like the Spanish singer Camilo Sesto (before plastic surgery—I mean the singer, not the priest). Padre VZ was entirely unaware how the faithful females at Montserrat (young to old) felt about his presence at our place of worship. And worship they did, boy oh boy, and Our Lady of Montserrat could not point a finger at them because truth be told, she herself more than likely counted him among her own favorite Padres.

CHAPTER 9

A Sense of Loss

Nineteen seventy-five arrived, sadly, with more worries about Grandpa. His diabetes onset causing various complications, and a couple of amputations. He was sent home to recoup, though we sensed the end was near. That year the summer was not very generous in warmth, and the start of school seemed to arrive earlier than normal.

Mom was worried sick about Grandpa, but she kept the care scheduling and all her soldiers marching to the beat. Grandma and aunt María looked after him during the morning to early afternoon hours when Grandma switched from nursing to knitting, and aunt María headed out to the beauty parlor for her daily hair and skin treatments. Meanwhile Mom would religiously make her way over each day the moment we finished lunch, she'd done dishes, and made sure our homework was well on its way to completion. She often offered to bring us along as well, and I'd agreed a few times only to notice the house was now kept at a much more reverent volume and pace, the curtains often closed to keep out the outside brightness which may trigger Grandpa's migraines.

Greetings and updates aside, Grandma sat comfortably in one corner, at arm's length from the tall footboard, the only sound, that of knitting needles clicking against each other, and her humming to a motherland tune. Mom sat next to Grandpa for hours on end, also attempting to distract her mind by reading, but often just staring into the dark corners of the room, between waiting on Grandpa's needs and wants. Anymore when he spoke, he did so very calmly, just for Mom to hear. And Mom would tear up and let the sad and warm moisture roll down her cheeks while Grandpa cycled through highs and lows and napped the afternoon away. He'd often tell her that anymore he could only sleep when she was around, teasing that Grandma's soft knitting no longer held the same spell. And Mom hurried to his side to hold his hand and nurse him, until the dark reigned again and he fell in deep slumber. Then, Mom headed home and one of her brothers took over for the overnight shift.

***

Grandpa passed away a cold and dark June afternoon, shortly after Mom left him resting under Grandma's and uncle Ernesto's ministrations. She'd felt Grandpa wasn't so responsive that day, but she needed to rush home earlier than usual to prepare for a doctor's appointment early the next day. She hadn't felt well as of late.

Wearily, she'd stumbled all the way to the bus stop, some blocks away from the Porta's house, letting the unsympathetic, sharp breeze, shower over her features as a means to cool her worried soul. All along telling herself that 'tomorrow' she'd make up for lost time with him.

She'd arrived half frozen at the bus stop on Avenida Sarmiento, and had waited endlessly under the shelter of the large entrance to the winery. Then the ride had taken about twenty minutes; but it'd felt like hours.

She'd made the trip home without feeling the chill entering the dilapidated bus at each stop, nor caring enough to mind the booze-filled breaths from the two young men sitting immediately behind her. As much as she'd always hated alcohol stench and drunken fools, she thought that perhaps drinking herself to oblivion this one time might help her mood. She was lost in thought when she realized her stop was coming up. Standing now, and hanging on to the grimy safety bar above her head, she built courage to face the elements again. She rang the bell, tires screeched, then the pliant door opened in front of her, loud and irreverent.

Winter and public transport did not mix well.

We were all seating at the table finishing up homework while Dad enjoyed a cup of mate and warm bread. She unlocked our front door, closing it swiftly behind her to stop the rush of wind chasing after her. She'd looked exhausted again. Or perhaps still.

The phone rang as she finished pulling off her coat. She turned and looked at it as if wishing that ignoring it would make it stop. Alicia jumped forward, asking whether she should answer it, but Mom smiled and waved her off, then took the one step that brought her next to the receiver, and picked up the call. We heard uncle Ernesto's voice on the other side. There was a pause. Then she turned her back to us, sobbing and pleading, *"No, please don't say that...please don't."* She cried for a moment covering her face, then puddled down on to the floor as we watched, still.

Dad ran to her, taking and placing the receiver back. Then he got down on the floor next to her, hugging her tight, telling her that everything would be okay. He whispered that he knew the pain she felt. And he meant it. He truly did. Then they cried quietly together, her head on his lap just like a child, while he ran his rough hands through her hair, and his fingers in slow circles over her back and shoulders.

He helped her to bed, to allow her to release her ache in solitude, and to rest. Mom was never the type to deliver excessive show of emotion in public. To her -much like to me- doing so can border on uncomfortable to spectators, hence should be kept behind private doors. Though extremely reserved and concerned about propriety, Mom was quite a sensitive soul. She wore her love deep under many layers of caution and toughness. I think she was molded so during her years as a young little hen caring for her numerous sibling chicks.

Dad covered her and left the room, closing the door quietly behind him. And donning his coat, he kissed the top of our heads and told us to keep an eye on her and handle dinner, while he ran over to the Portas' to see how he could be of help. He also said not to wait up for him.

We finished our homework battling tears. That evening Alicia deep fried scrumptious *Lampreados* (battered spicy beef filets), and she and I had eaten in silence, tasting nothing but the purest of sorrows. I couldn't imagine the family without Grandpa -we weren't prepared for it. How could we be? I thought about it for a while, and stayed up late trying to read though I could not get my mind to quiet down enough to focus.

Then I'd seen Dad finally return, also wiping tears, long, long…long after midnight. And my heart had twisted for him. My throat had the biggest, bitterest knot, when I'd seen his red and swollen eyes as I headed to bed. He'd told me that I better sleep soon because we needed to be up early, and ready to go. That we had a tough day ahead.

***

Grandpa had been the father figure Dad needed and missed his entire youth. They had loved and respected each other very much for twenty years. And Dad had now also lost his second loving father. He was so heartbroken, and only trying to keep it together for Mom because he knew this would be a hard hit to her.

For many years since, each time we visited Grandma's house, I saw Dad make prolonged visits to the room where Grandpa had spent a great deal of his down time: his shop and storage space. It held a widespread compilation of odd finds. Yes, any and all were guaranteed to locate one or another treasure within its walls -should one receive permission to go seeking.

El cuarto was dark. Thick, primitive lumber dyed by age lined the back wall which held long shelves. And thin columns of dust could be spotted swirling below the lonely low volt globe that lingered above a tall makeshift counter. Grandpa could always be found behind it, tending to one or another artifact, and to all visitors who dared enter. He exerted the pride of a tradesman readying to barter.

What I remember most was the scent of rusty—decaying— metal, oil cans, and the look of old, foggy glass bottles lined up against the walls tallest to shortest, fattest to thinnest. And the most intricate assortment of iron bars, leather straps, nuts and bolts, and many peculiar contraptions.

***

This is the coldest June I recall.

We all had quite a hard time accepting Grandpa was gone. Mom was consumed by a deep grief -she mourned long and greatly, to the point we all worried. She'd cared for Grandpa exclusively all those years while he worked alone to make sure the bulk of his children -and when possible, even his friends' children- had all they needed.

Even after married and away, she baked treats and called on her brothers to stop by, retrieve, and get them to Grandpa before they cooled. Like the little soldiers they were, she was never refused by them. They knew better than to challenge her requests.

Mom and Grandpa enjoyed the same things and had understood each other well, often confiding their deepest thoughts and hopes for the future. And shortly before leaving this world, he had asked her to keep the family united, always. That is who and what she had been to him: the glue that would hold them together.

***

Mortuaries did not exist, at least not for the poor. Back then, anyway. Visitation and *misa de cuerpo presente* (funeral mass) were held at private residences during the twenty-four-hour vigil.

This became the first of many viewings at Grandma's house. And though overtaken by sorrow and having always let "the men do as they wish" in all family affairs, to everyone's surprise, Grandma made sure she had a say in all arrangements.

All furniture removed to allow sufficient space, *el comedor* (the formal dining area, the first room of the house), was opened to the public.

Grandpa's casket was finished in dark brown lacquer, with heavy, lavish handles of shiny silver that comically reflected people's figures when they approached and retreated. I think he would have liked it, had he a say in the matter.

Centered in the room, it was flanked by six ornate walnut and solid brass candle holders, each taller and thicker than I was at the time. A live-sized solid-brass image of Jesus on the cross stood on the floor at the head of the casket; the cross' exterior edge donning incandescent purple lights.

And at the very entrance of the room sat a flamboyant stand matching the cross' style but resembling a voting booth, where folks in attendance could opt to sign their names on the remembrance book, or insert their personal cards -a common practice at the time.

On second thought, I believe Grandpa would have laughed at it all. He would have thought it very Spanish-like and would probably say the only thing missing was a small purse passed around for contributions to the cause. Grandpa was a simple man, but was being sent off in quite a grand way.

The smell of wax, flowers, and incense were overpowering, and generally meant to camouflage the stench of a decomposing body, normally the case in summer wakes, as bodies were not embalmed then (nor are they now in most cases). The scent assistance was not needed this time around though, given the season, and temperature. I must remark that none of this fore-thought was particularly done by us nor just for us, but as the time and custom mandated.

Shortly before the welders arrived to seal the interior metal box of the casket, tiny uncle Ángel brought Grandma forward for her to offer the first farewell. Then Grandpa's progeny stepped forward one by one in the order they were born, as they did mostly everything. Grandpa wouldn't have had it any other way.

I had never seen my uncles cry except when bursting into tears laughing at each other's silliness. Witnessing their deep sadness as they approached the coffin, I honestly believe that at the tender age of ten, I could hear my heart breaking. They each resembled little boys competing for his attention, gently caressing his hands, fixing his lapel, polishing his cufflinks, and finding any reason to stay close a moment longer.

Grandpa entered heaven in his best—though overworn—pewter winter suit. But not before each sibling solemnly stepped forward, kissed his forehead and cheeks, and murmured a loving farewell for only him to hear.

He passed on June 9th, 1975, and was laid to rest the cold afternoon of June 10th. The sun had shone brightly earlier in the chill of the day, but suddenly the skies turned their dark angriness on us. We were followed en route to the cemetery by a roaring chorus of thunder. A bolt of lightning struck the far end of the city as our car procession came to a stop on the bridge leading to downtown, before proceeding to the burial ground road ahead. Right at the precise point where the railroads crossed underneath, and also at precisely four o'clock, the time Grandpa's shift was normally over after his trips out of town, his coworkers led a repertoire of engine whistles marking his last ride by the station, and his final shift among us.

***

It was my first opportunity ever to enter one of the town's cemeteries. Grandpa, as a railroad worker, was laid to rest at Sociedad del Empleado, rather than at *Societá Italiana*, which was where half or more of the folks we knew were kept after passing. The remaining half went to *Sociedad Española*, and very few to the Muslim cemetery, unless the family owned a private mausoleum at the Israeli cemetery.

Sociedad del Empleado was one of the huge multilevel buildings erected at this peace field. The exterior bore quite a resemblance to a large brick office building or church, except there were very few windows. Inside, there were many levels above and below ground, with a wide center stairwell connecting all floors. Each level was divided by floor to ceiling hollow structures about twelve feet deep (two-caskets' deep). The structures stood in rows and aisles and while empty, could be accessed from one or the other side. The space within was broken into hundreds of cubbies, each meant to house one casket. Coffins were placed head-in into each niche, before elaborate marble plaques were cemented over, sealing each enclosure. These plaques contained the same details and photos a regular ground grave would display for visitors.

Upon entering the main level, most walls were already filled with caskets and sealed, first come, first serve style. As far and high as one could see, the caskets were artfully arranged in their allocated space. Grandpa had been assigned a space immediately below the main floor.

After that day I visited with Mom a few times. She always stopped by for Father's Day and for Grandpa's birthday. I don't think I ever got used to the eerie feeling that arose within me when I looked around and all I felt surrounded-by was death, side to side, above and below. Also, each time I visited I counted how many steps it took to reach the main entrance again. My biggest fear had always been to get locked-in at sunset, when the massive burial buildings were closed for the evening to deny ingress to unsavory characters that raided easily accessible graves during the night hours in search of valuables.

I also feared the electricity would go out while we were inside, without a window to light the way or secure an escape. All of it encompassed a truly remarkable sight and feel for an easily impressionable child.

Some years later, the cemetery had dug out so much of the ground and built up so much within its perimeter, the water level started to rise within the burial buildings. Eventually all floors below ground level had to be cemented in, though not before the families keeping loved ones within were notified and had an opportunity to retrieve and relocate their loved ones' remains. Many could not afford to do so, but Mom, Uncle Mocho and Uncle Juan had taken care of this on Grandpa's behalf long before she and Uncle Juan passed away.

I should remark that as I near completion of this story, Uncle Mocho is still alive. He is now ninety-one years old, to date the longest living Porta sibling, although he is not the only clan member still alive.

***

Alicia's 15th birthday was approaching. Mom and Dad had had many plans for a celebration, particularly rushing to finish up a renovation and expansion to the original house built by Dad. But Grandpa had just passed and all construction was halted. They were also in the process of postponing the gathering.

I recall a couple of my uncles showing at our home one late evening to "find out what the plans were". They pretty much knew what Mom was up to. She'd informed them she had already talked it over with Dad and Alicia, and they had agreed to delay it until mourning ended a year later.

My uncles advised her that the rest of the family had also spoken about it. They felt Grandpa would not have wanted to put a halt to our get-togethers. This was a time to cherish family more than ever.

It'd taken a bit to convince Mom, but the plan moved swiftly forward after that. There was no lavish Quinceañera celebration, but a rather cozy gathering. The whole family attended, as well as a few of Alicia's friends from school. The night was chilly. All attendees packed into the space, much of it still under construction, and had a real nice time together.

***

The rest of fifth grade went by fast. We were home at the latest by 12:30 each day. Mom had our lunch ready, and we'd eat while watching Gilligan's Island. Dad and I normally sat at either end of the table and chatted. When Grandma was around, the three of us told each other jokes, wiggled our brows, pulled faces, and laughed. The purest of innocence and silliness.

We gradually got used to Grandpa being absent from our reunions, though the conversation always kept him among us. No matter what we did, his memory was still so freshly embedded in all of us, we couldn't help but expect him to walk back into our lives anytime we gathered. Thankfully, his absence did not take away our eagerness to meet, reminisce, and continue to create memories.

Grandma and Grandpa's house would forever remain witness to the most cherished times of our lives. To this day, I often remember our visits and stays. Upon entering -although the house has undergone many renovations and changes over the years- there are still scents and sounds that bring me back to those childhood days. Also, when I visit, I almost expect Mom to appear, sending me to the corner store to purchase some forgotten item needed for an evening gathering.

The store was run by immigrants though I could not tell where they came from -they spoke a very different dialect. An old widow and her two bachelor sons. The lady was half deaf, but fully loud and mean, and both men appeared to have suffered polio or some sort of palsy. It often made me wonder how these folks passed the scrutiny of the immigration officers which were notorious for rejecting and sending back any number of people.

The eldest son was a short character who wore high-waisted pants reaching his armpits and highlighting his swollen belly and total lack of rear end; and a shirt always buttoned to the neck no matter how high the summer heat. Suspenders, and thick, grimy eyeglasses completed his ensemble. His legs were so bowed he waddled as he walked, almost on his ankle bone. He also wore so much cologne, I found it difficult to keep my eyes from burning when he approached.

His brother was a mean being, almost completely blind. He sported a makeshift peg-leg with a rectangular base, to which he attached a large shoe stuffed with something. He wore capri-like pants, though capris did not exist back then. His style of choice for bottoms was rather known as *flood pants.*

Their store always thrived, the family did well, frequently expanding to the immediately neighboring lots on either side as they convinced landowners to sell out their properties. Back then and still today, corner lots always were considered better (and more expensive), particularly for businesses, given the double road exposure. Those who could afford them, and additional expansion, were heavily rewarded financially. A far cry from the crammed courtyards of the slums where most immigrants started up and often remained for life, both in Argentina and abroad.

Passing by the Donato's home on my way back was another visual adventure. Another Italian family residing just two houses down from Grandma and Grandpa's. The father and his children were musicians employed by the town's philharmonic. Christmastime I recall standing directly outside their home, staring in awe at the beautifully decorated cypresses flanking the arched front entrance, and the always lively and well-maintained front yard where I marveled at the playful display of cactus and succulents, and the site of colorful flowering cauliflower and exotic species. In this I was not alone. My cousins reacted the same way when they walked by this wonder. In our dreamy faces someone could always read: *One day, that will be my home.*

Back at Grandma's house, the tidy flower beds were well kept (mostly by aunt María) but they were not fancy and plush, rather purely and satisfyingly sweet and proper. The bed borders were simple red bricks with domed tops, just as those used in the public squares throughout the city back then (and in many instances, thankfully, still today).

Interestingly, in my older years I found them everywhere in the older streets of Naples. And I knew, simply knew, how they had reached the furthest flanks of poor Argentina - their existence down there had not been coincidental.

***

As we attempted to get our lives back on track, I recall my parents getting into consecutive arguments related to Dad's work. The concerns Dad had been bringing home from work for quite a while by then, were finally spilled out when Dad decided to resign from his job. I overheard he'd been silent for as long as he could, after learning of embezzlement which utilized his shop in the outskirts of town to fund and store equipment that had no place at the shop premises. For what I understood (and in my youth and innocence I could be mistaken on this) Dad was aware of sham purchases made on the shop's behalf -a cover up for what was truly being acquired. But I do not know who was responsible, nor for what purpose had said scam been done. I do not know, and I suppose we never will at this point.

Mom understood his reason for wanting to walk away from his job, but feared it had gone on for too long and his resignation would put us all at risk. He'd said that, if necessary, he'd leave town to ensure *they* didn't come after him at home. I could be wrong, but I believe Dad kept his job a bit longer after this conversation had taken place. I think he was relieved that Mom knew.

***

January 1st. Sundown. We gathered outside Grandma's house, saying our numerous goodbyes before returning to our homes and lives until the next event that brought us together.

The adults conversed lively while the children awaited the last train of the evening. We'd sit in rows on the uneven sidewalk across from the tracks, making idle chat. Then at the sight of an approaching railcar, we'd all stand and cheer, full of excitement. The engineer and the folks inside also waved in obvious enthusiasm at the sight of us. The regulars knew us -we were often present as they hurried by. We always cheered and laughed, and reveled as the horn blasted and whistled, and the ground shook. This is a greatly cherished memory to this day.

Our attention was captured by loud voices a hundred or so feet away. The crowded sidewalk went still. Grandma's house faced East and the sun had started to hide behind us, hitting the back of our heads and shoulders with remarkable intensity. It had been a long, hot, and lazy start to the year.

I looked over as the voices appeared to come nearer, and although too young to understand their true meaning, what I heard was unequivocally an aggressive chain of insults; quite the extensive repertoire. I tried to understand what was taking place, but we were far removed. I couldn't quite make out what was happening and thought it a quarrel between drunken folks after a long night's worth of cheap cocktails.

Suddenly the train whistle blew, announcing its proximity. Dad and my uncles broke into a run towards the voices, which kept coming from a humble home on the opposite side of the tracks, kitty corner from us, about a block away or so. The railroad tracks sat directly across from Grandma's house, on a raised platform, about three feet above the road. We could now see the smoke from the approaching engine, and felt the tremors boiling under our feet. It was its last stage of daily runs before reaching the main station further downtown.

The voices grew even louder. Suddenly, a fully bearded man emerged from the house, dragging a little old woman behind him. She spilled soothing words at an attempt to calm him down, but he threw her aside, got close to her face, and screamed at her once more.

I heard Dad shout at him as he ran towards them: "Let her go, NNN-O-W." My uncles followed, all the while running towards the fast-approaching engine, calculating how close it was to their position. Mom and my aunts warned out loud to watch out. Meanwhile the old lady, now crying, struggled to get up by holding on to a patio table, next to a sewing machine where a younger woman usually mended clothes, commissioned by the neighbors.

The man yelled threats at her and disappeared, but quickly re-emerged waving a knife, his shirt undone now. He approached her, hit her hard on the head with the thick bone handle, dropping her backwards. He paused to look at the advancing train and at our men running towards him, and in a swift movement, he discarded the knife, grabbed and lifted the heavy sewing machine, and dropped it over the woman's head just as the train reached the intersection, stopping Dad and my uncles from crossing to the other side to aid the poor woman.

The few loud wagons went speedily by, yet taking sufficiently long to allow the murderer to escape. Mom and my aunts, crying in shock, managed to finally gather all the children and pushed us back into the house. As we walked in, we saw Uncle Ernesto split from the group and start to ran to the closest avenue, to reach the night patrol, and guide them to the scene.

That evening we didn't depart for home until quite late. We were the only witnesses to the poor old lady's demise by her son-in-law. Dad was silent and Mom shed quiet tears all the way home.

***

Never during Christmas did we expect presents. It was not part of our culture to give or receive gifts for that holiday. The only exception included dating couples. They'd give a gift, or surprise their partner with a proposal of marriage.

One of the only items we ever received and learned to expect as we grew older, was a pair of pink undergarments or pantaloons which old -unsubstantiated- tales said would bring us luck in the upcoming year.

And one of the very few times I remember receiving a different gift, was from one of aunt Alicia's boyfriends. He'd bought presents for all our family's children, which I've no doubt impoverished the heck out of him overnight. No one had been left out and we were all in awe, the kind you get on occasion and blindsides you for a moment, robbing you the ability to react in a normal way. Well, we weren't normal anyway. We were more of a wandering little circus marching at our own beat. At least so while we visited Grandma's house. And I don't think

Grandma and Grandpa minded it. As a matter of fact, I know they were quite proud of it.

We did expect a little something every January 6th (*Día de Reyes*: The 3 King's Day, or Feast of Epiphany) when wisemen Melchior, Caspar, and Balthazar gifted offerings to baby Jesus. As per the old book, they had arrived in town overnight on their camels. So, the evening prior we left out water and filled our shoes with grass, for the camels to feast on. Poor, unsophisticated, camels. I must note that this grass-in-the-shoes practice never made any sense to me, but I wasn't about to object to a custom that benefitted me as much as anyone else.

Some of the most remarkable of presents I recall receiving (because of its value, which we knew it had not been easy for Mom and Dad to afford) was a huge swing set, same style as those in the large parks in Argentina. We'd loved and enjoyed it for many years.

As we grew older Dad had patiently sanded it, repainted it, and advertised it for sale for an upcoming King's Day. It looked beautiful and brand new all over. He'd been so busy at it and had managed to finish it just two days before the festivity. Per Dad, there were many couples around with little kids and good income, and *someone* would bite. He had already planned on a long list of tools and improvements desperately needed for his shop. He'd even picked out and placed everything needed on hold, every penny from the sale already destined. And so, he waited.

As the evening of January 5th approached, three people called about it and wanted to secure it in word, but they would not be able to pick-it up and pay until the morning. Dad had told them he would only hold it if they'd at least make time to stop by and look at it before the 6th, emphasizing they'd have to pick it up themselves because he had no way to lift such heavy piece, nor transfer it to their home and yard.

The hours had passed and he'd become worried that he wouldn't sell it. He needed the money. Quite desperately, though he wouldn't admit it.

He'd taken a short break at six in the evening to come into the house and have his customary mug of warm tea and pastries while he watched a bit of TV, for which purpose one of us played contortionist and sat very close to the TV set, holding the darn antenna in some unnatural way so the rest of the family could watch a few minutes of television. Thankfully, the programming sucked enough and not all of us liked the same shows. This allowed us to take turns switching the set of ears around, manipulating or flicking the hardware, getting a kink in the neck, or an arm in pins and needles due to some odd long-held posture. All around a hazardous job, that of an antenna manager in the Ocampo residence those days.

He'd sat down, tired, exhausted really, and said to me, looking defeated: "I think I've been too ambitious, and such is why God has not sent me a buyer." He then started reciting his thanks for the food and for all the blessings we were showered with (he did this every day, with every meal -uncommon down there), when someone knocked on the shop door. He'd wrapped up his prayer and gotten up immediately. Then as he left the kitchen he'd happily expressed: "He listens to me, I tell ya…and there is my buyer!"

We never saw the purchaser, but after a while Dad came in with an ear-to-ear smile and giddy with excitement. He embraced Mom, pointed his index finger up, and said: "I knew he'd help me sell it if I was humble." Mom asked him who bought it, and he said that it didn't matter. That it was done!

Early the next day when his employees showed up at the shop, he helped them lift the super heavy swing set (that thing was solid), and they carried it along the avenue and around the corner to its final resting place. Mom heard them coming back and went out to ask again. Dad gave her a quick kiss on the cheek and handed her a small envelope with coins, saying: "Here, it's all yours. Buy yourself something nice."

Don Cardona, one of our neighbors, worked at the winery near Grandma and Grandpa's house. Each evening on his way back from work, he'd get off the bus a block away and passed by our home on way to his own humble one around the corner. He'd seen Dad's swing set advertisement and thought he'd take a look. He told Dad that he tried planning for the upcoming Holiday, wanting to get something for his precious little girls. But things were tough, so he stopped to see if this was the answer to his anxiety. He handed Dad a tattered envelope with a few coins -all he'd been able to save over the last many months. He also told Dad that if it wasn't enough to purchase the set, it was so late already he could not run back out to procure something else for his girls, so Dad could keep it all and use it to get the supplies he'd put on layaway. Dad could pay him back once the old swing sold. And Dad's heart had torn for him. He and his wife were the kindest of people, their little daughters nothing but sweet little big-eyed angels. There was simply no way the amount in the envelope could start to cover the cost of the set, but Dad said to him that he'd been waiting for him all day. He'd shaken his hand and let him have it for the coins he'd handed him, the full sum of which did not start to cover the cost of the paint Dad used.

He'd even told him not to worry, he'd deliver it in the morning before his babies were up.

And deliver it, he did.

Mom had tried questioning Dad again when she opened the envelope, and Dad said that if it was good enough for him, it was good enough for all of us. And that he got the rest of the payment the moment he and his helpers placed the swing on the grass and the three little girls had come out into the yard and gifted him with the biggest smiles those little faces could afford. Dad was in tears, and now so was Mom. Then Dad had hugged her and said: "No te procupes, Dios proveerá" (Don't you go worrying, God will provide for us).

Dad never gathered enough money to cover all the items he needed for his shop. But not once did he mention it, nor complained to anyone. He always faced challenges well, and often said that he'd never give into despair because that could only encourage *Satanás*. In his older days, Dad joined an Evangelical Church and started writing songs, although he knew nil about music. He made it up as he went -spent hours at the dining table, singing to himself and writing lyrics, while memorizing music to go with it. He kept loads of them in piles, next to his bookkeeping records. Then on weekends he'd go to church a couple of hours earlier, and asked the pianist to play and scribble them on music sheets for him. They were all songs of praise to Heavenly Father. He called them *Alabanzas*.

I have now been told numerous times that often folks thought he was blessed with the gift of healing. I don't know if Dad could heal physical illnesses, but I do know that evoking his name has brought me peace many, many times, during my ailments and personal trials.

Dad had the purest, most innocent soul; and the most giving heart I have ever encountered.

***

On another King's Day we received an above-ground swimming pool which we loved. Known as 'Pelopincho', it was huge, and not easy to set up. This was Dad's idea after the episode at the river. He enjoyed it even more than we did. But I remember even Mom and Grandma liked it, making it a considerable hit. I loved looking into it as it filled, but getting into it was an entirely different story.

Another great fun gift was a swing Dad fabricated by hand and hung from the tree that even today sits right next to the living room window at the old house. That was precious real estate, and one we often fought for a chance to reign over.

But what I liked the most was a bicycle Dad had bought for us to share. I LOVED it. On weekends Norma and I would take turns riding around the block in the coldest of winter afternoons. I wore my baby-blue bell-bottomed corduroys, a little orange-cream striped top, and my comfy dark navy-blue poncho. It was the outfit of freedom! I rode all the way around the block standing on the pedals, as fast as my wheels could turn, bumping along the ruts.

Back then, traffic was hardly an issue, especially on lazy Sunday afternoons, when most people passed a *mate* around while listening to *Los Chalchaleros*, after having sat down to *tamales, empanadas*, and a superb *asado* (Argentinian barbeque) or a *pasta* feast. Talking about pasta, no one -*NO ONE*- made pasta quite like Mom and Grandma. Inevitably Mom would get mad at Grandma each time she made ñoquis with us, because she flung the little dumplings up and off the rolling fork, and we'd end up with ñoquis all over the floor. When Mom complained, Grandma would say: "Mujer! You don't know how to have fun!"

When it came to food, there was something I did not like, no matter who prepared it. It was seafood. Of any kind, cooked in any way, no matter what body of water it'd come from. And so, Easter was a tough time of year for me, because belonging to a 99% Catholic community, the season translated into fish-eating. Living in a landlocked area, no fish was fresh unless it had been caught by the cook, and not many folks fish down there -at least not where we lived. So, the whole place stunk to High Heavens from the moment the fish was loaded onto the butcher's truck, to a couple of weeks later when people, and dogs and cats, were still burping it out.

It was so bad indeed that I would barricade myself in our bedroom with alternate food storage which did not need refrigerated. And came out of the room only to use the bathroom.

The air reeked of fish (very little fresh -most, not) when the entire country abstained from eating other proteins. It made me so ill, I vomited often and quite severely. And thanks to all of it, to this day I cannot come close to fishy smells or tastes of any kind.

***

I was now only two years away from high school. Note that in Argentina, High School is a combination of American Jr High and High School. It lasts five to six years, depending on the program...yes, there are different options, depending on the plans for postsecondary education for each individual student (though all school curriculums must meet certain requirements, institutions are allowed to place emphasis on different subjects, ie. some are technical or science based, some focus on accounting, some on humanities, and so forth -it has proven helpful to the students).

As a child, I rarely paid much attention to radio reports. Not that I would have truly understood what was being said, had I listened. There were no TVs or screens of any type to visually stimulate my attention, so I kept to the little tattered books, worn magazines and encyclopedias aunt Alicia passed on to me. And I carried them around from the couch to the table, to my bed, and so forth. She knew of my eagerness for knowledge and went around her huge pool of friends and coworkers, procuring and gathering printed material. And then passed them on to me.

My wonderful, sweet, aunt Alicia, who I love so dearly. She is now seventy-two!

Books held a special fascination in my world. Upon scanning through the pages, images of my own making flooded my senses and carried me away. By then, I had also acquired a whole collection by Louisa M. Alcott which I had read so many times, I knew the dialogues by heart.

I recall one chilly day quite clearly. Mom had tried to get me and Norma to hurry up and get ready for school, classes having started only a few days earlier. It was cold and grey outside. I was lugging behind, not looking forward to leaving the warmth of the house.

Early mornings Mom normally played a small radio she'd brought over from Grandma's house. She said it aided us in waking up (not really). But this day she kept switching stations, while they seemed to transmit the same announcement. Over and again. Norma and I had looked at each other, not quite understanding the meaning of it -we actually thought the unit was broken. Dad had been away for a few hours already, and Mom was sniffling, her back to us, as she prepared our snacks. We knew something was amiss, just did not quite comprehend her anxiety, until she'd let the transmission run its course. And we'd listened. It was an official announcement. Every person was being warned that as of that moment the country was under the control of the commanding officers of the armed forces. No gatherings were allowed. Beware! Then, military marches played back-to-back until the previous message blared again through the speakers.

President Isabel Perón had been detained. *She* (and only *she*?) had failed to deter the extremist movements popping up around the country for an extended period; instead, they had spread widely. So, she'd been removed by force, and the military had risen to power. And with it, they'd also taken control over all broadcastings…to manage the fall out and silence the masses. No individual opinion counted any longer. Our minds belonged to them now.

Mom had made us bundle up, and walked with us to school as usual, approaching a couple of teachers who were getting things ready for our flag ceremony. One of them spoke softly in return and advised her that classes were running in their normal schedule. And warning her not to worry, we would be safe at school.

There had been a lot of hush hush conversation and the morning had thankfully flown by. We fully sensed the fear the adults carried, and were concerned. Fear hadn't quite settled within us yet, but we weren't far from it. When the bell rang, we hurried home, only to learn the local government had also now set up *un toque de queda* (a curfew).

There were signs and rumors of riots and protests spreading all over the country, particularly by university students and different unions and groups surfacing around the various ends of town, though it was dangerous to rise in opposition. There were also several folks going missing, followed by swat-like teams entering residences to do *allanamientos* (police stakeouts and house invasions to search and detain).

Soon, bomb threats, kidnappings, and assassinations became a daily occurrence. At first, the only targets were well-known figures and celebrities who expressed disagreement with the new regime. Many of them fled the country. Sadly, the range of intimidation expanded quickly among all classes, to include even folks we knew. But most folks like us could not afford to leave, nor had anywhere else to go.

Our weekends became quite uneventful, except for Saturdays when throughout the day the church across the street officiated weddings. We'd sneak up close to the chapel doors to watch as the newlyweds were greeted by their loved ones in brief celebration of their new life together. Then Sunday mornings and evenings, the streets were graced by the faithful, who remained undeterred by *the law* standing around as they attended mass, the tall chapel gates wide open as the attendees spilled out the door and songs of praise floated in the air. A time when unfaithful souls converted by the mere need of something or someone to believe in. Times were tough. And getting tougher.

***

As accustomed, at the end of April, we celebrated the day of our Lady of Montserrat with a procession planned for the afternoon. All students made their way to the care center about ten blocks away (Hogar San José) where the city housed some elderly as well as mentally challenged adults and children. Some of them could leave the premises in the afternoons, and were often seen wondering the neighborhood; some, begging for treats during teatime.

The sterile space did not quite resemble a 50's asylum. Still, I could never shake the creepy feeling I got whenever I proceeded beyond the gate. It was not but plain-and-simple fear. A fear of the unknown, and a fear of somehow getting locked-in and not finding, or not being allowed to find, my way out. Seems I always felt afraid of getting locked-in somewhere...

This day the Montserrat students in our liveried school uniforms (*uniforme de fiesta* -different from our daily pinafores) followed along as *La Moreneta* was transferred back to her seat in our house of worship. Each of us three sisters in formation with our respective grade levels, walked behind the image of the virgin as we sang the Castilian Spanish version of the hymn, "El Virolai".

Following, a rendition of the hymn, from the Mont Serrat school at the abbey in Spain. ScolaniaMontserrat. 2012, November 26. *Virolai – Escolania de Montserrat.* [Video]. Format [Video File]. YouTube. https://youtu.be/7-Fkh3mUqWY?si=f-GZHkNzsACE-Sp0x

This was one of the rituals I followed for the twelve years I attended Montserrat. And I enjoyed it thoroughly. Not the rainy processions, nor the cold and windy times spent walking the dusty streets of our community, but the general feel of it. Although as we grew older, many of the guys and girls in high school showed only for one or both of the following reasons: to avoid an absence and then have to make it up with some sort of punishment by our Religion teacher. Or because either before, during, or after the procession they snuck away to have a taste of their *flavor of the day.* And I'm not talking about ice cream.

I had an exceptionally good friend at the time: Mariana. Her family moved into the area some years earlier and started a home business. They sold school supplies out of their living room window. Their business grew unpredictably fast, prompting their purchase of adjacent space, and the opening of a large and successful retail store. She confided that her mom inherited money and had poured every bit of it into what turned out to be a very profitable business.

The two of us got along well. We were always assigned to sit in alphabetical order and so, she and I ended up next to each other while she attended Montserrat.

This year our teachers encouraged group work, and often she'd be sent over to our house, or I'd go over to hers so that we could work together on our projects. The two of us cared too much about our grades, and often ended up with the bulk of the group's work.

Mariana's parents were younger than mine by several years. They were both very nice to me. As projects became due, we often worked long hours well into the evening. As they also worked late, whenever we studied there, her dad got us some fun dinner to go and once all done, I was sent home in their fancy new car, driven by her dad and older brother.

But one Monday morning she'd come to school in tears, refusing to talk to anyone or answer any questions. And after a couple of hours, she'd burst into tears again, and pulled me by the hand, asking that I followed her outside where she sobbed and told me that her dad was very ill. No doctor was able to figure what was wrong with him.

I had not been to her house for a few weeks, all our work together having ended for the time being. I'd not seen him for a while, but she said he'd lost weight, his teeth, and his hair. And even his sight was affected. He had finally been hospitalized the previous evening.

She had remained quite somber the entire day, and I did not know what to do, what to say, nor how to act around her. And that had been the last time I saw her, and heard from her. She no longer showed to class, nor was I able to get a hold of anyone at her home. The store closed, and both, house and business were left behind, a big SE VENDE (for sale) sign placed on the store front.

Some years later in reading the newspaper, I learned that her mother was serving time. She'd discovered that her husband was involved in an affair, and she'd poisoned him. The family had lost everything in the legal fight, and the paternal grandparents were assigned guardianship of the siblings -minors still.

CHAPTER 10

No Time Like Childhood

Way beyond the now gone firework factory, laid the slums, then some of the most dangerous and feared areas of town. On record as Villa Muñecas and Barrio Aguas Corrientes (both part of the former Aldea Santillán), they were initially populated by hundreds of impoverished families who'd lost their jobs due to the government closing of sugar cane factories.

Right through the aforementioned village, rose the railroad. The railroad system was long utilized by Perón (before he ruled the country from Spain, mind you...why would he live surrounded by poverty in Argentina when he could thrive in the first world, I ask?)

Perón, his late wife Evita, and his last wife named Estela Martínez (nicknamed Isabel), all had used the mentioned railroad for political purposes: to campaign, by feeding the poor.

According to Mom's own words about the Peronista movement, "The wagons would be filled to the rims with groceries and money, and as the train marched through the poor communities flanking the tracks, food and cash were thrown overboard to the delight of the starving masses."

This inevitably gained Perón millions of votes. While often regrettably fomenting a lazy way of life which would scar the land for its remaining existence. But you couldn't argue this with Peronistas. To them, he was "a godsend."

As the Secretary of Labor (before his stunt as Vice-President and ultimately President) Perón had understood the masses, and sided with the labor force. He spoke like them and acted like them. He helped them organize and progress, thus gaining *huge* support. But with the end of WW2, then Argentinian President Farrell understood his vice-president was seen by the U.S. and Europe as a distinctively Fascist leader in Argentina. Farrell turned him in to the authorities. His supporters, however, brought him back.

And in 1974, about a week before Independence Day and the start of our winter vacation, Perón had died in Spain. It was July 1st. I recall Mom crying as the announcement was made on TV. And as we watched, we could hear the train horns whistle loudly from the Muñecas station. Far, far, beyond the end of our avenue.

Mom and Dad had been raised under the general belief that Perón had been a most suitable leader, as far as understanding the needs of the poor. His second wife, Estela (initially his personal secretary) was puppeteered into the presidential seat in order to keep the party and the plans moving forward.

Eventually, Peronist militants organized to oppose a quickly forming military regime sworn to oppress the masses with the intent to squeeze them dry of their ideology. But ultimately the military took power, incarcerating Perón's widow and the remnants of Peron's cabinet. This set forth a path of destruction to obliterate the Peronist philosophy and any resistance.

It was an era of deep uncertainty, and clandestine detention centers scattered around town. Folks of all walks of life disappeared, many were tortured and released, but not all ranked among the fortunate that saw the light of day again. At the end of it all, relatives of those who never found their way back, formed the movement *Madres de Plaza de Mayo*, to voice the pain and anger of the mothers, wives, and daughters that never saw their loved ones return.

Today, historical data confirms details about implementation -by the Argentinian military- of what they called "counter-revolutionary warfare" which included concentration camps, kidnappings, and terrorism tactics to torture and murder *guerrillas* and their presumed supporters. Pregnant prisoners were kept alive until they gave birth, then were murdered, and their babies given in adoption to military families. Meanwhile adult bodies of both genders washed-up on Argentina's Atlantic beaches. They had been thrown off planes, from flights organized by the military.

***

As the railroads were laid out, many small communities emerged and grew along its path.

My Grandfather and some uncles, along with several acquaintances, were all part of the railroad family. My uncle Ángel and his family eventually moved to one of the small towns serviced by the railroad, *Tafí Viejo* (native terminology meaning: a place where the wind blows cold). The town had originally been born as a summer resort, on the 3rd of May of the year 1900, under the name San José de Calasanz.

I loved Tafí. The fastest way to reach it was by train as the roads were not physically laid out yet. And even less, recognizable, as attested by the wild vegetation which occasionally stood in place. The lightest of storms could get an experienced driver in deep trouble and severely stranded in the middle of nowhere.

One Friday a month, the entire Porta family made their way to their closest train station and took the train departing at five pm from the main station to Tafí Viejo. As the train passed through the city, Mom's parents and all her siblings accompanied by their spouses and children, and often cats and dogs and any friends that were up for an adventure, gathered onboard as the train made its way over San Miguel's tracks and stations. Each family member brought along enough food, clothing, and excitement for the entire weekend.

La Estación de Villa Muñecas, built in 1898, was about a thirty to forty minute walk from our home, in the very intersection of Viamonte and Ave. Francisco de Aguirre (I think). The trip always appeared so long to me then, when it was not in reality. Age is a funny thing.

Mom, myself, and my sisters boarded at the Muñecas Station. I think this was the last stop the train made enroute, but I could be wrong. Dad always stayed behind to work Friday evenings, then joined us on Saturday.

The train conductors and inspectors were all family friends and enjoyed seeing the Portas onboard. Our clan alone took over most of the wagon chain which ran the daily route from San Miguel to Tafí intended to transport laborers back and forth, although said folks found themselves in a pickle each time the Porta clan chose to do their monthly tribal relocation.

While Grandpa was still alive and well, he visited with the conductors in the first wagon, while Grandma crocheted, and my many uncles read the paper or napped, arms crossed, a newsboy cap over their faces. The boy cousins looked at magazines while munching on *sweet tutuca* (popped corn covered in honey), tangy kumquats, and delicious mortadella sandwiches in warm, soft French bread. And the girls played checkers (always a bad idea as we inevitably lost pieces that scattered each time the train jerked), so some of us opted to play with our Tiki-Taka (clackers) until we were sufficiently bruised in the hands. Finally, the aunts watched the passing landscape and chatted lively over the chukka chukka chukka chukka chukka chukka chukka, whistles, and rattling of the engine. Another innocent, and truly unforgettable experience.

The train emptied on arrival at Tafí. And we again walked the dusty -unpaved- mile to reach uncle Ángel's home. But as the main crowd marched straight to their destination, Grandpa and Mom brought my sisters and me to a home on the main avenue, just steps away from the station's entrance. There lived some first cousins of Mom's, daughters to her uncle José Pio, one of Grandpa's brothers who'd also been a railroad worker. I only seem to remember a Tía… Irma (?).

Our visits were brief, nevertheless as loud as any Italian event. They included the always present squeeze to the cheeks on arrival, and slap to the bum on the way out. And often also concluded with the sometimes expected -and sometimes not- bite of homemade treat jammed into our mouths...often worth swallowing, I must add, though in a few opportunities all we got was a good gag, at which my little sister responded by throwing a serious fit and raising a spastic right fist at the host as we walked away to our destined getaway. And Grandpa got a good laugh at all of it.

Finally, off we were to our adventurous weekend, which inevitably ended on Sunday evenings with our procession back to the station for departure on the last train to the city. Unless Dad was feeling brave and brought a car over for the weekend, which needless to say was not always well received by Mom though very occasionally appreciated if she felt ill and preferred a quieter ride home. More often than not, he loaded Mom's brothers on it, and there they went on yet another adventure of their own, which they always made sure to turn into a real escapade.

Our times in Tafí were grand -to our taste, anyway. Tafí was (still is) the national *Capital del Limón*, its streets then lined with citrus trees, and roses, the scent marvelous to the senses.

Uncle Ángel and Aunt Norma's home (the married first cousins) had an abundance of space, with the most awesome and largest enclosed patio perfectly fit for family gatherings. It also had a mid-sized, inground swimming pool that couldn't possibly accommodate us all. Many, many, many fruit trees, and a giant tree specimen from which a strong rope hung, and was used by my uncles to swing over, and jump, into the pool. Wild men. Wild times.

Aunt Norma was an expert baker, and we, thank goodness, had the metabolism of hummingbirds, or else we'd all look like

Oompa Loompas now. Some of us do, but please don't tell I said this. She had no formal culinary training, but her skill was unmatched, and she was often hired for catering services. Undoubtedly a talent we all appreciated each time we stayed over—tea teatime was presented to us with a long table covered in baked goods to delight the most finnicky of palates. The tantalizing scent and feel of a hot oven, lemon and vanilla swirling in the air.

They were great hosts, my aunt and uncle, willing to accommodate however many of us came to visit and chose to stay. It was always a time full of nature walks, games, and excursions to the small theater in the main street. We piled like sardines to watch movies several years older than ourselves; even mute short films featuring Charles Chaplin and the like.

There, the weather was always kinder in the summer and cooler in the winter. We felt so dignified strolling through the main avenue, playing the part of tourists, looking our best in "city dress."

However, back into San Miguel, the capital, the unrest continued, now including food and gasoline shortages, and other rationing. Thanks to my grandparents, Mom and her siblings were well (and even extensively) connected, and managed to get large quantities of flour, rice, sugar, and *yerba* (local tea) to split evenly among all our households. Our family never went without the (local) essentials.

***

Mom had a soft spot for a neighbor, Consuelos Pilar, two houses down from ours. Her father also lived on site but we hardly ever saw him. His name was Benjamín, and he was blind in one eye, which always made me stare.

Consuelos was young, unwed, and had seven children. The kids often wandered around half clothed, bare footed, and sporting runny noses. There was an agreement of sort among the immediate neighbors who took upon themselves the task of sharing with them meals, clothing, and anything they could spare.

Mom knew from a young age the relief of having enough to feed a little troop of children, and always said she would not close her eyes at night should she not share her bounty. She made it a point to reserve for them a portion of whatever we attained. And Dad did the same. He said it was "nuestra responsabilidad moral." That we were far from wealthy, yet above from destitute.

Consuelos' kids attended public school, and during summer vacation they were all given chores to keep busy and out of trouble. Their dad was a young lad named Marcos Asturias, a decent guy of humble means. He did not live on site, but stayed over every now and then, and never failed to bring the children clothes, food, toys, and money for their daily needs. He treated them well, and for what I understand, it was Consuelos who lacked interest in marriage, though he'd proposed many, many-a-time.

Their oldest daughter, Soledad, was my age, and my closest -steady- friend at the time. Soledad was gorgeous and almost an exact replica of her mother, with a dark and lustrous complexion, beautifully slanted dark eyes, and brown hair with naturally reddish highlights. As she grew older, she was quite the exotic beauty. But boys always showed misguided interest. And regrettably for her parents, such interest never went unappreciated by dear Soledad. She was a stunning girl and understood the value of her natural charms.

As a child, she was never free to come to our house to play because she was expected to help care for her younger siblings. Her days were fully scheduled; as I suppose my own mother's days would have been when she was herself a child helping Grandma and Grandpa care for their large family. So, in our home there was great respect for Soledad's responsibilities.

I only saw her often during hot summer siestas after she placed her young siblings for a nap. She'd then stand under the shade of a tree washing dishes and hanging bucket after bucket of clean laundry -no such thing as Pampers then! We talked a lot while she completed her tasks, and I watched, amazed at her ability to handle it all like a mature mother looking after her household, though we were very young children still.

Consuelos' next daughter, Vega, was Norma's age and a good friend of hers. Vega was small for her age, but gorgeous regardless. She was darker than the rest, but her hair sported caramel highlights, and she had the most striking green eyes. She was also the sweetest girl.

All the names of their other siblings run together in my mind today, except for the eldest boy, Santos, because he had told Mom that he'd marry me when he grew up, and she never forgot that. He often stopped by our home to watch TV, exactly at teatime, and always left with a belly full of tea. And bread and treats crammed into his pockets.

Mom always expected him, yet always got upset when he showed up. She always hoped that *never again* he'd need to lie or pretend to secure a meal. The TV excuse was just that, an excuse. He showed up religiously day after day, and thankfully, once Mom opened the door, she forgot all about her upset and proceeded to spoil him, always first making him wash his hands, then join us at the table.

Consuelos and the kids lived in a handmade *prefabricada* type of home. Its frame made of a weak mix of 2x2s and 2x4s, and inexpensive shiplap that barely stood up to the wind and rain. It served only as a partial block from the burning temperatures of summer and the freezing air of the then opressive cold months.

The roof was corrugated tin which in summer made the covered area so hot it was difficult to breathe inside, and in winter it did nothing to shield the space from the blasting chill and freezing rain. And after a few years it sported so many rotted areas, the kids had learned exactly where to place tin cups and old paint cans to capture the unavoidable leaks resulting from downpours. They also placed bets as to which would fill the fastest, their prize an extra slice of bread. Then as they grew hungry during the afternoon hours, they used their winning to spread with a thick layer of cold, greasy stew, just as you and I would the most indulging homemade jam.

Indeed. Luxury is relative to your customs and circumstances.

The house was comprised of three rooms: two bedrooms and a dining room. The floors were nothing but packed dirt that often-needed moistened in the highly trafficked areas to tame the unsteady earth. The beds were holey, soiled mattresses, laid directly on the dirt, frameless. Sheets, covers, and pillows, all laid around in total disarray, also dragging onto the loose, powdery mess.

There were no chairs, and the table was missing a leg, hence the children had pushed it against a corner of the room, under which they piled bricks stolen from the various neighbors' yards, still in the process of building their homes.

The cooking was done outside, over a firepit fabricated from an extra-large *tarro de LECHE NIDO* (a Nestle baby-formula tin, back then thick and sturdy, opposite to today's cardboard or plastic containers). They'd managed to attach legs to it, to keep it off the ground. Then they'd fill it with coal and splash it with gasoline before throwing a match at it from the distance. Yes, I said they were poor, not stupid.

When the flames were too large to contain within the can, they dumped the red and white lumps of coal into a large ceramic base laying on the ground, over which they cooked their meals, baked bread, and roasted meats, sometimes on racks or containers, and others directly over the flaming coals.

These fire cans (*braseros*) were also used to warm up the rooms overnight and even during the day in the freezing months of June through August. Amazingly enough, between this practice and the fact that all the adults smoked, none of them *ever* suffered from lung or upper respiratory issues, though their skin and clothes reeked of nicotine and burning coal. Explanation? Anyone?

They washed all clothes by hand using a faucet coming out of the side wall that marked theirs and their neighbor's property line. I wouldn't be surprised to find out they tapped into it without asking, so in all truth their water bill was paid by the neighbors all along. Not done out of blatant mischief, but rather out of pure necessity.

Clothes were hung to dry, but they had no budget for pins, so they knew to be swifter than the wind when it started to blow, the only way to ensure their hard work did not end up on the ground, or in someone else's yard.

The bathroom shift was left to the imagination. You could literally *go* anywhere as long as you did as doggies do, and covered it with dirt. If you hid behind the house to do #2 (which was not favored because the window on that side carried the scent into the master bedroom) you had to be careful not to drop over -or leave behind- your id, or eventually the CSIs would come after you.

***

At the very back of the property there was a large shop where Marcos made floor tiles by hand for the large *corralón* around the corner (a primitive version of today's warehouse stores). There was a large mechanical wonder in the center of the giant space, which had rotating trays in the shape and size of the tiles to be fabricated. Marcos mixed, poured, and manipulated the grainy pudding-like material by hand on each tray, which yielded 8x8, 12x12, and 16x16 tiles, as well as their bullnosed baseboard companions. He somehow managed to *manually* replicate the exact pattern and color combination over and again, ultimately placing each piece into a press to set the design and squeeze the extra liquid out. They were finally moved into a bath of salts to cure. Later, he removed, dried, and prepared them for delivery. He made hundreds of tiles each day, sun-up to sundown, all by himself.

I remember sitting on the side of the saltwater pool watching him along with Soledad and being spellbound by his work. The contraption he used suited his manufacturing needs, with partial modifications and repairs of his own making. My crafty mind was fascinated by it all.

The plot of land where the shop and prefabricada sat was long and expansive, with a huge -unkept- side yard where their numerous pets peed and defecated, and also where a couple of chickens hung lose. And it reeked so.

At the very front of the lot, near the sidewalk, were four large rooms and a huge yet primitive bathroom, built a century prior in brick and mortar (most-probably leftovers from the orchard's owner dwelling).

It had been a house in ruins when the next-door neighbor, the corralon's owner, had acquired the property (or assisted in its acquisition) to help Marcos set up shop. The man was of Middle-Eastern descent. He was successful in his business, and genuinely cared for the Asturias -he felt a strong responsibility towards any neighbor in need. He was a Catholic convert, a fervent believer, and a congregation member of Montserrat by choice -he lived further west, in another community and parish.

Most of the plaster fallen, most of the brick bare, the space reflected the harsh burden of age. Marcos and Consuelos hadn't set-up house within its walls in fear the ruins would collapse over their children's heads. But eventually Marcos needed help, and Consuelos called on two of her brothers, Armand and Ardiles.

Ardiles, single, had welcomed the chance to start anew. He took over one of the dilapidated rooms, grateful to have a roof over his head.

Armand worked elsewhere at the time, but also took the opportunity to use the lodging as his newly found shelter. He hadn't come alone though. He'd moved in with his girlfriend.

"Too young to really call her so," Mom had said. And she wondered how he got away with it. He appeared over thirty, and she barely fifteen-ish. But he did not look friendly, and no one dared pick an argument with him.

The house was generous in size, had cement floors dyed burgundy, and an overall airy feel (which could have been the result of all doors and windows being long-gone). The space resembled an intriguing ruin rather than a house. The clay roof was almost intact though, and after each rain when the loose dirt washed down off it, it showed an intricately laid-out (heavy and handsome) Spanish pattern.

Soledad and I attempted to clean the rooms when we learned about her uncles' arrival. The water was still running, and so was the power, but the small bulbs hanging low from raw cables presented more of a risk than a solution, and needed addressed. She and I had used an old and dried-out straw broom to break through the dense spider webs hanging heavily over the space, and we found ourselves staring at the beautiful ceiling. What people would pay for it today! It had wonderful beams, the type you saw in Jesuit buildings of old. Then Marcos whitewashed the walls, and honestly, the space looked a million times better (and safer) than their own home.

When the two brothers finally moved in, we learned that there was justified reason for them never to be confronted by neighbors or family. They both worked and mostly minded their own business, but they also liked booze, and often got tipsy beyond sensible and then picked fights with each other and the rest of the world.

***

Armand, a large and mean looking fella, delivered construction materials to building sites. His means of doing so included a *carro* (uncovered, hand-built buggy) and four horses, which he sort-of sheltered in the side yard.

I must mention that said side yard was loose dirt-on-dirt about twenty-four inches deep. Once Armand started coming and going with his buggy, and the rainy season arrived, the wheels and the horses turned the space into a swamp difficult to navigate. And as long as they remained there, it was never a space any human could walk over without sinking to the knees. The potholes could swallow a child whole.

His carro and the horses would get halfway buried in mud, the wheels would spit out all over creation not only the mud, but all the accumulated horse manure he never cleaned, and he would go berserk and start swearing and punishing the horses for his own foolishness.

Dad, twice the age but only a fourth the size of Armand, had gotten so fed-up one day hearing the poor horses being beaten and yelled at, he ran over, grabbed the horses' leads and challenged Armand to dare lay a hand on him instead. Armand looked at Dad, ready to plant him a facelift, and Consuelos heard the exchange (thank goodness) and rushed out at the precise moment Armand raised his fist. She'd stepped between the two of them and planted her right knee in his genitals, and he'd fell and made a splash on the filthy soil as she proceeded to warn him to never dare fantasize again about hurting any of her neighbors, or she herself would see that he was thrown in jail. Armand had managed to mutter a colorful assortment of insults that would have made any woman blush, though she'd remained unmoved by it.

That was the end of that argument. She then asked Dad if he would like to help feed and clean the horses. And she hurried to offer to pay for it, but Dad gladly went and did it for free while her brother laid on the mud, temporarily subverted. Dad had enjoyed every minute of it, including Consuelos's disabling of her own brother. And that night he had been wired about how well the horses responded to him.

***

Armand's girlfriend was a very shy teen. A child herself, she did not read nor wrote, and normally stayed in her room, away from people and all type of socializing.

Spring had sprung and they'd welcomed their first baby, a very healthy boy who greatly resembled his father. He was a darling, happy child, and a model baby. He had started to crawl early, and at six months he'd become quite the explorer, managing to get himself into superior mischief.

There were no kitchen cupboards to open, nor doors of any type to keep him corralled. The only room separations consisted of old sheets barely held atop the tall door openings; the rusty nails pounded over the cloth corners barely held them in place, but had successfully torn the quasi-curtains to shreds when the baby pulled on them in futile attempts to raise himself to his feet. His mother, young, inexperienced, and always slow to chase after him, often found him after he'd reached the filthy mud of the side yard; an unknown fascination in his determined little mind. He giggled and shrieked as she followed in pursuit.

And one hot afternoon as mother and baby napped and not a soul was seen or heard around, Ardiles heated water at the far end of the large and open receiving room, atop a brasero full of burning coal, while preparing for his afternoon round of mate. He'd left the water readying while he hurriedly showered.

Meanwhile the little chubster awoke and crawled out of his parent's room to once more make his way to the cooling mud of the side yard; but had been distracted by the whistling lid of the tea pot, as the water spat in its boiling dance. His attention now captured, he diverted his tracks and crawled slowly towards it. His mother, now also awaken by the whistling pot, suddenly jumped-up from the mattress, realizing he was gone from her side. She came out of the room to see her baby, wearing only a cloth diaper, reach out for the iron base of the brasero, attempting to stand by it. In his attempt, he tipped the already engulfed can and full kettle of boiling water over himself, falling backwards. The baby started to scream and seemed to try turning on his belly, to crawl away perhaps, but almost immediately stopped and went into shock. His mother leaped towards him, reached him and had tried grabbing him, but he already laid on the floor in a pool of boiling water and hot coals, instantly blistered from the back of his little head down to his little heels, not one square inch of skin spared, but for his sweet face. She'd splashed into the hot water herself without feeling it on her bare feet, and lifted him. He'd then started to scream again at the mere agony of her touch. And she was then also squealing out loud like a wounded animal.

Ardiles came out of the bathroom hastily wrapping a towel at his waist and stopped at the sight, his eyes bulging out. He'd then snapped out of it, and ran out to pound heavily on our door to ask Dad to please help getting them to the nearest hospital.

There were no other vehicles around, not a soul drove at this hour in the blasting sunny siesta. As Mom always used to say about our hot summers: "Ni las lagartijas andan en este calor" (even lizards don't come out in this heat).

Dad told him to bring them immediately, and while readying the car, he had Mom call Padre Cucala across the street to ask that he too came along to bless the baby on their way to the emergency room.

Ardiles gathered mother and child and had come, his pants only halfway up his legs and jumped in the front seat next to Dad, who drove his car like a maniac, blinded by tears and all along barely seeing the road, one hand locked to the car's horn to keep other vehicles at bay as they reached the most highly travelled roads. He was sobbing for the baby that was now barely breathing, covered in such giant blisters. Years after, Dad referred to this moment as *"the longest 20 minutes of my life."* He hoped the child was still alive when they reached the hospital. The preacher had prayed out loud all the way, and they all grieved along with the desperate mother and the misery surrounding the little soul.

Upon arrival everyone at the hospital was terribly affected, and the young girl-mother was ready to faint at the increasingly horrifying sight of her child, who barely hung on to life in her arms. She was treated for severe burns on her feet, shins, knees, hands, and forearms. My Dad felt such anguish at seeing the young mother had not given any thought to her burns, even when the nurses had peeled the child off her arms and chest.

The baby suffered severe burns over most of his body. The poor girl was so brokenhearted, no one could figure how she managed to endure it. Dad and the priest returned home much later, after having made sure Armand and his girlfriend had whatever they needed. The priest had spoken with doctors and taken upon himself the burden of informing the couple that the baby was in God's hands. The doctors were doing all they could, but now it was time to pray and ask the Lord to help the child bear the suffering, regardless the outcome. Reverend Cucala hugged them, once more brought down to tears himself -the brusque man that many feared in our neighborhood.

About three agonizing weeks later the child was sent home. The damage to his vital organs was severe enough the doctors did not believe that he stood a chance at a dignified, enjoyable life. The weather was quite hot, so he was kept on a cloud hammock donated by the hospital, near a window opening so that any breeze available would gently cool his now thin-as-paper skin.

Mom had cooked a dinner for the parents and brought it over along with the tall fan she kept in her bedroom so the child would not suffer further in the heat of the night. When she returned home, she had sat to cry after seeing the baby still suffering with every breath as his mother daubed soothing oils all over him. Mom had become literally ill from the sight.

After a few days his blisters broke, and he'd gotten a horrible infection. Soledad, who loved her little cousin as a sibling, asked if she could look after him at times, and she invited me to come along and help. I had been not only horrified, but the infection smelled putrid and I had just sufficient time to excuse myself and reach the sidewalk, before I had to crouch, take a couple of deep breaths, and calm myself down. I wondered why the hospital had sent the little infant home. Why hadn't they cared for him right there; until he improved, or otherwise.

To everyone's surprise, the child made improvement and survived. He remained in a stroller the first few years of his life. They did not think he'd walk -some of his tender leg bones had been weakened by the intense heat that had eaten his skin raw. He also suffered from constant ear infections -his body too weak to fight them off. He would nearly faint screaming of pain when the pressure and fever built up and threatened to finally carry his poor little soul to the heavens.

In silence I observed his young mother (my senior only by perhaps three or four years) and wondered whether at times she didn't wish that his assigned guardian angel would just let his little soul float up and meet him at once.

I remember Dad was often called to perform the pressure release ritual. That of inserting a cone made of paper into the child's ear, then lighting the very top on fire and keeping it in place until just before the fire reaches flesh. It is supposed to work miracles, though I know for a fact I do not have the required dexterity to do this myself. But it was common practice as I grew up, and even performed on me a couple of times.

The child's parents eventually separated, and both moved away just before his third birthday, but not before Armand engaged in several fist fights with his brother over the child's condition. And when Ardiles would no longer listen to him or be affected by the blame placed on him (plus the guilt he carried and tried to drown with excessive drink) Armand would turn on his girlfriend and scream, and proceed to throw around and break anything within his reach. The poor girl could not stay there much longer.

***

These were times when Grandma stayed over with us much longer than at any of the other family homes. When she arrived, she'd tell us that she had walked all the way from her home downtown. And faked being so tired from it that she needed an urgent nap. Reality, though, was that she'd spent the previous night gambling until very late, then had taken a bus or cab over and asked the driver to drop her off a few blocks ahead of our home, from where she proceeded to walk. We had witnesses!

She was quite the accomplished actress, so we let her get away with it. Often (but not always).

I loved sitting next to her while everyone napped. And even after Mom and Dad and my sisters went to bed at night. Grandma taught me to knit and crochet, and as she did, she shared many stories with me about her life. Particularly about their Atlantic trip. Though she'd been quite young at the time, the family spoke often and extensively about their experiences aboard the ocean liner. And as they had, Grandma had acquired quite the repertoire about it.

She was funny and often predictable, but she'd a nick for storytelling, and all of us grandchildren often found ourselves riveted by her imagination. I also don't think I've ever laughed quite so much as I did around her.

I vividly recall one night when she'd gathered us in the main room at her house, the adult women cooking while the men played cards and argued about sports. Grandma laid several blankets on the floor, sat at one corner in a squatting pose, all the grandchildren gathered across from her in half-moon formation. She turned the lights off and proceeded to make up a scary story that ended with some dead paisano digging himself out of his grave to claim his widow back on the night she'd taken a new husband. As the end of the tale approached, she had us screaming and scattering out of the room like rats in a sinking ship, our hearts racing so, we weren't but able to laugh afterwards. And so, we did. Anytime she was around.

Everyone at home said that I was around her so much, I had started to act a bit like her, and once when Grandma was away and I had unsuccessfully attempted to replicate on my own the stitches she'd taught me earlier, Dad had been near, and told me to watch it, "knitting should not involve profanity!" Again, point taken. When I told Grandma about it, she said she'd never intended to turn me into a *"boca de conventillo"* (tenement mouth).

***

It was also Grandma who told me the story of the town doctor. And this my friends, was a true story (according to her). One a bit eerie, and it went like this...

Dr. (Juan Domingo de la Cruz Páez) Garmendia was educated in Seville. He was barely out of university when he lost his mother -his father having long-before left this world. Upon his mother's demise, and amidst the turmoil surrounding the old continent, he had given up all his possessions in exchange for a passage to *Las Américas.*

About all he afforded to bring along were his new medical degree and the clothes on his shoulders. Luckily, he'd managed to keep his medical bag and all its prized content, guaranteeing he'd be able to start seeing patients just as soon as he established residence somewhere.

Upon arrival in Buenos Aires, he got word of much needed help up in the newly formed northern provinces. Buenos Aires was busy, larger, and noisier than he'd expected, and the idea of leaving it behind had meant no heartbreak. Anxious, he hired a room for a couple of nights before departing again on his trip inland.

The journey had been long and difficult, and on arrival in Tucumán long-due tiredness set in. He made quick work in finding a guest house that catered almost exclusively to lonely male immigrants. The food was great and tasted and smelled quite like in the homeland, fact in which he'd found priceless comfort.

Before long, the doctor became acquainted with his surroundings and in only a matter of weeks began to settle into a humble apartment which would become his home and office for the foreseeable future. The space was located in a corner building, overlooking the crossing of two main roads, Sarmiento and Mitre avenues. It was surrounded by a series of rowhouses in both directions and sat directly across from what eventually became the *Plazoleta Mitre* roundabout (still in place today). It was nothing to brag about, but he did it regardless -he was quite content with its location. The folks he'd met so far were kind and caring, and life was at last looking up.

Once his humble sign went up, it took no time for his clientele to begin pouring in. And it also expanded beyond expectation, to the annoyance of the local *curanderas* (healers) who would now need to figure a different way to supplement their income.

A couple of years into his practice, Dr. Garmendia was a well-respected physician who often traded his services and counsel for food, house cleaning, clothes washing, and whatever else his humble patients could afford to hand him in exchange for care.

Dr. Garmendia never married. Never had progeny, his only pride being the many great friends he'd made along the way. He had a live-in housekeeper and confidant; an immigrant like himself, though considerably older. A mother figure, it could be said. She stayed in his employment for many years, becoming his caretaker through the illness that eventually ended his life.

During the long months before his passing and fully knowing that his time was running out, he tried to engage her in conversation as to what would happen when he was gone. But she refused to hear any of it, waving him off time after time.

Yet knowing that his chances to inform her were swiftly coming to an end, he intensified his attempts, able only once to get through to her that he'd made sure she wouldn't be left in need of anything. That she needed not to worry nor search for other employment, but just present the document that assigned to her name all he was leaving behind. She'd dismissed this again, but he'd felt better after having had a chance to speak of his plans.

Dr. Garmendia died that very evening. His faithful servant Sra. Valenzuela was overtaken by grief. She also hadn't had other soul in the world, having dedicated almost thirty years to caring for him exclusively.

When the gentlemen from the *servicio fúnebre* arrived to take the body for preparation, she sat gently next to him, searching for the right words to offer him her private farewell and thankfulness. And all that came to her mind was the overwhelming wondering of what her life might be like going forward. He'd been a loyal employer and a great friend. The son she'd always wished for. She couldn't have asked for more. He'd come to her help when she'd arrived and never once questioned her abilities nor doubted her character.

Her emotions had taken over only seconds after, when the local priest arrived to assist. Noticing her distress, he'd asked her which suit she'd like to see the doctor wearing during visitation. In tears, she'd directed him to the doctor's closet, saying he'd always looked his best in blue. The priest had honored her wish, and had afterwards given her a much-needed blessing of peace and comfort.

The next forty-eight hours had been a calvary, worsened only by the arrival of county solicitors as soon as the casket had been covered in dirt and its mourners separated at the cemetery gates.

The solicitor's visit was not unusual, but a standard procedure at the death of well-to-do immigrants without known heirs. But it wasn't until then that she really thought about the message her dear doctor had so insistently tried to convey in his last few moments on our earth.

The solicitors demanded that she pack her bags and leave soon, or show documentation confirming her to be the sole recipient of the estate. Otherwise, all she possessed -an extension of the doctor's wealth- needed returned immediately to the county's purse.

Sra. Valenzuela asked for the maximum time allowed to look through the doctor's belongings. She'd been granted two days during which she once again engaged the assistance of the priest. But by the end of the second day, they'd nearly turned the house and practice upside down without success.

When all hope seemed lost, the priest asked if she knew the attorneys who'd prepared his will. She did not. He'd asked her when this would have been done. She'd no idea. He'd asked when the dear doctor had been out and about last. Finally, something she knew. She'd said: "Ten months ago." Then he'd asked what he'd worn, and she vaguely remembered it as a very rainy day after which he'd returned febrile and unable to eat or even strong enough to talk. They both thought he'd caught a bad cold. It was late, and he'd wanted only a cup of warm broth before heading to bed. She'd been upset and asked that he take his drenched raincoat and hang it to dry in the small covered patio. This chain of events alerted her mind to check in his closet, the only space still left untouched. The raincoat hung in its usual place, and it smelled of him. A tear slowly dropped down her cheek as she checked all his pockets, and then scrunched the cloth lovingly in a soft caress. But she'd come-up empty handed once more. She proceeded to examine all other clothing items in the same manner. Not the slightest sign or inkling had come to mind. The priest returned after a second round of checks of the library and the admitting room at the back of the apartment. He asked many questions again, none of which had triggered clues either.

The young cleric appeared to surrender all hope and said there was then nothing to be done, all the while offering her lodging at the church until they could figure the next step. This time as he spoke, her mind again remembered the doctor's plea for her to listen. It allowed her to realize that all but one suit had been inspected: the blue ensemble he'd worn in his casket. It'd been his and her favorite. The one she suddenly recalled he'd worn under his raincoat the day he'd gone out to catch his death.

Upon mentioning this, they'd looked at each other at a loss for words. The suit was the only possible chance, yet it laid around the doctor's shrinking bones inside a wood box, under recently disturbed earth. The priest expressed his concern about violating the grave of a body just laid to rest. He understood the importance this document carried, acknowledging also the doctor's intentions had been noble; he'd not have desired for the product of his hard work to sit in auction while she was left in need, her only option begging for handouts in the streets of the city.

The following day, before the solicitors had an opportunity to knock at her door, she and the priest obtained an order to have the sarcophagus unsurfaced and the doctor's pockets emptied.

They rode in a hired car, speeding all the way to the cemetery. Once there, she chose to stay a few yards away from the vault as the laborers started the awful task of digging to remove, rather than to place. The diggers had been initially reluctant at the job at hand, forcing the priest to summon support from a couple of police officers. The priest said a solemn prayer as the last bit of dirt was removed and the silver cross over the casket came to light. At that precise time, in the distance, he'd noticed the county solicitors running towards them. Upon arrival at the main gates, they realized they'd almost missed the entire development.

It took six men to lift the heavy wooden lid, and two welders to undo the soldered edges. But something had been wrong. A long silence spread as all eyes were horrified at the sight of the bare metal lid, which had pushed the welders to act rapidly.

Once they accomplished the task of breaking the seals, everyone around the dugout donned a large handkerchief which they all tied or held around their faces at the precise moment the final divide was lifted, revealing a most dreadful display. The body had luckily been in the ground for only three days, and in the blistering cold of winter it hardly had any opportunity to decompose. However, it laid not in the same order it had been positioned to rest.

Dr. Garmendia had been among the few schooled medical professionals for several miles around -doctors had been spread thin through the vast territories. He'd been the one called when someone was born, ill, or had passed. He had been the one to confirm the passing of many-a-fellow. When he died, there had been no one to check and ensure he had truly gone from this world. Ceremonies aside, the casket had been welded shut and later placed in the dampened earth. Not long after, the doctor woke up and found himself locked in the dark box, running quickly out of oxygen. He checked his own pockets for something to stub at the lid of his coffin, running only into the document he had hoped his housekeeper would find and use to execute her ownership over his belongings.

He'd pounded hard on the metal top, trying to alert someone. But no one had been around. While on his back, no amount of whacking or kicking the lid allowed him to reach the bowed wooden top that held the earth above. He succeeded in making considerable dents on the thin metal and even a puncture a bit later-on by kicking it repeatedly with the heel of his right shoe, after successfully turning himself upside down within the tight box. Then tiredness had given way, and he'd ran out of air in the confined space.

He thought hard but had no idea how long he must have laid there for the coffin to be sealed already. His most concerning thought had been that of Sra. Valenzuela never knowing how, nor where to claim her inheritance. An inheritance she'd only known about because of all his attempts. Now he could not even die in peace -she'd no way to claim her rightful bequest.

The doctor was found facing down, holding tightly on to his will. The priest saw he held something in his hand and had gently unstiffened it to retrieve the document, after which the doctor's old bones seemed to finally relax. Everyone had seemed horrified at first, then touched by the doctor's obvious concern even as he laid alone under the earth. He was rearranged on his back, and his eyes gently closed again, two large coins replaced over his lids. The final sealing was completed while a gentle prayer was elevated for his generous spirit.

Sra. Valenzuela never had an opportunity to see what had occurred. No one had allowed it. Not even when she tried running over, knowing that something had gone wrong, as reflected in the horror-filled looks of those present. She wasn't privy to the shocking sight the priest and diggers had uncovered in the fresh crypt.

She was known to have survived several years beyond the incident; and to visit the tomb of her benefactor every week for the remaining of her thereafter lonely life.

In further reference to this occurrence, you may discover more details by researching an earlier comparable incident -the case of socialite Rufina Cambaceres, who was pronounced dead on her 19th birthday in Buenos Aires, 1902. She had suffered an episode of *catalepsia*. Rufina rests at the Recoleta Cemetery. Her story I only learned about when checking whether there had been similar instances recorded.

***

Grandma was great company. And loved it when our friends gathered for short parties in early afternoons when we weren't allowed to congregate outside. We put on plays and tried to karaoke; except we didn't own any such thing as a karaoke machine (nor had we heard of such contraption). But we had a makeshift microphone Dad had fabricated for us, to hold-up to our lips and pretend, while the music blared on the speakers he'd connected to our turn table. Norma would always get mad at me because I wouldn't pass the darn mic to her right-away. But whenever I did, she'd get mad again because she could not remember lyrics.

Several Spanish singers had entered the Argentine music scene at the time. Among them: Camilo Sesto, Julio Iglesias, Dyango, Joan-Manoel Serrat, and José Luis Perales. Their fame rose, and with it, Grandma's admiration -they were her *paisanos, pues*! As their singles came out, Grandma swung by downtown to buy them, brought them to me to play and learn, and subsequently sing for her. Actually sing. She even taught me how and where to emphasize the accent so that I sounded like her paisanos. We had lots of fun.

Camilo had many beautiful songs -his music sounded gypsy-Moorish. He was talented, and unlike many singers that gave concerts in Latin America, he actually sang (rather than lip synced). He quite resembled our own Padre Vicente Zueco, and this gave Padre Zueco quite the following, particularly among faithful (and even unfaithful) females.

Grandma LOVED Julio Iglesias; a former soccer star who'd been involved in an accident that kept him from returning to play the game. During his long hospitalization and therapy, he'd taken up songwriting, and risen to fame. It is said that he sang in many languages (or at least attempted to). Truth be known, it didn't matter if anyone understood what came out of his mouth. Just looking at him made even men swoon. But we noticed that he did not, or could not, move very fast -as he walked, he appeared to drag his legs. Again, no one seemed to care, even though at the time Julio hadn't yet grown into the fine specimen he matured into -boy oh boy, as he aged, he had us all eating out of his hand. He was all attributes -his voice was just a perk.

He wrote many songs to -or about- his children (which he'd scattered all around the world -the children, not the songs…like poppy seeds in the wind, actually. And after so many world tours, who could be blamed?).

Mom was enamored with Gianni Morandi and Domenico Modugno, though eventually she veered to the American side and became infatuated with Bruce Springsteen. Dad on the other hand, remained loyal to Rafaella Carrá and Charles Aznavour. So, I had to offer some of their songs as well. Quite the selection I tell ya, and though I had solid votes, I knew I'd never win Entertainer of the Year. But I also knew that as long as I offered something Mom liked, she'd let us dress up in her gowns and stilettos from her younger days. The dresses were dreamy, petticoats and all. The shoes hurt quite like hell though. Yet, we never passed up on a chance to indulge in feeling like grown-ups…oh, to be that young again!

***

Mom and Dad made several good friends in the neighborhood. As one of the first families in the area, they'd witnessed first-hand its growth and expansion. This was a tight community working towards the same goals: a safe, productive, and happy environment for all.

There were several small stores popping up to cater to the rising demands. A supermarket, two butcher shops and two bakeries, a barber, seamstresses and hair stylists, a tire store, a mattress factory, a paint shop, and the school had taken in a couple of folklore dance teachers. Businesses were run in the respective lot fronts or side yards, a humble and hopeful dwelling always rising in their shadows.

All in all, the community started to thrive. Everyone was proud of their own contribution and overall growth. The plan had been to help the colony boom, not just survive. Most families purchased a lot, built their store up front or in their patio, and resided in a sturdy *prefabricada* while they planned construction of their home, or, more appropriately said, saved money to start building a proper home. It was what you may call: *The Argentinian Dream.*

In Argentina, if you owned a butcher shop, bakery, pharmacy, or an event venue, you had it made. Literally. People down there, no matter their income, won't go without beef and bread. Then, everyone is bound to get sick. And parties abounded -the more miserable and deprived the government managed to make their lives; the more people turned to gatherings to quench the need for a respite.

Mom liked both butchers. The one immediately around the corner from our home, Don Falicce, was *Italiano.* I'd always wondered if his name hadn't been Faliscii and changed at the Office of Entry (not unusual).

And here comes another brief deviation from the story.

The Faliscii were a tribe of Italians which included Oscans, Sabellians and Umbrians. I'd discovered this on a little encyclopedia-like magazine I subscribed to when I was seven years old. I thought I'd get in trouble for it when Mom found out. When she had, she'd asked "Por qué, ¿decime por qué? ¡Eso cuesta plata!" Indeed. It wasn't cheap. I'd told her that I was running out of reading material and did not want to bother her with my worries. And that I'd saved the coins she gave me for school every day, together with the ones Grandma always hid for my use in my night table.

Mom had actually laughed and told me she wished she'd been so gutsy when she'd ended up memorizing her books because she couldn't get new ones. She also said that she wasn't aware Grandma had started a savings account for me with all her gambling winnings.

Now that my secret was out, she'd asked that I loan her the magazine collection (which I'd been hiding under my mattress). And she liked them too - well, she'd liked the series about the Etruscans. And then when Dad found out, he'd also asked to see them and had sat down to read for hours one Sunday. They had both sacrificed education to help their families. And both craved all things educational -only then I realized that mine had been a good venture. They'd been so nice about it, and I'd felt so relieved. And that very same sunny afternoon, Mom had walked Norma and me to a newly arrived amusement park a block away from home, and given us tokens to use at the different rides, and told us to stay together until she returned to get us, in short. I'd approached a little stand and won a prize, and instead of getting some ugly stuffed animal that Norma was begging me to get for her, I'd chosen to get a beautiful white ceramic tea pot for Mom to repay her for not giving me a belt to the bum earlier in the day. Norma got so mad at me because now not only we couldn't stay and get on rides while holding the darn pot, but we had to walk back home to drop it off.

She'd slapped and pinched my arm all the way home in rebellion, making it hard to keep my eyes on the uneven sidewalks and steps up and down to ensure the silly pot got to Mom in one piece (btw, each neighbor built their own sidewalk -there was *no* uniformity). My arm hurt so much by the time we got home, and Norma's mouth was all over the place, so the moment Mom took the pot from me, I grabbed Norma's darn ponytail and dragged her to the bedroom and told her to shut her mouth or I'd tell Mom she'd run away from me and gotten on a ride by herself. Thank goodness the threat had worked.

Now back to the butchers' story...

Mom preferred Don Falicce, but would occasionally visit the shop a bit further down into the orchards, ran by a beautiful girl from Spain (Carmela something or other).

Fabbio Falicce was a simple man with big vision. He was also a bit of a playboy, though not exceedingly handsome himself. He had a short torso with very long and muscular legs that produced a long—exaggerated—stride. He had pale skin, a wide square jaw, straight nose, thin lips, and jet-black hair…lots of it, too. He looked quite like a dreadful Roman guard and though his looks were often softened by a modest smile, each time he waved his colossal knife with such confidence and dexterity among the oohs and aahs of his typically feminine patrons, I could easily imagine him as a great warrior in armor and cape.

He'd been long married to an Italian lady no one dared mess around with. She looked quite like the statue of David, as I recall it -wavy hair and all. When she wasn't helping him right behind the counter, she could be found sitting in a corner, observing. And many-a-time she'd catch him flirting with the customers and would call him to attention, but Don Falicce was an incorrigible tease and never failed to make his way into trouble, over and again. By the way, no male was ever found among his clients.

I did not mind him; the butcher man. I thought he was quite the character. But I couldn't stand going there with Mom. Or with anyone else for that matter. I gagged each time I entered *carnicerías* (butcher shops). He received fresh meat from the central market each day, but the smell of fresh meat turned my stomach more so than decomposed meat, which on occasion I had smelled when our darn dog would escape to go rub himself on some dead animal's carcass lying in a nearby vacant lot.

Falicce's shop was always full, a line forming for half-a-block each day. If you shopped there, you weren't just guaranteed fresh meat. No, no, no! The real bonus was that you never needed a subscription to the city paper. The man was pretty much the ground zero of news and gossip. I dare say he must have had a broad network of informants because his ability and accuracy for breaking news would challenge the BBC. So, the shopper who did not bring in the news, took it home, and it was apparent that *she* was also responsible for spreading it home-by-home on her way home-sweet-home.

Sometimes when Mom had other errands and made the grocery rounds too late to get the best deal at Falicce's, she'd take us, or send us, to Carmela's shop. I liked Carmela. I even remember when she got married across the street at Montserrat. She was beautiful and had been a gorgeous bride. But some years later one day, Carmela's hand had gotten trapped in the grinding machine. I could never again approach her shop without getting a queasy feeling in my gut. I did not want to imagine, nor ever see, a mangled hand and missing fingers spilling out onto the mount of ground beef below. Yes, I've always had -and still have- a vivid imagination. If I were to tell you my fears of the sea, I am certain you'd think twice next time you got your feet in the water. That, my friends, is entirely another story.

***

And so, the Falicce butcher became quite wealthy. The house behind his shop displayed all the signs of it. They lived quite *la vida loca* and his two sons were considered the catch of the decade. I only remember the oldest, Aiello, about ten years older than I. He was tall and handsome, quite like his mother actually, though I never thought her good-looking. Confusing, I know. But Aiello was quite a realistic looking David. Michelangelo would have been impressed by the resemblance.

Their home was super-duper fancy inside and out and had the biggest inground pool. Falicce had also bought acreage further down the same dusty street, as a surprise for his boys, only to find out that the younger generation was not planning on remaining around, but rather possibly returning to their mother country.

Regardless, the old man decided to put the naked space to use. He had the land cleared, leveled, and covered by a thick layer of *aserrín de cedro* (awesomely scented cedar dust). Then, the whole property had been surrounded by a very tall brick fence with a privacy gate. We thought he'd rent it out for parties, but instead he started sponsoring what eventually became his legendary annual *fiestas de carnaval*, during the month of February.

All neighbors were invited to partake in the celebration, for free. By then there were hundreds of them (our family among them). He'd built a full wall worth of grills and would cover them with every beef delicacy imaginable, hiring teens to serve in all-you-can-eat-and-drink style. Even the priests would grace his tables -no surprise there though, our poorer than mice priests were not the type to turn down free food and drink.

Tables were set all around the center of the space, which was reserved for dancing, and, at the very end, a water balloon fight. But before the balloons were introduced to the crowd, Grandma (who never missed a good party), made sure to dance a couple of *Pasodobles* (the Spanish double step) with Don Falicce and the priests. They had fun. And I think Grandma was the only female Mrs. Falicce didn't mind dancing with her husband.

The entire party was financed by the Falicces in honor of the community that had helped them into fortune. It was outrageous and such good fun; the neighbors would talk about it for weeks.

***

Carnaval in Argentina takes place in the hot month of February. And is celebrated pretty much as New Orleans celebrates Mardi

Gras. When we were young children there were large groups of folks (*Cumparsas*) that came from Brazil to parade in the downtown streets. It was quite interesting. I'd never seen so much flesh on display (excepting my aunt Alicia's bedroom art).

In the neighborhoods, members of the community would hold water balloon fights in the street, particularly during the hotter hours of the afternoon—noon to five or so. It was not a planned activity, but a rather spontaneous thing. When girls got off a bus and walked home, a younger guy would start a chase or something that would evolve into a block party, and it wouldn't end until people ran out of balloons, someone fell and got hurt, or someone got upset due to a ruined outfit.

My sweet Dad liked keeping a bucketful of cold water and ready-balloons by our front door. He was clever and picked people who enjoyed getting into water fights.

There was a family in the next block, the Torranzas. They were great neighbors, all but one of their children older than I by several years. One of their daughters became a teacher and eventually taught at Montserrat. She was quite beautiful, and a sweet, classy woman. She never minded when chased with a bucket -she was always game. Her name, Carola.

While still single and dating, she'd come and spend hours chatting with us during tea time. Her boyfriends called her at our home, the only phone available nearby, other than the church's and the pharmacy's, neither of which would really do for dating.

She was fascinating to listen to, had the brightest of smiles, and a fantastic voice that exuded sexiness. For a while she dated one of Grandma and Grandpa's next door neighbor's youngest son. Small world, but not surprising. Tucumán wasn't really that large back then.

Last time I saw Carola was on a bus ride while I visited Argentina in the 90's. She'd married a military man, and had two sons. The three men in her life were her pride and joy. Sadly, she died in her forties, of pancreatic cancer.

Dad *loved* attending the famous *Bailes de Carnaval*, but often Mom would prefer to stay home if she wasn't feeling well. He'd drive us from one club to the other, to show us the folks going in and out in interesting costumes. And we listened to the loud festive music and announcements blaring from the speakers. Live bands often visited and performed for a while.

I remember one particular year when Grandma had stayed with us during the season. She had helped Dad convince Mom to attend a dance at Club BMM which was at the time a decent spot for families, though today I'm unsure within which category it falls.

The day wasn't very warm. Balloons, buckets, and you-name-its were all allowed and people often got wet even when the splash was meant for someone else, so we'd been wrapped in covers to avoid freezing in the cold, late-night breeze, and catching something. Grandma, who loved a party as much as Dad, had agreed to sit at the table with us while Mom and Dad danced.

Dad always had the time of his life at parties. But a guy had sprayed Mom with *nieve* (foam) or whatever they sold for people to harass each other with. Mom's eyes were immediately irritated, so Dad had started leading her towards a restroom where she could rinse off the nasty stuff. But she'd wiggled herself from his grasp, ran back, stole the can from the sucker, and in her own words, "Smashed it on his daft forehead." Yup, her signature moves were still alive and kicking.

We'd witnessed the entire ruckus, fully knowing that signaled the end of the night. While she was finally secured in the restroom rinsing her eyes, Grandma had walked us near the entrance. And as we waited for Mom and Dad, we observed a couple dancing across from us, near the stairwell to the second level dance floor. He was considerably younger than she. And she was beautiful. I recall she reminded me of my aunt Alicia because she was rather short in stature, but my-oh-my, well-proportioned and muscular.

They were so into the music, CCR's "Traveling Band' -the song playing wherever we went that year. They looked great together, a joy to watch, and since this was the end of our evening, it made for a great end.

They were awesome dancers and knew all the right moves. And all had gone well until he lifted his leg to swing her under it, without noticing his fly came wide open. They couldn't have predicted that her big blonde hair would get caught in his zipper and be pulled right off her head. Yes, ladies and gents, the term *off her head* is correct. She'd been wearing a wig and hadn't realized her mane had been pulled off until she faced him and saw her locks hanging from his crotch.

An entertaining finish indeed.

***

Occasionally, power was shut down sporadically during the evenings. With this, the military expected to slow down the growth of the antigovernment movement. Darkness reigned until the weak light of day softly touched our roofs, and the town awakened.

During the still hours of night, military trucks rolled along the streets, patrolling for unjustified traffic and gatherings. When they thought they detected clandestine assemblies, they sent police units to investigate, often utilizing the blinding lights of military helicopters to catch rebels, compelling those snooping through their windows (much like me) to stay away from the slightest idea of insurgence.

Their tactics always bordered on intimidation. The military marked the areas they controlled by sending groups of soldiers to trim sidewalk trees -all identical in shape and height, their trunks painted in white from the ground up to about three feet, in the exact manner they had historically marked military zones, near and within bases.

They also sent menacing notifications to each household they felt needed to address the front façade of their homes and spruce up the sidewalks, pressing them to conduct the necessary repairs within an allocated time, or face severe fines. But these fines mostly went uncollected as no one could really afford the repairs nor the set penalties. After their initial warning, their attempts would turn into harassment. It was easy to tell the neighbors who did not handle repairs on their own. All such homes' paint jobs looked identical: a shabby hand of watered-down white paint applied by a handful of soldiers.

We lived in all sense of the word in a police-run state. We were restricted in so many aspects that some folks grew accustomed to this practice and continued them indefinitely. Some, even to this day.

The country in turmoil, people fled the big cities, bringing several new families into the area. Most of the children attended Montserrat, but some could not afford it and walked or rode the bus to public schools.

The school year had been running for only a couple of months when a new family moved-in around the corner. They appeared quite nice. The couple had two beautiful children, both younger than I. Sometimes they were allowed to play with us, however they were mostly kept indoors, their only guaranteed outing was a daily ride to a private school downtown. Their dad drove them early in the morning on his way to work, and picked them up on his way back. They were rather well to do, the father having *some sort of business* the children were unable to describe. Their mom was a radiologist of sort on maternity leave, ready to give birth in the coming weeks.

I remember Norma on this one day, particularly, because the previous night she'd gone to sleep with gum in her mouth and had woken up with it webbed all over her long hair, causing Mom a big upset while she attempted to get us ready for school.

Mom had tried quite unsuccessfully to get rid of the sticky mess with ice and conditioner, however she'd run out of time and was unwilling to let Norma miss school (a request Norma would often place). So, Mom, all out of options, proceeded to cut out some of the worst clogs. Norma ended up with a fashion-breaking haircut. And although Mom and I kept telling her that it looked nice (because it actually did), she'd walked to school all upset about her mane and the minute-maid chop-chop-hairdo she'd received in a hurry.

It was May 20th, Mom's birthday being the next day. We expected grandma to arrive early afternoon to help Mom who'd be busy prepping fill for *empanadas, pre-pizzas* (pizza crusts) and *kipes* (Arab finger food Italians love). All these for the extended family to enjoy when they stopped by for a quick bite in the most frequent and traditional celebrations in our family. The house was already in full prep mode when we'd left for school. Upon our return we were to help Mom make *pastafrola* (Italian tarts with quince jelly), her dessert specialty.

At school, the release bell finally rang, we completed formation, and were free to go. Norma and I met at the school patio as usual and headed towards the avenue where Mom normally awaited. But this time as we approached the curve, there was no traffic, nor parents waiting. Nothing and no one, except for several police cars and military trucks approaching from the base.

They were moving slow, almost silently. And a block away from where we stood observing, soldiers started unloading. As they saw the children emerging from the school, they signaled us to remain quiet and to run, run, RUN! as they began placing themselves bellies-to-the-ground, flanking the curb across the street from our home, along three blocks, all the while pointing their *fusiles* (guns) at the doors facing the avenue. Ours included.

Norma was turning blue and not moving. I grabbed her hand and pulled at it like our lives depended on it. I felt they did. She'd finally snapped out of it when I started running across the road, dragging her along.

We got to the other side panting and just about losing our overloaded school bags.

We are about to reach the door handle when Mom -running a bit late due to party preparations- opens it, sees what is developing outside, and pulls us in, scared. She locks the door swiftly and tells us to crawl under her bed. Then she joins us on the dusty, cold floor, placing herself between us. She trembles while holding our hands tightly.

Everything has gone silent. But suddenly there is a small explosion followed by several shots. It's all taking place on the property behind ours. Mom lets our hands go, and places her own spread out over our heads, keeping us down. No sooner, a shootout breaks.

We hear people scream, and others clearly being shot at. There is a lot of yelling. The shooting goes on. And on. And on. They are so close to us the racket is overwhelming. Mom is lying between us, holding on to us, terrified. Then she looks up and we know what she is thinking. From our position we see the wall clock in the living room, near the front door. Then hear the final bell for the high school students -they are about to be released, and Alicia is among them. Mom whispers at us to stay put, then belly crawls through the bedroom floor and into the living room to reach the phone, while bullets fly right over us.

In her attempt to grab the phone, the cables get tangled, and she drops the tall and skinny phone table. Undoubtedly the commotion could be heard from outside and must have alerted someone. I close my eyes tightly and hope such is not the case. Once she secures the phone, while still lying down on the floor, she dials the school to ask them to please keep the highschoolers in place. I know Mom is wondering if the school is aware what is happening on this side of the avenue. They can surely hear it? On the other side, the phone rings numerous times while on our living room floor Mom sobs, curled in fetal position, with the receiver held tight to her ear.

The soldiers out front go silent for a minute, then start another round of shooting in our direction. All that separates Mom from them is the street, our front yard, and our living room wall. She is crying hard now, still down and next to the phone, looking at us while still attempting to reach the school. We can see her from under the bed while the bullets keep rushing over our heads.

There is another break and almost simultaneously someone attempts to open our back door, which we always keep locked. Something tells me that the table falling has called attention to our home, and I start shaking uncontrollably, then I reach out to grab Norma's chubby hand to steady my own. She is now crying, tears rolling down her little round face.

Mom signals us to remain silent, then tries to crawl back towards us, but the back door into the kitchen is kicked open before she reaches us. Knowing we are watching her from under her bed, she looks in our direction and closes her eyes softly, signaling us to do the same and remain still. The door slams against the side wall, and in come four men in civilian clothing, wearing bullet proof vests and holding *metralletas* (machine guns) pointing in Mom's direction. From the kitchen they yell at her, asking how many people are in the house. Her voice breaking, she says "Just me and my two little daughters, please, please don't hurt us." She is now bawling, and an indescribable feeling of panic has Norma and me pinned to the floor.

They ignore what she says and walk around -from our vantage point we can only observe their foot movements. One points his gun at Mom while the others open and slam shut the drawers of Mom's dresser. Then they approach the other bedroom and ransack our wardrobes, turning mattresses upside down, also including the one above our heads. They are startled when they see us, but at the same time one of them finds a revolver Dad kept in the bottom shelf of his night table, inside a shoe box where he also kept his gun license. That seems to take precedent in their minds for a moment, but they hand it back to Mom. Then one of them looks at her and says "It's almost over. Stay down right where you are, and don't come out until you hear sirens." Then they communicate by radio, and they are gone as quickly as they'd arrived, leaving through the front door, confirming they were not the people being looked for, but those doing the actual searching.

The shooting resumed then, and went on for another interminable moment while Mom crawled back to her bedroom and waited with us on the floor, with relief, but still sobbing. And when we thought it was over, and had started pulling out from under the bed, we heard one final string of shots some feet away from our home, followed by our neighbor Consuelos' scream, at which I saw Mom wince in a praying attempt as she squeezed our hands.

Then there was calm for a while. And then the sirens finally approached…

Right behind our property sat a nice home owned by a railroad worker, Don Augusto. The house was always leased out. The latest renters had moved in from another province.

It was common for these tenants to receive out-of-town visitors. But what in our innocence were acquaintances, had turned out to be radicals—government opponents—a broad term that also included many civilians around. Of course, most folks didn't dare make it known. We had just witnessed what happened to the opposition.

The military had heard from an informant and busted into what they defined as *a cell meeting* at our back neighbor's house, exterminating most as they sat, planning their next move.

Some had attempted to climb privacy fences to escape through neighboring yards. Consuelos, the woman with all her children inside their little shack, had come out of her home also thinking the gun fight over, and as she approached the patio where she'd hung blankets to air, a man about to jump over her back wall to reach freedom through her yard, was brought down by the last chain of bullets, falling to his death, entwined in a coverlet.

Several others had been killed inside the various neighbors' backyards and homes as they'd attempted to flee. The one I recall most was downed crossing over on to the yard of some little old folks from Spain who ran a small store from their home on Pasaje Holmberg, the side street north to my parents' house. The couple were Carmela the butcher's grandparents. I used to stop by their shop every other day at precisely this time to buy *Mirinda* (apple soda), *Granadina* (raspberry syrup for Italian sodas), or a handful of sugared gummies and a *Bananita Dolca* (banana fudge covered in dark chocolate) for my breaks at school.

All said and done, this operation went down in history as the *Masacre de la Calle Azcuénaga*. One of the dead, quite influential in the group (killed while attempting to reach Montserrat property), was one of the founding fathers of Descamisados -later fused with Peronist guerrilla Montoneros-, aristocrat Fernando Saavedra Luque (also known as F. S. Lamas, "Damián" or "Culipanza"), grandchild of the first Argentinian Nobel prize winner, and direct line descendant (great-great-great grandchild) of the Argentinian first junta president Cornelio Judas Tadeo Saavedra.

Mom had finally allowed us out of the house after she believed all was clear, but Norma and I witnessed young soldiers dragging a bloody cover wrapped around the last of those who'd met their fate that day. He was hauled across the uneven ground, bouncing over the curve on each side of the street, and once reaching the truck parked at the church entrance, they'd lifted it, swung it forth and back, and finally slung it onto the truck bed, dropping it on the steel floor of the vehicle like a sack of trash. The chilling sound of flesh and bones hitting metal still rings in my ears.

It was rumored that, that very afternoon, our newest, pregnant neighbor, had been captured as part of said radical movement. While the operation went down, she'd been home alone. Her husband and children had not returned home yet, and were never found, nor heard of, to my knowledge.

Thankfully, this raid *sort of* marked the end of the guerrillas in Tucumán.

My understanding of the causes and reasons for all of it then was nil, and even today when I attempt to read what really happened and how things intertwined and got so out of hand, it is impossible to keep track of who did what, why, nor how many players -and victims- were involved in the atrocities that took place.

I believe the extremists/guerrillas/Montoneros/ERP, or however they are referred to today, saw themselves as the only party defending the lives of civilians and the rights of the union workers that Perón had aided. In many instances, their actions went beyond reason and were inexcusable. But I also believe that the menacing military dictatorship itself fanned the flames of the militias.

Some actions by the military were indeed disguised as that of 'extremists,' only to suggest that the revolutionary forces, or radicals -whichever term the reader may prefer- were the actual perpetrators of said crimes. Then a reasonable individual wouldn't be inclined to support or join them. Yet, word around is that tunnels in and out of the city—dug out by Jesuit Priests long ago to escape the wrath of the Spaniards and Portuguese—had been reopened by the military and utilized as torture chambers.

Once again, I am not claiming to fully know nor understand the reasons or various facts and actions, nor to favor one or the other side. In their defense -which many of them will need for salvation purposes- I would dare *guess* that most, if not all, felt they fought for a fair cause. My only purpose in this writing is to convey the feelings and circumstances I experienced as a young and vulnerable child, in hopes that my children and grandchildren learn about these events through my very own words rather than through someone else's perspective. I also hope they themselves are never forced to live through such experiences.

Although I witnessed these events in the flesh, you don't have to believe my words. Historical facts reveal that between 1976 and 1983 military forces and what is known as the triple A (Argentine Anti-Communist Alliance) tortured and eliminated anyone believed a sympathizer of *The Montoneros* and other guerrilla organizations, Peronism, and Socialism.

All in all, between thirteen and thirty thousand people were killed, or disappeared. It is hard to know the exact number, as it encompassed not only activists, but students, writers, artists, and even folks that had remained un-involved, but represented in some way a political threat to the Junta. The extermination plan was known as Operation Condor, not exclusive to Argentina, but also conducted in other regions within South America.

Some of the master planners and executors of the numerous deaths and disappearances during the dictatorship were eventually indicted for crimes against humanity and genocide. Some were convicted to serve life sentences. In Buenos Aires, one of those indicted though not convicted was Jorge Zorreguieta Stefanini, Secretary of Agriculture during the military regime, and father to Máxima Zorreguieta Cerruti, who married Prince Willem-Alexander in 2002, and eventually became Queen of the Netherlands.

Zorreguieta's contributions to the cause had generated quite the stir in Holland prior to Prince Willem's nuptials. But the wedding bells had rung regardless, and Zorreguieta's actions even silenced (in Holland, home to the UN's Int'l Court of Justice, and fierce protector of human rights) though former Argentinian President Jorge Rafael Videla (Zorreguieta's boss) wrote a book describing in detail his own involvement, citing his cabinet members as able and willing participants, though they were *only following orders.*

It is also a fact that Máxima ran in upper class circles and was too young and altogether sheltered from exposure to the crimes her father was accused of. Still, when Máxima and Willem baptized their heirs and the Dutch press portrayed Mr. Zorreguieta as a tender grandfather, the tribute to Mr. Z. hadn't exactly sat well with many Argentinians. Folks down there were livid, and wondered where his loving trait had been during his stint in the notorious dictatorial government. To my knowledge, that is not something the Dutch answered, nor acknowledged or further publicized. It wouldn't be surprising to learn that Dutch monarchs had a hand in his charges being literally erased.

***

Seventh grade was not particularly eventful. Mom decided that each of us would attend an English Academy for a year before entering high school. Alicia had done it, and now it was my turn. Mom felt this would prepare us for our high school English classes starting in eighth grade.

She had accompanied me to the academy once, to show me where to get off the bus, and where to take it back to return home. I clearly remember my first day, coinciding with my first time traveling to and from downtown by myself. I had just turned twelve, and was simply terrified to be out on my own.

I also recall the tests I went for after each trimester. I had a teacher who'd lived in the States for five years, and I loved listening to her speaking to a couple of North Americans who also taught at the academy. I had classmates who already knew quite a bit and had traveled abroad with their families, something I never expected I would be fortunate enough to do. Ever. I listened to them and honestly thought I'd never understand English at that level. I also could have never imagined I'd end up spending my entire adult life in the U.S.

I excelled in all my classes again, and as much as this brought me a few friends, it also brought me a few enemies who got a thrill at making me feel inappropriate for my efforts.

The only thing which had at least temporarily deviated their attention from those of us that applied ourselves, was the rumor, and later confirmation -sadly- involving our principal, a spinster, the strictest yet fairest of educators. And the newest priest to grace our little community, Padre Ulises Ainza, who'd just arrived from either Spain or another parish.

The relationship had begun innocently, on the expectation that the church and school's leadership worked closely on both, discipline and curriculum. But it had unequivocally gotten out of hand, resulting on Ms. Iturbide leaving her job to join a convent, and Padre Ainza being literally thrown out of church. But I heard he'd left his secular life joyfully. The young man discovered he liked the opposite sex too much to keep himself at arm's length. And after a few years it was again rumored that he'd married a young girl from the congregation.

Other than this pivotal moment in the otherwise quiet existence of our little religious flock, most of what I recall was being bullied by a classmate, who also happened to be a close neighbor. Her family had moved into our neighborhood from Tafí Viejo (the same city where uncle Ángel resided). She had several brothers and a sister, all older by many years. Older even than my own sister Alicia, five years my senior.

They were truly an awesome family, however Narcisa, in my grade, and no bolt of lightning herself, did not know how to deal with competition. As the youngest of many siblings, she'd been spoiled rotten and believed no one could, should, or would, better her. Anyone receiving praise from a teacher or excelling at anything she could not, or did not, was an immediate target of her envy and anger.

Narcisa was much taller and stronger than I. She was pale, with green eyes and soft freckles, and wore thick square glasses with black acrylic frames that resembled Army-issued eyewear. This, when thick square glasses with black acrylic frames were *not the thing*. Her light brown thick hair lacked shine and care, and that year she'd had a butch cut that made her look like a jail warden.

Her arms and legs were too long for her torso, and her large hands gave her yet a further air of discoordination. She was almost the purest definition of a pre-teen boy. She wore mechanic's overalls over stretched tees, no bra, always preferred to play with the opposite gender, and often acted quite like them, too.

In many opportunities when our paths crossed, she had been orally rude to me and physically forceful, often sneaking behind me and whistling loudly in my ear, or stepping over my feet, and even pushing me down a flight of stairs (a couple of times, actually). She stared at me in a weird way, often scowled, and I couldn't help at being altogether uncomfortable around her. All in all, I can say with utmost certainty and in no better terms, that I was literally scared s**tless of her. She was unpredictable -I did not trust her. I was also considerably smaller in size, insignificant really. A matter of genes, for sure.

***

We were in our second hour of class one day when one of Narcisa's siblings arrived at school to pick her up. Her father had been ill, and we assumed things were not well if she was being pulled from class to return home.

That evening I learned the sad news. Upon much thought, I realized what a scary thing it would be to become an orphan at such young age.

Mom asked that I go and spend time with her. Her own family had requested this because Narcisa did not have many (more like *any*) friends, and was quite lonely among all the adults and gloom surrounding her.

They lived only a block away. I liked their home, a nice Spanish façade with deep arched walls and exposed brick work. Their backyard had also been part of the old local orchard and had never been cleared -the lemon trees still sat in rows by the large windows. I loved the overall feel of it.

Our parents were good friends. Dad had repaired their vehicles several times. By now the family owned a small general store they operated right out of their home, and whenever their sons ran into trouble during their daily trips to the grand market downtown to pick up merchandise, Dad was only a call away to assist. It can be said our families got along grandly. Then again, most everyone got along with my parents.

Doña Milagros, Narcisa's mom, had done my hair the day of my first communion. I loved the way she did her own hair, her nails, the way she talked...there was a slight accent to her musical voice. She was a sweet, refined lady, had beautiful green eyes, and was quite an accomplished baker. Her breads and pastries sold for a pretty penny at their store. I was particularly fond of her fluffy *pan de anís* (anise bread made with *anco* -similar to butternut squash), and *rosquetes* (the same dough, cut donut style, baked rather than fried, and covered in a sugary glaze while warm, the anise seeds bursting with flavor inside your mouth...un-for-get-ta-ble). It is because of her that until today, my sweet bread recipes call for anise seeds (not a very common staple in Argentinian baked goods, though anise liquor is quite popular in winter).

Anytime I could gather a few coins by saving my lunch money or leftover change that Grandma gave me from her bus rides (and gambling) I'd make my way over to the Laras' to pick up warm treats. Doña Milagros would always sit knitting at the far end of the store, but when I entered the shop, she'd always run up to help me in such graceful way, telling me she'd missed me and wondered if I'd forgotten her rosquetes were due out of the oven in a few short minutes.

The family was tall and on the larger side, their hips and thighs massive. Grandma always said they were "Spaniards of good stock, and surely came from a well-fed ancestor." And because they were so tall, their display case and countertop were also too high for my reach in my younger years, so she'd always come around the corner cabinet, open the little gate, and hand me the stuff herself. She always made sure I got some warm, freshly-out-of-the-oven treats in a bag to take home, and one extra (for free) to eat on my way back. The woman spoiled me. She knew how much I loved her baked goods and could not help giving me a big smile each time I walked in—religiously every Wednesday—as the loaves emerged from the oven. The heavenly smell twirling around the neighborhood marked my cue, leading me straight to the store front.

Doña Milagros was among the few truly faithful that NEVER missed mass, nor did she mind or tired of donating time and goods for any church activity the priests fancied. She always walked to church, bible in hand, her little black Spanish *mantilla* on her head. And also, always after church, she'd stop by to chat with Mom. On occasion, Grandma had teased that her visit was the closest she'd come to a bible since her own running with the Madre Superiora.

Doña Milagros liked Grandma very much. Herself the daughter of Spanish migrants, they used to talk about *the old country* and the paisanos they commonly knew. They laughed together and enjoyed each other's company.

***

The sun was going down as I made my way over to their house, bringing along some of the class work we'd covered during the few hours Narcisa had missed. On arrival, I did not ring the bell out of reverence. Through the windows above their front garden I could see the inside movements, just as they could observe anyone approaching.

Doña Milagros saw me at the entrance gate, came over, gave me her usual warm welcome, and asked me to go in and wait for Narcisa in their dining room. I entered, noticing the family was gathered in the large living room to the right, surrounding the casket. I was not particularly fond of home viewings. In truth, they were somewhat frightening, and they reminded me of Grandpa, the large candles, and the giant *crocifisso* at the head of his coffin.

I avoided looking in as much as could be helped, and marched straight to the dining room at the back of the house, where they had coffee and mate ready to serve. I sat there for a minute in solitude, then Doña Milagros had approached me and asked if I had had *merienda*. I hadn't. She served some mate for me, and after disappearing shortly through the door to the store, she reappeared carrying a tray with *rosquetes* and other sweets. She smiled and told me to go ahead, and that Narcisa would be over shortly after she finished bathing.

As she prepared to leave the room, I heard voices. A constant stream of people had entered the house behind us to pay their respects. She arranged a few shots of coffee and strong liquor on a fanciful tray of *plata real,* the customary refreshment and serving utensils during visitation hours. Then she readied to go. She asked if I minded being left alone for a bit. I said "*No,*" and she left.

After a few moments, Narcisa arrived. She immediately seemed upset that I had started our merienda without her. Right then one of her brothers also entered the room and served himself some coffee. As he prepared to leave the room, he set his eyes on her and said *"be nice"* while pointing his chin in my direction. It was comforting to learn they knew she could be mean.

We chatted for a bit. She seemed disinterested, withdrawn, and once again, I wasn't sure what to say. She made no mentioning of her current situation and I assumed she preferred not to talk about it. So, we spoke about random stuff. Still struggling to find a subject to focus on, I pulled out and showed her the work we'd done during her absence. She scowled at me and told me she had no intention of making up the missed work, so I closed my workbook and asked her what she wanted to do. She invited me to play a board game. I am not a game lover, but I figured I'd try if that made her feel better. We played for a while and time passed easily.

It was nearly nine pm when I finally picked up courage to tell her I needed to get back home. I had already heard all visitors leave. Her siblings had gone home to their families, and her mom was in the shower. Only an aunt and uncle remained, now also in the kitchen, getting a quick bite.

She offered to walk me out. The living room, to our left as we exited, sat empty except for chairs perfectly arranged around its perimeter. The room had been chosen as the *capilla ardiente*—the casket, candles, and crucifix sat in perfect coordination in its center. All lights had been deemed except for the candles and cross, all of which burned bright. It was peaceful.

But instead of continuing onto the front door, she veered to the left and made her way into the room, approached the casket and looked-in, almost spellbound. In that moment I thought she should be devastated. I knew I would have been, had it been me in her place. Instead, she looked distant.

Without turning, she asked me if I had seen him yet. Standing to her left and slightly behind her, I told her I had when I'd arrived -though I hadn't really approached the room then. She turned towards me, her right hand grabbed my upper right arm forcefully, hurting it, and in a swift movement her left hand went straight to the tender hair right above my neck, pulling hard yet pushing down 'til she'd brought my face a mere inch away from her father's, inside the casket. Then she hissed: "Yeah, but not like this, HAVE YA?" She then pushed my face even closer to his -almost touching it-, then let me go, laughed loudly, and walked past me, headed right back to the dining room. I was left alone, my only company her father in the casket.

I flew out of the room, out the front door, my hands struggling to open the front gate. I ran home at such speed, tripping over the ruts on the road separating her block from mine, all the way imagining she was chasing after me and dragging me back. I dared glance back once and was grateful to find she was not in sight. I reached our front door, snuck in quickly, locking it right behind me. And though going against *keeping friends close and enemies closer,* I swore never again to allow myself to be left alone with her, no matter in which of the mentioned categories she fell.

Even through the explosions and shootouts, and every other act of violence I had ever experienced or witnessed, I had never -EVER- felt so helpless and terrified of any one person as I had that night at her hand.

Soon, the end of the year approached. We were graduating from seventh grade. It was decision time as to what school we'd chose to attend in the upcoming stage of our lives. I'd long before decided to complete my twelve years at Montserrat. And was beyond myself with happiness when I learned Narcisa would not be returning to *my* school.

***

Around this time, a new family had moved into the neighborhood. The nicest people. The couple also had three daughters, the middle one younger than Alicia, the youngest, younger than Norma. Their oldest daughter lived away from home, which was considered quite progressive at the time. The parents were lovely people and in time became Mom and Dad's great friends, and one of their best neighbors.

Dina was a schoolteacher. She was such a loving, genuine, and attentive friend to Mom, particularly when Mom's illness started taking a hard toll on Dad and my sisters. She would offer to cook and do laundry, and to help out in whichever way she could. She was a fervent Catholic. We often saw her pass by to attend mass -every evening and weekend. She meant a lot to my parents. Her whole family did. Their oldest daughter never married. The next did, and had a daughter herself. Their youngest was employed as a nanny for an older single man from Lebanon. He had two children from a previous marriage. Dina's daughter was young and patient, and in no time became a mother to those children, and eventually even married her employer and shared a couple of children with him.

***

My first year of high school was interesting. A different pace and too many subjects to juggle. I excelled at my classes still, although not without a complete lack of sleep during school days, which I desperately tried to make up for during weekends.

During elementary, we'd had a horribly obnoxious and harassing gym teacher from Buenos Aires. She taught the girls, while her husband taught the boys. In high school, luckily, we had a different instructor. But I still did not enjoy the class.

I've never been the athletic type. I'd much rather sit some-where by myself reading if not memorizing stuff, any subject, anything that kept me away from the torture of doing any ath-letic activity in front of the opposite gender (we did P.E. in the afternoons while the boys attended school, then during their breaks they'd line up by the gym area to watch us...ugh!).

What I enjoyed even less was any type of gym activity in our ridiculously short gym skirts. It did nothing to build my self-confidence...all the mixed Italian and Spanish blood graced us with booty-licious girls all around. I matter-of-factly knew I could never match their looks, even when some of them had a face only a veterinarian could love. But I knew too well it was not their faces the boys gathered 'round to watch. Do not misunderstand me, I could appreciate and admire their offerings, but realistically speaking I did not do myself a favor by standing around next to them. So, my strategy was to stay away from boys, or hang out with ugly chicks. Just kidding! I was a very studious and insecure teen, and it could be said I never got over this awkward ugly-duckling feeling. Never felt pretty. Never felt

I looked good enough to be noticed. Never felt an ugly person could get away with breaking the rules.

Perhaps all this was the result of not growing up around boys at home. I saw the difference in the classmates who had brothers -with it came a revolving door to a parade of the male species, and an acceptance to them always being around.

I should however note my annoying awkwardness did not seem to affect either of my sisters or friends. Just me.

***

I had watched soccer repeatedly over the years with both Mom, and Dad. Mom was quite vocal as we watched teams confront each other. Dad was a bit more playful and disciplined, smart man that he was.

The winter of 1978 shaped up to be another crude one. The most exciting event during this year was the World Cup. It was held in Argentina, among overpowering military presence evident throughout the championship -music for the opening ceremony was dominated by military bands, and marches.
Edu Seijas. 2017, June 30. *A78TV – Mundial 1978 Ceremonia Inaugural.* [Video]. Format [Video file]. YouTube. https://youtu.be/Wig-ylchN-c?si=wAeupyj-78_rsas5

I had become quite familiarized with every name on each of the many competing teams, together with stats. I enjoyed it all. My brain craved details, so my parents had me running calculations and the likelihood of this team beating that one -it'd turned out to be a very fun winter.

But none of the games were played in Tucumán. The closest game was held at the largest stadium in the province of Córdoba. Grandma, who practically lived with us by then, never cared much for soccer though this time she joined forces, and our enthusiasm. This was the first entirely televised Soccer Cup we were able to watch. Luckily Argentina shone, beating the Netherlands 3 to 1 in the final. We were champions – it was a great feeling.

The blistering cold on the afternoon of June 25th did not stop fans from celebrating. All Argentina was a grand party. The sky was lit by fireworks as the last goal was scored, marking the very end of a long game rendering us a victory the country was very much in need of, psychologically. There was a lot going on in our world.

My family stood outside by the curve waving the *Albiceleste* at the passing cars loaded with fans, honking their horns non-stop. And before we knew it, Mom and Dad were loading us on the bed of a giant truck of a family friend, who'd stopped to pick us up on their way to the massive downtown celebration, which even in our police state, had been advertised as *allowed.*

The truck was loaded with fans and flags. Even the quiet good-looking guy that often wore suits to work and took the bus across the street was in the truck with us. I had always wondered why he never wore his suit jacket all the way on, but rather hanging off his shoulder, and only then I realized one of his arms was missing. Later on, I was told that he'd grown up on a farm, and that as a toddler barely learning to walk, he'd been attacked by a large pig who'd torn off his tender limb.

And off we went. My voice was already gone by the time we arrived at Plaza Independencia. We'd sang the World Cup hymn all the way into the city at the top of our lungs -such euphoria. We parked as close as possible to the town square, already in full party mode. There were already thousands of fans waving flags and chanting the theme song again, as giant screens played the numerous goals our team had scored throughout the tournament. Mom and Dad sang out loud, holding Norma by her hands, and waving flags in the other. Alicia and I held on to Grandma, who'd always argued she was Spanish to the death, but this day she sang the Argentinian National Anthem alongside us, tears rolling down her reddened cheeks, while she smiled at us. What a fantastic memory.

With this win I came to understand the fact that soccer (Fútbol to Argentinians) is imprinted in every being carrying Argentinian DNA upon their entrance into this world. Though it seems that by the time my second born made his imminent approach, my inner printer may have run out of ink (wink wink).

But this wasn't all as far as 1978 went. We also saw three popes grace the gates of St Peter's Basilica. This year kept the College of Cardinals busy as they worked to decide who'd step up upon the death of Pope Paulus VI on the first week of August. By the end of the month, John Paul I had been chosen to preside over the Catholic Church, however he passed away only a month later, forcing the Cardinals to reconvene for a repeat of the process. And two weeks later, the chosen cardinal was Karol Jozef Wojtyla, Polish, who took on the name John Paul II, and was head of the Church and Sovereign over the Vatican City State for over twenty-six years, until his death in April of 2005.

Pope John Paul II was a most personable and humble servant. He'd lost both parents and only sibling by the time he was twenty years old, and aided numerous people during the Nazi occupation in Poland. He was truly adored by the masses, beatified in 2011, and canonized in 2014.

***

After such eventful year, 1979 did not deliver much excitement except for a time just after our winter vacation, when our Syrian neighbors next door and down the road (both owners of the then staple home-run general store) prepared to host a *promesa* (Spanish term for Ramadan), a celebration held at the culmination of their long Muslim fasting. The best recollection I have of it was that of males with thick accents and bushy mustaches, and females with stunning facial features and gorgeous curvature.

One evening, Mr. Mohamed had invited us to take part in the feast. But Mom and Dad already had another engagement, Alicia wouldn't attend because she aimed at staying away from Mr. Ale's son's inquiring looks, and I felt intimidated by the fact that all guests were male. Hordes of them had arrived wearing simple white robes, and some of them even a scarf or head cover. They doubled and tripled parked along Viamonte, making it impossible to transit along the avenue, upsetting neighbors and drivers-by alike.

They were quite lively. But the music (or prayers?) had been beautiful. Mr. Mohamed and his daughters had wanted to share this with us, however noticing our apprehension they'd brought tray after large tray of food. Some savory, some sweet, all so new in taste and appearance, and all to die for, really.

The prayers, and evening feasts had gone on for days, during the whole while the road leading to our home had been littered by expensive cars. And once over, we'd finally met the Mohamed clan. Their daughters, one prettier than the next.

Only the eldest was married then, to a man her senior, Dante Porciello. He was an Italian immigrant, a wealthy business-man, and one of the kindest and most distinguished men I've ever met. He and Cristina Mohamed had become acquainted through a mutual friend while, I believe, she worked as an extra in a soap opera being filmed in Buenos Aires. *"My Dante"*, as she called him, was the love of her life. At the time they'd just returned from a long honeymoon abroad, and anxiously expected the arrival of their first child, who would be their only one (Diego Porciello, who grew up to be a sports anchor and automobile aficionado in Florida, rubbing elbows with Jay Leno and other celebrities).

The Porciellos were happy. I always hoped I'd be so blessed to find that same kind of love one day. They had eyes for each other only, and shared a very special bond.

Anecdote by Diego Porciello -Miami, Spring '24: "When I was a teenager, and while visiting my grandparents in Tucumán, one of my cousins and I had been loaned a brand-new Ford sedan by my uncle, to go around town and impress the girls one weekend evening. We were young, wild, and careless. We'd wrecked the car and didn't quite know how to avoid getting in trouble when we brought it back and showed our families what we'd done. I was leaving town a couple of days later, but there was no way of hiding the facts, so I'd called your dad and asked him how fast he could fix the damage and make the nightmare go away. It was just past midnight. I knew I was asking for a lot, so I'd promised to pay whatever the price for an immediate solution. He asked that we bring the car by immediately, sheltered by the cover of dark. He worked on it all night and had all issues literally erased by morning. The car looked brand new again by the time everyone was up next day, and no one ever learned, until now, what had transpired. Your dad was a pro, a genius, and a good friend!"

The Mohameds had only one son, Yusuf. Or José, as most everyone called him locally. José was in his late twenties and was a playboy in the true sense of the word. He was a headache to his parents—a rake and a rogue, and conceited to boot. He was his mother's and older sister's favorite, being the only reason Don Fares did not kick him out -permanently- from the family's home. When his older sister came into fortune, she showered him with presents and play money which at times he managed to multiply by means of honest work, but more-often-than-not, he wasted it all at casino tables. Yes, I knew a true playboy.

José eventually settled down with a sweet young girl named Marta, about my age. She was several years younger than him, and came from another province. She had been made to marry a young, promising boy from the very small town she'd grown up in. But the marriage had been over as fast as it started…when Yusuf rolled into town on his new wheels. She'd walked away from her commitment and never looked back. But she often felt lonely during their first few months together though. And such is how Marta and I became quite good friends. She adored him, simple as that, though his parents were not fond of her. But her patience prevailed, and she was in time accepted into the family, and appreciated by them all. She and Yusuf shared three sons and two daughters.

Next in line of succession came Mirta, a doll of a woman. Small but sassy, voluptuous, and overall perfect. She lived in Bs. As. and owned a successful medical emergency business. Anytime she graced us with her presence in town, she could not be missed. Drop dead gorgeous in all sense of the word and clueless about it. One of her cousins had tried her best at marrying her to some wealthy relative -not uncommon in the Islamic community. But Mirta would not have it. Eventually she fell madly in love with a young guy from Armenia, they married, had one son, and moved to Montevideo, Uruguay.

And last in order was Graciela, who'd ran away with her high school sweetheart because Mr. Mohamed did not approve of him. She was the last chance for the patriarch to get at least one of his children married into the faith, but he'd failed at it one more time. Eventually the Mohameds allowed their wedding once their youngest informed them their opposition didn't matter. They intended to marry no matter what it took, nor how long. And she was married right away to dreamy Tito Cangró, with whom she ultimately shared half a dozen children.

***

Every once in a while, during winter, there were fundraisers either by the school or church. The offerings included a beautiful sunny day spent at the huge school playground, enjoying the best of Argentina's food and music. There were singers and *cantautores,* both amateurs and well-known performers like the famed *Tucu-Tucu quartet,* plus *gaucho* parades, folklore dancers, and *malambo* experts -Argentinian male tap dancers that show off skill in the use of *boleadoras* (leather and stone hunting weapon) while performing pirouettes and knife fights.

The food was fantastic, including *locro criollo* (a sort of Argentinian jambalaya), tamales, empanadas, asado, and warm breads and desserts to enjoy with a nice cup of warm mate. And there were also fun prize drawings. Dad used to enjoy this very much, and would often attend. Mom did not like this type of event.

*****

Mom and Dad had married at an old age for the era's standard, hence some of their siblings - particularly on Dad's side- married and bore children much earlier than my sisters and I made our debut into the family ranks.

As our cousins on Dad's side came of age and started marrying off, Alicia, Norma, and I were paraded and introduced around to the mass of folks becoming attached to the family by means of marriage. And one thing I recall making a lasting impression in a sad and scary sort of way, was having met one of the in-laws-to-be to one of my cousins. It was an engagement party of sort, though my memory plays tricks on me now and again (beware of age, my friends).

The groom and two of his brothers were wonderful to us. He worked for Xerox Tucumán and did well for himself. He was marrying an equally sweet girl who ran a catering business she'd inherited from her mother. We'd been invited to a lively gathering to celebrate their joining together, and it had been lovely prepared and executed. The bride-to-be had made all the wonderful food, and merriment abounded. She was either the youngest or only daughter to the family, and everyone in attendance seemed thrilled for her.

I sat right next to this sweet old lady in a wheelchair. I remember she'd been introduced as one of my cousins' aunts-to-be. Her hair was entirely silver, and her eyes a soft grey, quite resembling those of my own grandma. She had such sweet smile and voice, with a musical Spanish lisp. Worth mentioning is that though surrounded by many Spaniards, it was always refreshing to hear their very proper accent -a bit like when Americans come face to face with an England native.

An air of aristocracy engulfed her persona, and there was a manner of robust warmth radiating from her. She was handsomely dressed and groomed, and wore a layer of beautiful uneven pearls around her neck.

In a world where most folks spoke with their hands, I noticed she kept hers on her lap, with great effort, and covered by a mantilla. All had gone well until the multiple siblings summoned folks to the tables and made toasts to the new couple and invited everyone to share in their happiness. Then several of the younger relatives had approached her, selecting and separating drinks and hors d'oeuvres as she requested. It had all been carefully dished and placed within her reach. Then they'd again murmured in her ear until she had finally risen a hand to wave them off. And then I saw what she'd so sensibly disguised under the lacey cover.

To my young eyes, her hands were mercilessly deformed. So twisted and shaky, she struggled with the food that had been so elegantly laid out for her. She'd hopelessly also attempted to hold and raise a glass of bubbly to her lips, shortly thereafter giving up on her endeavor.

Her joints twisted and turned in the oddest angles, mimicking intricate corkscrew willow branches. I could not tear my eyes away from her hands, and my mind had gotten caught in thinking she couldn't have gone through it without excruciating torment. Nor could it have happened fast enough to lessen the agony of the process. I didn't know her, but I had already grown fond of her in our short acquaintance. And I'd felt such sorrow for this lady, I suddenly had a knot in my throat. I was weak that way when I saw someone in pain, and Mom had noticed, as usual, and had come to me, and told me to calm down. And that she had the same illness as aunt Hilda, which had shocked me.

I had known all along that uncle Juan's wife was affected by rheumatoid arthritis, but we hardly ever got to see her anymore. The ailment had only represented a scientific name to me until this moment, though I knew aunt Hilda's illness had kept her from outings, and by the time I was ten or so, she'd become a recluse. Though we heard about her suffering, we hadn't witnessed the cross she carried. Little did I know that in my fifties I would myself become intimately acquainted with the menacing effects and life sentence of R.A.

***

There were many weddings taking place. Cousins, neighbors, you name it. Mom would always scrutinize her gift giving, and struggled to obtain items she liked sufficiently to give away -within her budget, that is. She had a good source for her findings though. His name was Tito (from either Ernestito, Albertito, Robertito…one would guess?). He was a Spanish merchant married to a lady many years his junior. They shared one child who eventually became a professional figure skater.

He travelled around, sometimes by car and others by train, dealing with craftsmen and importers, and purchasing oddities among some quality merchandise hard to find in our isolated podunk location. He ran a one-man show, but business must have been decent because he drove a large, expensive vehicle, which he filled with goods he offered around to the masses, after his repeat customers had had a chance at them first.

His success was all word-of-mouth. And evidently lucrative. Often when Mom needed a present or quality items for the house (bed covers, blankets, winter coats for us, etc.), Don Tito was only a phone call away. The man was the primitive version of Amazon...the very best deal, delivered to your front door.

CHAPTER 11
The Eighties

Nineteen-eighty was a year I could seldom forget. It was also my turn to sport long and primal looking arms and legs, quite in disproportion with my short torso. And my skin and hair were simply awful. Puberty sucked.

Unlike winter breezes that brought along the scent of roasted peanuts that were sold in every corner, summer evenings smelled like burned sugar cane. The air was thick and sticky, making for a long and lazy close of the day. Sleep always took its sweet time. It was merely too hot to lie down on the rudimentary foam of our thin mattresses. The sheets rarely cooled, and then, remained so only for so long.

We prepared for my 15th birthday party. It would be held on January 26th. Mom had secured a venue from the railroad society, a large brick building with handsome thick walls and quite a great open area out back. It was party-fantastic!

I had invited my class from school, and some of the boys in the mirror class from the afternoon hours, many friends, and our huge immediate and not so immediate family. I had also asked my classmates to bring their boyfriends and older brothers. We expected about two hundred guests, the big mass of them made up of family.

Mom and Grandma made some of the food, but the extensive banquet was mostly catered by a neighbor of ours, Doña Juanita Carrizo. She was an amazing food crafter who occasionally prepared yum-yums for the Porta's big events. There were dozens of very large trays with empanadas and all the goods that were the staple of large celebrations at the time. The cake and petit fours were nothing short of amazing, and I had made pretty souvenirs to give out. Dad's brother René (at the time a weekend DJ, and radio talk show host) was in charge of the music and quick announcements. His stage name was Carlos Galé. Finally, one of my classmates' dads, Don Ladrón de Guevara, was our photographer.

The party was a great hit. We had a huge group of kids on the dance floor. I still carry in my mind the image of everyone dancing to 'Rasputin' (song by Bonney M), and to Donna Summers' 'Hot Stuff.' The older folks had also joined-in once the Bee Gees had entered the DJ's repertoire. Everyone had such fun and the gathering had gone on until the wee hours, which by the way was no exception -Argentines are night owls by nature.

Towards the end—early morning already—some guys walking back home from a popular dance venue further up the road, happened upon us and asked if they could come in. Most older folks had left already and loads of food remained still on trays, untouched. Mom agreed to let them in, telling them to feel free to enjoy some of the food. The music was still going and one of them—the pushy one of the group—invited me to dance. He was the handsomest guy I'd ever laid eyes upon. Quite tall, on the larger side yet well-proportioned, well-spoken, and best of all, he had the most perfect lips, and a gorgeous face. He was quite a beauty from any angle. And he was asking ME to dance. I accepted. I was no fool.

As we walked to the dance floor, my classmates looked at me as if saying "What did YOU do to get HIM?" And I didn't know. This was a time when I felt quite awkward, clumsy, and overall unattractive. And my friends' looks made me further doubt myself. I already couldn't picture anyone liking me enough to want to spend time around me. Further acknowledging my lack of sophistication hit me with full force. I was young and innocent. I had NEVER had a friend that was a boy, let alone a *boy*friend, nor could I imagine anyone would want to call himself *my* boyfriend. For sure I wouldn't know how to react to someone asking me out. And the fact that this guy appeared interested blew my mind and made me feel … grateful?

We danced to several tunes. He was fun to be around. Uninhibited. Silly. Very, very cute. But I needed to sit because the shoes

Dad's sister had gifted me for the party hurt so very much. He then asked permission to sit with me, and again I couldn't fathom what was happening.

We spoke a bit. More actually than I had ever spoken with any boy all my life, even my boy cousins. He sat immediately across from me, so close I had to turn a bit so my legs would not touch his. He seemed genuinely interested in what I had to say. And as I brought my foot up to rub my sore sole, he suddenly got up and disappeared for a second, making me wonder what I'd done wrong. But he'd quickly returned to my side with a drink in hand. For me. My jaw clicked open, my chin dropped, and there was no hope of him not noticing I was about to drool. Then he'd smiled at me and I could only imagine my idiotic face looking back at him like a cat staring at an open can of tuna. I knew I looked foolish. He was too easy on the eyes, and I couldn't help the heat I felt when, in taking the glass from him, my hand rubbed against his. The touch had seared.

We talked. The conversation flowed easily and I felt accepted. I had no clue back then what was occurring to me, but I noticed he knew how to play along.

He was of German descent on his father's side. His grandfather had migrated to Argentina leaving behind a land at war. His mother was of Arabic descent. He said he had two sisters that he adored, and mentioned he was about to start his senior year at one of the technical schools in town. He also said more. Much more. I only caught that he wanted to attend university to study Engineering. BTW, did I mention he was gorgeous? He really was. And not just in my imagination, but truly, truly gorgeous. With perfect eyes and lashes, perfect lips and nose, a perfectly square jaw and a whole lot of perfection spread thick throughout the length of him. He made me think of the soldier with whom Liezl von Trapp falls in love.

After these odd feelings in my otherwise complete lack of expertise in matters of the heart and the male mysteries, I wondered whether someone feeling emotionally slutty could claim to be respectable...because that was me in that precise moment. I was unsure what the priests at school would have said about that, but I felt the tug towards convent life loosening up. A few of my best friends at school had always dreamed of a life of service in perfect reclusion. But after my newly awaken sentiments, I knew I no longer genuinely could, or would, consider such destiny.

A handful of relatives remained at that point to help us clean up the venue. Everyone looked our way but said nothing nor asked me to help, though I expected someone would. There seemed to be an agreement among everyone present not to bother me (us).

He inevitably noticed he and his friends were about the only non-family guests left. In chatting, our eyes locked for a bit, and foolish of me, I stopped breathing. Our conversation had come to a pause. Then he asked for my phone number, which I wrote down in a piece of paper he facilitated, simultaneously -yet silently- praying he'd call me back. He took the paper, came close enough to make me faint though I didn't, and gave me a soft peck on the cheek. Then he busied himself gathering his friends, and started to leave. He turned around, looked at me from the entrance gate, waved, and was off. He was quite a gentleman, and good-looking to boot. And saying he was good-looking did not do justice. He was perfect...had I mention he was gorgeous?

With him gone, I felt my Cinderella story had come to an abrupt end, so I removed my crystal shoes for good, and helped Mom and Dad finish the cleaning.

We finally made it home as the sun started to rise, and hurried to fill our two refrigerators with food we were unable to give away. Plenty was taken away by the last strugglers that helped bring order back to the venue, but there was still lots left.

We staggered into bed as the sun rays peaked out in the sky. That Sunday was the hottest day ever. We got up later in the day to hydrate and feast on leftover food and deliciously cold, moist cake. We were exhausted and not in the mood for much talk that evening. Until a call came in. For me.

***

Karsten started calling on me at home the following week, at least twice during weekdays, but each evening from Friday through Sunday.

Today I recognize he knew he had me wrapped around his finger, and wonder if he ever noticed that each time he came close, my knees knocked against each other and I had to find the strength to prevent myself from melting into a large puddle of stupidity. I bet he knew. I think I know he knew.

But I also knew then as I do now, even in all my innocence, that he was genuine and that I meant something to him, because he was a genuine dreamer when I did not dare dream. I couldn't help feeling I was only taking part in an imaginative bubble about to burst at any minute, though all the while he made plans for a shared future. I wish my brain succeeded at communicating those fears to my heart. I wish my brain had won that battle when I started, and continued, to fall into puppy love.

He had started coming along with us to family get togethers, asking to go along. He'd also eventually asked that I met his family, which I agreed to, though quite apprehensively. I felt it was too soon, and I was nothing short of terrified, knowing fully well in what category my family fell, class wise, compared to his. I was also of European descent, but my background was no match for his Germanic ancestry. And then, there was the middle eastern bit. The potential for his parents to find differences between us was massive.

During my first visit, his father was very sweet -an older version of Karsten. His sisters were lovely, one much older, the other much younger. They all were very hospitable and made me feel genuinely welcomed. They seemingly adored Karsten, and gave all indication that life in their household revolved around all he did and wanted to do.

Then his mother arrived home and from the start she showed she was not keen on me. She used every opportunity available to make sure I heard and understood that at eighteen he was "too young to be involved in a serious relationship." And I agreed. I, at fifteen was not looking for a 'serious' relationship either. I was not looking for any relationship at all, in truth. He had initiated the relationship, fact of the matter. I wouldn't have known how -nor would have dared do it myself had my life depended on it. But she repeatedly showed and expressed disdain. And I felt insignificant. Inept. Her eyes always insinuated that I did not measure up. And I inevitably felt tongue-tied around her.

I knew that in some circles Mediterranean bloodlines were perceived as vermin. And I believe that was exactly the point she was attempting to get through. In her eyes, I was no match for her only son. Now looking back, I can't deny that I had also sensed subtle signs of condescension from him a couple of times, mainly when she was around. But each time I had pushed the feeling aside, telling myself I was too soft and vulnerable. And that I was only imagining it.

Thankfully, I've learned by now not to overlook red-flagging behaviors. But back then, before Narcisa from elementary school, and again until Mrs. Haas surfaced in my life, I hadn't experienced explicit condescension towards me, with the exception of a handful of girls at school. Though in said cases, I considered the source. Those girls mostly came from money and kept to their little clique. The remaining majority of us were kept in a very embracing and accepting environment.

So, Mrs. Haas' dislike, in particular, hurt in ways I could not express. Discrimination in Argentina was -and is, still today- not so much focused on skin color, but rather in close relation to the differing socioeconomic classes, and to the last name some folks are privileged to carry.

Down there, always present is an economic elite made up of 1) traditional families stemming from the colonists, and 2) a capitalist class who owns most of society's wealth and whose pockets keep inflating to the further detriment of the lower classes worldwide (typical). On one side, traditional/colonist families, though aristocratic, have a better understanding of their standing, while somewhat respect the lesser classes. But the capitalists' presence is felt, although it represents only a shy two to three percent of society. And their disgust for the rest of us was (often still is) simply apparent.

As we grew up, age brought wisdom, and with wisdom came the sad realization of where we stood in the world. In roman dogma, I belonged to the plebeian class. That was—and still is—Argentina: very few patricians; very many plebeians. Not much in between.

But there, many folks believe that racism and discrimination only exist abroad. Racism and discrimination there, are perhaps manifested in a different way than traditionally seen elsewhere, but they exist regardless.

***

This year most of my classmates turned fifteen. And each were celebrated by their parents in sometimes small gatherings, and sometimes in outrageously lavish parties. We attended numerous of said get-togethers. Alicia, by then twenty, was sent along as chaperone, and she took her job as third wheel quite seriously, though her rigid enforcement of what was -or was not- appropriate seemingly only applied to me.

I was naive enough to never dream about breaking any rules. But the fact is, I could not go into a bathroom without her standing by the door as if it were a citadel. Even less walk away to get a drink or even walk out the door from the stuffy venues to get fresh air; or dance with Karsten unless we were in her full view. None of it was allowed unless I remained in her full line of sight. We could not even talk without her involvement, and the suffocation choked the life out of me, particularly because Karsten and I did not intend to hide or do -nor get away with- anything.

Karsten went along with it until he no longer could. His solution was to bring a classmate a few years older than himself to pursue her, and hopefully this would give us room to breathe and properly talk and get to know each other.

His plan worked, and Alicia started to date again, thank goodness. The guy had repeated his high school classes for years and hadn't managed to graduate. By now he was considerably older than the rest of his classmates, but the general consensus was that he exuded sex appeal and it appeared that -that alone- granted him ranking within our clan. The deliberating committee (my ten aunts) had seemed to gladly -and openly- approve his acceptance.

Alicia liked him, so I couldn't care less if the man had the lowest IQ in the southern hemisphere, as long as the two of them did not give me idiots for nieces and nephews. Yup, you got it...críos were not part of the plan.

Karsten's sisters came along with him to visit us at home, and we had a great time together. They were sweet, well educated, and did not show any apprehension about associating with us. They were wonderful to be around, genuine, happy, stunning girls. He loved them dearly and protected them so.

This year he would also graduate from high school, and as per local custom their senior class would take a one-to-three-week trip somewhere -their last hurray before they turned adults and started fending for themselves. It was interesting to see that Karsten's mom appeared particularly excited for him at the prospect, while most other stuff he'd ask to do away from home was met with hostility.

The time for his departure arrived, and though at this point we did not spend many evenings away from each other, I was grateful he'd gone away. Not at the small farewell before they loaded on a chartered bus and departed for Brazil. Not then. But a few days later, when I fell quite ill, unable to keep food down, and was diagnosed with a severe case of chicken pox. Though I had been vaccinated as a child, the infection and high temperatures gave me convulsions for a few days, and it took several others to get over this bout.

Luckily things improved, and he'd been finally allowed to visit well after his return.

And the difference I noticed between the darling boy I'd waved good-bye to some weeks earlier, and the one I was seeing now, was quite striking.

***

In August Dad's mother passed away on uncle Rene's birthday. The proceeding was awkward, since we had many times felt unwelcomed around that side of the family. Karsten attended with me and I was glad he was there. It distracted me a bit from the difficulty Mom always felt when around Dad's family.

But we learned that the only reason that feeling had existed was because of Grandma Ocampo's dislike for Mom. Now, everyone felt free to welcome us, and the rest of them were great people we hadn't had an opportunity to know.

But this had been Dad's turn to feel the pain of loss once more. He had now lost both fathers he'd known, and his mother. So, the Portas stepped in to offer him comfort -they really cared about him.

***

With so little time left in the year, I could not wait for it to end. I had missed so much school due to being sick, that catching up in a hurry was a bit overwhelming.

Karsten visited now as often as before, though something was missing. Something had changed and I could not quite put a finger on it. I was too naïve to figure, nor dared think, that this was the beginning of the end. I loved him with everything in me, and the pain seeing him slowly pull away from the small world we (well, he) had created, started to scratch the surface like unrelentless, nagging claws.

My heart, so pure, started to slowly hemorrhage, right up to the moment he looked at me with painful, unforgettable humility and sincerity in his eyes, and told me that he had to stop seeing me. And then my heart had skipped a beat, and it was no more. It was torn so deeply by his words that I felt the full blow of it splitting my chest, head, and soul in a million pieces.

I don't think I heard much else he said for a while that evening. I was sobbing, and hurting so badly I could not manage a word. I couldn't stop looking at him in one more attempt to memorize his face. He'd cried with me too, because the bubble had finally—truly—burst.

I'd finally looked down and rested my eyes. My vivid imagination brought to mind the sound and feel of a freight train fast approaching in the dark of night. I could hear it, and though I could not see it, I could visualize the full extent of it dragging my heart across the tracks.

Karsten said that his mother had hoped that going away for a few weeks would have made him forget about me and want to start anew. And when it hadn't, he was being given hell at home day after day. He needed to go away because he had nothing to offer if he asked me to marry him. And there it was. He was the first male -yet not the only one- who would make important choices on my behalf and to my benefit -so they all said- without consulting me.

So rather than waiting for his turn to be called up for conscription a few months later, he'd leave as soon as allowed -*if* allowed. I saw this as a glimpse of hope, and he read it on my face, telling me not to. He said he could not remain in contact. That if we were meant to be, we would eventually find our way back to each other. I thought and hoped that nothing and no one could undo what we shared.

Then he had hugged me in a deep, loving embrace. And left. Walked out of my life almost as casually as he'd walked into it. And I learned what devastation felt like. My brain played havoc, and my tender heart jumped into the abyss and sank, fast and deeply.

***

I'd never done anything to contradict my parents' teachings or principles. I actually agreed with all they taught and expected of me. They knew this, and that I was one hundred percent vested in school, and in the relationship that had just ended. They knew I was deeply hurt through no fault of my own, and did not know how to make it all go away, though they tried.

Night after night I cried myself to sleep, all the while trying to muffle my sobs, covering my face to avoid being heard. But

Mom had heard me, and had come to me saying that her heart was shattered for me. That she knew what it felt like to have the mother of the person you love push you away because you are not good enough for her son. I realized what Mom had gone through every passing day. I wanted to keep that in mind and not feel alone in my pain. But the aching remained. Relentless.

To my surprise then (though not today as a parent myself), Mom and Dad became really upset by the whole issue, and what it'd also meant to them that I be treated in such manner. And one evening they'd driven to the Haas residence to have a chat with his parents. Mr. Haas had been home alone upon their arrival. He'd been kind, understanding, and apologetic. But his wife had arrived mid-conversation, and had acted entirely the opposite. Karsten was away and arrived just as Dad was driving off. "Might as well," Dad had expressed. Though he thought he would have probably been disgusted had he heard his mother's biased—humiliating—response.

I sincerely doubted it would have changed the outcome.

Later that month, Dad decided he'd travel to Bs.As. for the first time ever, by himself, to visit his siblings, and be present at his niece Iris' wedding. I wished I could go along and be distracted from the hell on wheels my life felt like. But I knew there was no chance. There was no money for it, and me asking would make him feel further sorry for me.

This made for a difficult start of that summer. I always expected Karsten would call or simply show up at the door, but my wish never materialized.

***

In March of 1981 (the beginning of fall season in the southern hemisphere) I started my junior year in high school. I made sure to pack my days and get involved in any and all things happening at school, thus helping the time fly by. And it did. My grades were great, and the fundraisers I picked proved quite profitable. My class (boys and girls combined) were gathering funds for our senior trip. I worked quite well with some of the boys and found that talking and dealing with them now was not as hard as it had been in the past. But the boys I worked with were also excellent students, not the wild ones most of my female classmates associated with.

This year our Chemistry teacher arranged to take both classes (boys and girls) to Altos Hornos Zapla, a mining complex in Palpalá, Province of Jujuy (six or so hours away), to witness fabrication processes. And to a cement plant, to observe safety practices in their day-to-day operation.

Since our school was godfathered by the Army, instead of spending money in hotel rooms, she'd arranged for us to be housed at an army barrack. And although everything was "ready" for our arrival on base, and they had even planned to feed us and prepared a space for such a purpose within the large building, they hadn't separated the sleeping quarters so that boys and girls did not share the same space. The boys were rowdy as heck and did not mind the teacher one bit, so Ms. Calderón shared her bunk with one of the parent chaperones, and placed it right between the boys' and ours, to maintain some sort of order.

We were high up in the mountains in the crisp of winter, the barracks were cold and humid, the food was horrendous, and the weather outside was freezing; sleet falling during our entire stay.

We were made to get up at 04:45 together with the rest of the base at the sound of a clarinet, given time to make our beds, take a cold shower (no hot water to be had), and ready ourselves for the day. We then stood outside the building at formation by 05:45 to observe the flag-raising ceremony, while the breakfast team dished our food into tin dishes which inevitably set like cement by the time we were released back into the building to eat it.

After a few days of school related work, we were bound for the small villages of Purmamarca and Humahuaca, in the high planes that border with Bolivia. I loved the views, the food, and the people. It was a different world void of any superficial, unnecessary fluff. Truly amazing.

But the trip back into the city was long and dusty, followed by our immediate departure from Jujuy. We'd continued straight from there to the highway that would bring us back home.

Between our failed attempts to sleep in the cold building, eating cold breakfasts, standing in the freezing rain with freshly washed—dripping wet—hair, and remaining in the damp environment each day for a week, most of us caught some horrible bug, and slept, high on cold and flu medicine, the six hours that took to get us all the way back.

We'd learned a lot. Primarily, not to enlist.

***

After winter vacation, I started with a nagging pain in my lower right side. It'd gone on for a couple of days before Mom pressed for a visit to our doctor.

Our family physician informed us that I needed an immediate appendectomy. I was terrified. I had never had a single stitch put on me and the idea of it scared me out of my wits. This was back when an appendectomy scar was bound to heal at about six inches in length, and only so if the doctor cared enough not to scar the patient too badly.

Note that the first laparoscopic appendectomy was performed in 1983, and did not become common until the early 90's. In first world countries, that is. Quite far from our neck of the woods.

I had surgery the evening of July 28, 1981, at Sanatorio Galeno, a newer private medical facility that housed the office of our family doctor. This went to become one of the worst days of my existence. Even in retrospect, I know being stuffed into a coffin would have been easier.

They'd assigned me to a room and sent-in the only nurse available to assist and prepare me for surgery. A gruff young male. And prepping me involved shaving me completely from my belly button south of the Equator. I wanted to DIE—and I actually thought I would. I was sixteen and entirely self-conscious.

He'd asked me to undress from the waist down and lay on a stretcher. And I'd asked God repeatedly why didn't he -God, not the nurse- take me right then and there. I was already on the stretcher and willing to go six feet under, pronto.

The son of a gun -the nurse- went to work in silence with what today would be an old-fashioned half-sharpened Gillette blade inserted in a metal shaver. Lying there, I closed my eyes, clenched my teeth, and curled my toes tensely, making fists so tight I could feel my nails biting into my palms.

It took so long I could swear I'd miss my next birthday, half year down the road.

But suddenly he'd announced he was done, handed me a robe and a handful of disinfecting towelettes, and pointed me to the bathroom, instructing me to go clean myself. He then exited the room.

I jumped off the stretcher in such pain, and dragged my feet until I reached the bathroom door and pushed it open. Once inside I locked myself in. I thought I was simply traumatized by having had a boy look at -and work on- me, but next I understood that the pain was real, and why. I looked down and saw he'd sliced and broken skin everywhere, and I was profusely bleeding in several places. The pain hit a high note then, and I choked in a burning bout of bile rising to my throat. I felt emotional and somehow broken. He hadn't touched me inappropriately, nor said anything to embarrass me, but I felt violated regardless.

I'd barely finished cleaning myself when I had to turn around, drop on my knees, and allow my arms and face to hang over the toilet. Then violently hurled my lunch into it. Sitting butt naked on the cold tile, tears running down my face, it felt like a lifetime went by.

When I returned into the room, he sat on the guest chair waiting for me and smiling a crooked smile. As if we'd just shared a milkshake.

He helped me get on the bed, then put an IV into my arm and lifted the side rails, all the while telling me that I'd be going to sleep soon. I felt him pushing me out of the tight space, and saw the bright ceiling lights all the way to the operating room. Once there I saw our physician. He'd sounded funny when he asked if I was getting sleepy. I don't think I lasted awake long enough to answer.

Next time I woke, presumably an hour or so later, the bed was being pushed back into the room and the wheels bumped over the floor divider at the door. I felt a sharp throbbing pain in the lower right side, and started to shake uncontrollably, learning that as I moved, the pain intensified. But I could not control it. I then saw and heard my doctor ask the nurse for additional covers. He'd then approached and told me he'd increase the medication. I think I passed out once more, quite promptly.

I slept long and woke up thirsty in the middle of the night. Mom slept in a small (very small) sofa near me. She'd heard me and had come to my side, bringing along a small zippy cup of sort. I tried to drink from it, unable to stop tears from rolling down my face once more. I didn't dare sob though; now aware, and afraid I'd pull the stitches out. Mom did not quite know what else to do to help, and softly tried to calm me down, shushing me.

It was a horrible night. I felt pain, cold, hunger, and above all, once alert, I still could not shake the feel of embarrassment and total upset washing over me. The morning finally arrived, but the pain didn't go away. The wound was dry, tight, and pulling.

Mom helped me get up to use the restroom. I could not find my balance, so she came along with me. I didn't dare look down for fear of what I'd see. Trying to urinate was a struggle -I could feel the movement and sting of the very large suture. It made me nauseous and afraid. I did not want to think what number two would entail, hence from that day on until the time I was due back to get the stitches removed—a whole two weeks later—I didn't dare eat solids.

Early morning I was given enough medication to put a dinosaur down. I finally felt better. More like wonderful! I was half starved, so Mom got me some tea and crackers. Never before nor after was I so grateful for tasteless warm water. Still, the large wound pulling in different directions made me queasy and I would have preferred to sleep it off.

I lasted awake quite a while so Mom and I watched the royal wedding live on television, with all its fantastic pomp and ceremony. Prince Charles was marrying Diana Spencer. The enchantment of the fairytale helped me find sleep eventually, but not before I'd wished my breakfast had resembled the pertinent crumpets, bangers and mash the day called for.

While the bride and groom sat next to a couple of nuns (double-agent look-alikes), I thought royals were smart to start bringing commoners into the realm…can't disguise everything under elaborate hats now, can we? Then, as I was being numbed by the sweetness of a pain-killer cocktail, and after observing an abundance of aristocratic smiles during the proceedings, I dared one more thought: if you were looking for job security, becoming a dentist in England could render quite profitable.

A couple of days later I was released from the clinic. I was glad that never during the rest of my hospital stay, or ever for that matter, I had set eyes again on the male nurse.

***

One fall evening, as sleep started to claim me, we were awakened by our neighbor pounding on our front door. It was the middle of the night. Mr. Mohamed's heart issues had worsened, and his wife was asking Dad to help take him to the nearest hospital.

Dad had not been feeling well himself but would never turn down a call for help. He dressed quickly and loaded Don Fares onto the back seat of our car, with Mrs. Mohamed's and Mom's help. And there they'd gone, Dad and the Mohameds, rushing through the dim-lit avenue.

But Mom told us they'd be back soon because his body had been lifeless. Which had sadly been confirmed within the next hour.

Then had come a time of reverence as his widow grieved alone while Mom contacted their four children, all residing far away. And Dad was asked to send for Mr. Ale a few blocks away.

Not long after, an ambulance had delivered Mr. Mohamed next door, and the elders, already present, had gone to work, cleansing and shrouding the body. It was a very solemn ceremony. He was held in wake at home as done customarily for the rest of us. But I understand this had only been done so, because his children were away and enroute, so they could hopefully see him once more before he was taken for burial. In brief.

Mom and Dad had been with her as the ritual was performed. At day break, groups of folks were allowed to enter and visit every few minutes. I had gone to convey my condolences once a couple of the siblings had arrived, but no one present spoke, rather, they all sat in silence near the family. Once again, as in most viewings I attended, I was afraid of looking directly into the casket. I wasn't sure I would have been allowed to do so, in any case.

There had been no candles or crosses to impress me this time, but I recall verses being read from the Quran. And a never-ending parade of men in robes.

***

We attended school from March through December, as I believe did, and still does, the whole southern hemisphere. Summer vacation went from mid-December through mid-March. And our two-week winter break normally started on or around Independence Day (July 9th).

Alicia attended the University, Faculty of Humanities. She had good friends from out of town who crashed at our place during their class breaks, cancelled classes, and anytime they had late night study sessions. One among them was Silvia Medina, who during their five or so years in attendance at the university had quite frequently stayed with us, and felt like part of the family.

Silvia and Alicia attended classes at the u-branch right across from the park Grandpa Jesús had helped landscape and maintain. Grandma María loved her. It was mutual. She was welcomed anytime and for as long as she wanted or needed, and more often than not, she was found at our table partaking of meals and jokes, good and sad times. Most everyone in the family liked her. She'd taken part in most of the Porta's celebrations for years and was well known by the clan.

On summer vacation we often made plans for her to visit us. No study session, but purely for fun. But on occasion she had to cancel due to her dad's work commitments. They relied on her help at home during the summer. She would then ask that one of us visit her instead. When there had been no takers, she'd insisted I made the trip. And I'd done so, come Carnaval (February).

Silvia lived out in the country, in Bella Vista, a small *poblado* about an hour away (in good weather) from my parent's home. It took a couple of bus rides to get there. Her parents were separated -her mom lived in Bs.As. When she left their town, Silvia had remained behind with her father, brother, and a couple of cousins, all male. She held the home together by cooking, doing laundry, and whatever else they needed looked after as they worked.

I'd never traveled anywhere far by myself and had taken the offer with apprehension, particularly at being around so many males. And I'd found myself on a bus to nowhere. And when it seemed we'd passed nowhere, I realized my stop was still further beyond. And I thought the driver was drunk to boot.

We'd agreed which bus number I was to take from downtown, so she'd know exactly when and where to wait for me at the bus stop nearest to her front door. Directions had been easy enough, or so I thought. But along the way I'd seen so many folks get on and off this bus, when beyond the stop there was no sign of civilization. I could not figure where people came from or went to. They all seemed to simply vanish after getting off the bus.

The roads not yet paved, the entire stretch to Bella Vista was nothing but dirt and gravel. The weather was hot -it hadn't rained for several weeks. The dry, barren land was coarse and full of ruts with no sign of vegetation. And each time the inebriated driver put a screeching halt to the tires, they lifted a substantial column of dust, most of which permeated inside as the pliable doors opened to allow more riders in through the front, or let some poor soul off through the back opening, near which I sat, in fear of missing my stop and getting lost in unknown territory.

I was already a hairspray advocate and could bet that by the time I got up to ring the bell and be graced by the final dust baptismal, my teased bangs resembled a hen's nest complete with sticks, straw, and dried leaves. Even rocks.

But bless her sweet soul, as promised, Silvia waited for me at the precise stop. I was so glad to see her at last. We'd then walked three blocks to her home. On high heels, and over -you guessed it- more gravel.

She had the largest room set up with extra beds for friends to stay over. I had remained four days and had a remarkably great time. We visited some friends of hers and went out to a club with her three best friends, all males playing the part of bouncers around us. Her dad, brother, and cousins were quite polite, but I hardly saw them. They ran a tire shop near the freeway and worked at all hours of the day and night. Knowing I was visiting, they'd told Silvia not to worry about meals or laundry, so she'd have more time to spend with me.

The entire time I was there, Silvia only cooked once for the big mass of men, and we all shared the big table in the dining room. Then they offered to bring us to the river, which we took them-up on, and enjoyed very much.

I was a bit sad the day I got back on the bus to return home. They were truly amazing people. Silvia graduated with Alicia in 1987 and remained a good friend of the family. She married a neighbor of hers she'd fancied for years (Alfredo), and remained in the little town of Bella Vista. They had one son, Joaquín.

***

Once home, things fell back into rhythm as the season started to change. I was excited that after this year I'd be starting at one of the local universities. Also, a year and a half had gone by since I'd seen Karsten last. And I was doing well, sooner than

I'd expected. I think the wound had finally started to heal. He was now a tender glow in my heart each time memories came to mind. I loved him dearly still, but did not expect to cross paths with him ever again. And I almost wished it'd be so, thus avoiding all the sadness and painful awareness his mother had purposely brought into my life.

***

For many years, more than ten I believe, Alicia dated a kid from a nearby neighborhood.

Fausto was a few years older than she. They'd started dating when she was either fifteen or sixteen, so he'd seen Norma and me grow from children to teens. He was pretty much a member of the family.

He attended the police academy and all along he'd been "our" Fausto. We were proud of him. I remember how each time they briefly broke-up (and there had been many such instances), I felt a loss. He had been coming by for so long, I did not recall anymore a time without him in our lives.

His father had been a police chief, and both Fausto and all his brothers (a whole half-dozen of them) had also joined the force.

Upon graduation, Fausto was assigned to escort VIPs that came into town. Around this time, there was a band from Buenos Aires who was THE band to follow. Their name was Virus (how fitting they would have been today), and they were stopping in Tucumán during their multi-city tour. No sooner than an upcoming concert was announced, we learned that Fausto and his brothers were assigned to work the security team, so after much begging from our side, the brothers had agreed to let us into the venue. And they'd managed to place us in the first row to watch the entire concert while they worked crowd control.

Virus…I'll never forget it. They played a few loud and wild songs, but the concert had gone on for hours on end, and afterwards I had had a kink in my neck and a ring in my ears for a whole week. Crazy times those, when you are young and stupid.

Eventually Fausto and his brothers were assigned undercover work and he'd show-up at the weirdest times at our home, his long hair and beard making him quite unrecognizable, which was the intent -I get it. But I did not like this side of him, particularly not after his clean-cut years at the academy. And anymore, he always carried a gun, as required of all police and armed forces in Argentina, even during their off hours. This also made Mom uneasy around him.

Then one late night someone had knocked on our front door quite frantically, and Mom had not wanted to open it, but Dad heard someone crying outside so he'd gone out to check, and found Fausto hiding in the shadows. He'd been beaten, had cuts and bruises on his face, hands, chest, and back. At least, that was all I was allowed to see. He and his brothers had been running away from thugs to reach a safe shelter, and they'd become separated. Mom was very upset about the whole thing, though sooner or later we got somewhat accustomed to this kind of situation.

Eventually, Fausto and three of his brothers were working the drug contraband entering from Bolivia. They ran undercover operations on the railway, riding back and forth, buying and selling, setting up and capturing criminals. The brothers had gotten a taste of all the money to be made on the midnight trains, and it had been too sweet to pass up the earnings. They'd eventually ended up serving time for drug trafficking.

And with it, Fausto and Alicia's romancing era came to an end. For good.

***

The 1982 school year started. My senior year. It was relatively easy, and now as seniors all of us who'd worked hard, were seeing the fruit of our work, having gained the friendship of our teachers, many of whom had taught our older siblings, and even some of our younger parents. This last year they encouraged us to continue to try hard to meet our goals. My biggest mentor was Ms. Figueroa, our English teacher.

I had many classmates without a clue as to what they'd do come next year. I don't think I ever doubted that I wanted involved in some sort of law enforcement, although I did not want to be part of the Argentine Police force, which in many instances were more corrupt than the outlaws. I would have loved to join the military, but knew that my forte was not physical endurance, and after having lived through civil unrest in my younger years, I rather cringed at the idea of carrying a weapon or using one. I'd decided then to go into Law.

***

As previously established, Britain had intended to get at least a little piece of Argentinian soil way back since the 1700's. And they ultimately did. Fast forward to 1982, the islands of South Georgia and South Sandwich in the southern Atlantic (Falkland Islands, or "Malvinas" to the Argentinians), taken by force by Imperial Britain in 1833, were being sucked-dry of their oil and marine wealth by the loyal British occupants.

Argentina sat back and observed the exploitation exponentially grow; the land positioned immediately next to Argentina's southern Atlantic coast. There had been tension for a long while. And Argentina could do nothing about it, simply because the country was not properly equipped with funds, in troop numbers, nor in training. Even less in access to reasonable and necessary weaponry.

Gral. Galtieri from La Junta (The Joint Chiefs of Staff… the then Argentinian military dictators…but for this purpose let's call it *government*) gave-up on never-ending negotiations to have the islands returned to Argentinian jurisdiction, and declared war on Britain, launching an invasion of the islands.

Galtieri, just as most post-colonial military forces in Latin America, had simply lost his mind. How could a well-educated, career-military man, fully aware of our lack of capabilities, believe that Argentina could resist an aggressive response by Britain? Or that Britain would just sit back and watch as we'd been forced to do for a century and a half?

In truth, the decision to invade was political regardless the outcome. La Junta was in trouble for having committed human right abuses, paired with assisting in plunging the country into economic chaos. They thought that attempting to recover the islands would bring out the country's patriotism and we'd together rise in triumphant elation while they got the credit, and sought forgiveness.

Regrettably, some of the populace fell for it, applauding and encouraging, because sad but true, *dictators thrive when their prey is in state of ignorance and gullibility.* And so, a regime without moral compass and conscience continued to push forth in this and many aspects, literally pledging, and practicing, retaliation against anyone who dared contradict their philosophy.

As the reader may hopefully realize, there is a concerning resemblance between the dictatorship mentality, and the style and doctrine proposed by our newly elected president. The man has an inflated sense of self-importance, just as the dictators he admires and plans to emulate. Has even managed to manipulate the system in advance, placing himself in a position of unrestrained power, full immunity, and surrounded only by 'yes' men.

He is a textbook case of oppression. His plan undermines all the progress this country has made over centuries.

We declared independence from Great Britain to now invite the same predicament and vow to another king?

No one who has lived under political subjugation would ever choose to place another Hitler in power. Nor another Mussolini, Stalin, Hussein, Noriega, Pinochet, Videla. The list goes on. Once again, don't believe what I say; just ask someone else who has lived through restrained freedoms. Then ask yourself, why did we aid in the termination of the biggest democracy on earth? Why take away rights, ban books and vaccines, but allow more guns and rampant ignorance? The country is being shaped into the next authoritarian estate.

History is full of great lessons and speeches. A *virtuous leader's words*—like those of a good parent—are kind, compassionate, unifying, and above all, protective of freedoms. They are not self-serving and incendiary, aggressive and insulting, meant to promote fear, incite violence, hate, and disunion.

Awareness is vital.

***

The Argentinian military had few troops fully prepared to engage in a battle of magnitude. We had some Marine, Air Force, and Navy Officers. Lower ranks were made up of eighteen-to-twenty year-olds joining the compulsory two-year military service, which in reality, served only to instill discipline and fear into young men. It was not real training for live battle. Not as known to us here.

Gral. Galtieri had miscalculated so greatly, that many boys my age were sent to war without preparation, loaded onto trucks and literally shipped south, on to the frozen battlefield. Luckily, among them there had been some experienced military personnel called back in a hurry, who could somewhat guide them.

Argentine Marines (Navy Officers) invaded Port Stanley the 2nd of April, 1982. I remember the day as if it had been yesterday. The sheer fear of it, I mean, fully knowing it was taking place far away from our home, but not far away enough. The Argento-Marines took over a small Royal Marine unit. Argentina suffered some casualties in the surprise take over, yet our troops obeyed an order not to kill or injure British soldiers, only to capture.

The following day Argentine forces took over the Island of South Georgia, and by May second, Argentina had stationed about 10,000 troops on the Falkland Islands. The poor soldiers (teens, really) sat waiting, completely unprepared to ride the icy conditions without shelter, equipment, sufficient food, medicine or medics to care for them. And waited. And waited.

Prime Minister Margaret Thatcher wasted no time in rounding up an expert response team, headed by one British Prince today in trouble with the law, and with his brother The King. They did not realize in all their warfare and geographical wisdom, that the Argentines, if left alone, would shortly begin to expire thanks to the horrific environment surrounding them.

Most European countries sided with Britain, and most of Latin America did so with Argentina. Except Chile, who does not know how to get along with its own three next-door neighbors -a fact! Instead, they sympathized with the UK, because they were themselves also better at taking by force what they didn't have and wanted most: land (another verifiable fact).

But the biggest blow to Argentina came when the U.S. was expected -by Argentina- to remain neutral because we shared a continent. Too naïve of the Argentinians. The U.S. declared their partiality to Britain -a move Argentina never got over. At the time, we were faithful followers of the U.S. *in everything*. Our clothing, vehicles, movies, music -among other items- came from the U.S. Those were not necessities – they were luxuries. And they came from the U.S. because we so preferred it. We were fervent fans. We didn't take a single step without the U.S.' approval.

Heck, even Operation Condor (yes, the coup d'état followed by the mass killing squads) did not commence in Argentina until the U.S. was made aware of the plan to depose the president. The U.S. was also aware of the genocide the same maneuver was causing in other South American countries; and knew that it could -and more than likely would- occur also in Argentina as a result of the *new government*. And the then Republican White House had still agreed to recognize and support the Junta as a legitimate government.

That is factual – it has been revealed through declassified documents.

So, the very moment the U.S. advised they fully supported (and even offered aid to) the United Kingdom, all English and American merchandise in Argentina was pulled off the shelves, and there was a complete boycott on all their products. It also took away much from TV and radio programming, hence the space available to instead broadcast the war for hours on end. Live.

By the end of the month, the British arrived on aircraft carriers and on a nuclear-powered submarine, the latter sinking an Argentine cruiser. This occurred outside the war zone, I must add.

Britain also captured a vintage submarine we'd purchased from the U.S. Thankfully, earlier on, Argentina had acquired a newer German submarine, and our sailors gave the Brits a run for their money. Argentines lost a fourth of their planes, but ultimately our pilots sunk a British destroyer during a missile attack. The damage to the British was considerable.

Argentina did put up a fight. They sunk British frigates, destroyers, container ships carrying helicopters, and a troop carrier. Still, our troops were unable to stop amphibious landings scattered among the various islands. They were quickly surrounded and cut off from assistance from the mainland. After heavy gun fire, and ultimately even fighting hand to hand, they were exhausted, wounded, and freezing. They ran out of food, and starved -sheep grazing nearby became their only hope for sustenance.

Then Great Britain engaged Gurka mercenaries to quickly annihilate our teens on the battlefield. Indeed, to do the job they themselves would or could not.

Argentina surrendered on June 14th, having lost approximately 700 servicemen (half in the sinking of the cruiser Gral. Belgrano), with nearly 12,000 troops having been captured by Britain. Britain's overall loss did not add up to 300.

I remember the fear and sadness these boys brought along on their return. Many went back to their regular lives, able to put the ugliness of war behind them. But many could not. Argentina was not then -and even today is not- part of a culture accustomed to partaking in wars. The country does not have an excessively large fighting force, nor the mental preparation for it, or the support required post deployment.

This was a conflict which *could have been* -and should have been- avoided. A short stint on the battlefield, yet so much damage done to a generation. Loss of life is tough, particularly when it can be prevented but it's not. I feel it should be a requirement for all world leaders to have a child serving in the military while they are in power. Perhaps if they come close to experiencing the fear and pain a parent feels on a child's deployment, it may change the war panorama a bit. Because no war ever has brought-forth only benefits. Even in victory there is loss.

***

With half-a-year gone, and life somewhat back to normal, my class had managed to gather enough funds for our senior trip in the fall. We'd travel by coach to Carlos Paz, a small town in the Province of Córdoba, about nine hours southeast of Tucumán.

I had many good friends I had known since first grade. We'd literally grown up together, in the same neighborhood and schoolroom. I could not wait until our trip.

But my lack often played games with me, as it did this time. At the hotel, I learned that I'd be housed with a very well-to-do group of classmates, one of which brought along a friend and a cousin, filling the spaces from girls whose parents could not afford to send them at last minute. I felt out of place once more, and wished I could be with my own friends, but the chaperones emphasized that we should always stay around our roommates, entering and exiting the hotel together, always keeping an eye on each other. Inevitably this did not work to my benefit.

We were accommodated in rooms with two triple bunks. And starting the first night, my five roommates escaped the hotel after everyone had gone to bed. Twice the chaperones had entered our room while doing rounds in the middle of the night, to find me sleeping alone. They were upset that I didn't let them know, while I had been so tired, I hadn't heard the brats leave. But surprise-surprise, when they'd returned, they were met in the back lobby by the parking lot. Furious, the girls hurried to blame me for telling on them. Thankfully, not only had they snuck out, but they'd returned tipsy, and the chaperones had had it.

Ultimately, the girls were split-up for the second part of the trip, but not before their parents had been notified. And I finally got a chance to stay and travel with my own group. That part of the trip had been great.

***

In 1983 I turned eighteen. As everyone back then, I had to take an entrance exam for the public University – not a chance my modest pocket could pay my way at Sto. Tomás de Aquino, then our best-known private university.

I attended the four weeks of prep and passed the initial exam with flying colors. This was the initial thinning-out of the masses, as the career I had chosen had three times the applicants for the limited available slots. Then I went to the second round of testing, which I passed as well. But in the final phase, although I'd scored higher than a passing grade, it hadn't been sufficiently high to place me among the lucky ones who got in for the year.

It was my turn to learn the meaning of academic disappointment. It was the first time ever I had no control over my own situation…in my studies, that is. After finding myself in the long list of names posted at the University, and seeing in disbelief my name crossed over, I'd returned home feeling deflated. *"Sad and sorry like a tango,"* my granny would have said.

At the time, my sweet friend and neighbor Marta had an infant baby—little Fares. Fares was a darling baby I loved being around. Marta struggled being a new mom while helping her mother-in-law in their business -the typical general store that carried anything and everything for the home, school, office, clothing, and even car filters and anti-freezing fluid. The store was popular and made substantial amounts of money, daily, while others barely survived. It was an all-cash establishment.

In conversation, Marta asked if I'd watch her baby while she worked for the remainder of the year. Her partner Yusuf, my neighbor's son, had already endorsed the idea, and they were offering to pay me a small fortune. I would have been insane to turn them down. I was glad for it, though it didn't really present enough challenge to keep me interested. But Fares was a doll of a baby, and he'd hold up his arms to me any time I approached. He smiled a lot and hardly ever cried. All the purest of incentives.

But my arrangement with Marta did not last. Doña Yola Mohamed, Marta's mother-in-law and store owner, wanted me to help *her* instead. She still offered the same money and hours, so I was happy to join the household for most of my day, and do whatever they chose and assigned. They were all truly wonderful to me from the first to the last day I was employed by them. I helped wherever was needed and everyone was happy and pleasant to be around.

But Mom wanted me to study, though there was not enough money for me to attend a private institution, even with my newly found income, or rather, the income which had actually found *me*. Then aunt Alicia suggested I started a teaching degree at a local community college taking evening classes, and in time decided what to do about the University. And I'd done so. I registered in the Social Sciences program and started classes shortly after. I could still work at Mohamed's during the day, and attend school at night.

I continued to work with the Mohameds mornings through mid-afternoons and headed downtown each day at 6 p.m. to attend classes from seven to eleven. This kept me busy all day, every day, except Sundays. I maintained this schedule for just over one year.

I also got involved with the Partido Radical, hopeful to help bring back our democracy from the claws of the military. I took part in registering folks for voting, assisted in the local campaigning, and ultimately at the voting tables. It was the first time I was of legal age to vote, and it felt empowering to witness the party candidate, Alfonsín, win the presidential election.

***

Nineteen eighty-four rolled in. During summer vacation, I'd retaken the entrance exam and this time I scored quite high and was able to start at the University, which forced me to stop looking after little Fares. I had an overwhelming amount of studying to do, and when not, I found myself attending classes and walking between the Community College and the University, both downtown, some blocks away from each other.

I missed the baby tremendously, particularly in the mornings when he had been so attached to me. Fares (in his mid-forties now) has not changed much in appearance over the years. To this day when I see him, I can't help remembering the babe I helped care for.

***

Norma had met American missionaries, and she wouldn't stop talking about them. All I knew was that people referred to them as Mormons, and that Mom wasn't exactly thrilled about her making their acquaintance. I had seen a few of them around the neighborhood years earlier, though I'd never spoken to them.

Norma, as per usual, did exactly what my parents asked her *not* to do. She was quite the pro at contradicting them. She'd even started attending meetings at a church building downtown. I was invited to come along, which I eventually did, although I couldn't help but feel I was letting Mom down.

During my visits I felt welcomed by everyone present, but it still felt wrong -Mom's opinion was important to me. We were Catholic, born and raised, baptized, and confirmed so. I'd attended catholic school for twelve years, had religion classes all along, an additional catechism course before my first communion, plus another set of lessons prior to my confirmation ceremony when I was fifteen. But now that I had something to compare it all to, being Catholic, it seemed, mainly entailed memorizing the mass' prayers and repetitions, without thoroughly understanding the meaning of some practiced rituals.

I had lots of questions. Yet, what had me sold from the start on the LDS church, was the promise of eternal families. That was a concept I'd never heard of, and I could not appreciate more. I loved my family. And hated the mere thought of ever losing any of them.

So, I had also started to attend regularly, and although I felt a warmth as I never had in Catholic mass or other religious gatherings I had attended on occasion, Mom seemed upset each Sunday when we spent hours at the downtown church building. And I felt at fault for making her feel so.

Considering Norma and I were still underage (full adult age in Argentina is twenty-one, not 18), and should we choose to baptize, we would not be allowed unless Mom and Dad signed an authorization. Dad didn't have an issue with it. But Mom did. She'd told us we could continue to attend, but she'd never agree to sign a permission.

She'd also made us aware that what she feared most actually, was how to explain our change of mindset to her siblings and to Grandma. And what their reaction may be. And I could not blame her, honestly. Mom and I had always coincided on the importance of how people perceived us. We always cared about reputation -something I can still be found guilty of, though many times I've been told I'm a fool for thinking so.

I stayed busy with my studies, simultaneously attending the second year of my teaching degree in the evenings, and the first year of university during the day. But I felt awful asking Mom and Dad for money to travel to and from school, plus the numerous expensive books I needed. So, I found a receptionist job posted in the classified section at the U's student center, had called, set up an appointment, and had made my way over for an interview.

It was a new law office in a not so popular side of town. Two young attorneys ran it. They offered a low salary, but full access to their codes and textbooks plus all transportation costs—these benefits alone more than I had expected. They had offered me the position and it was tempting, but I could not shake the vibe these guys were sending me. I had felt undressed in their presence.

Once at home that evening I had a talk with Mom and Dad, and they both suggested I pass on it, even though finding work anywhere in town was difficult to say the least. Mom and Dad felt I'd most probably end up regretting working for, or with, the characters I'd met.

I often had study sessions with one of my former high school classmates. She had a tough situation at home and after telling her my experience, she showed interest in the opening. I explained to her exactly what they'd said and offered, and how uneasy I felt around them. She resolutely told me she did not care, met with them, and got the job. In time, she became an attorney and even stayed as an associate to what grew to be a larger firm.

***

This autumn turned out eventful.

One Friday I arrived home a bit earlier than normal, completely exhausted from a full week of classes, testing, walking, and carrying around a million books. This attempt at a double career was really catching up with me. I couldn't wait to make my way to bed.

The house dark and empty, the phone rang as I unloaded my belongings on the couch. I lifted the receiver and said "Hello" a couple of times. Dead silence. As I readied to hang up, I heard my name. The phone back to my ear now, I said "Hello" once more, and the familiar but now mature voice coming from the other end answered "I'm glad YOU picked up. It is so good to hear you again..." And I froze. It was Karsten. He noticed I wasn't reacting and went on to say he'd like to meet next day, if possible. Quickly yet hesitantly, I had agreed to his request and terms, unable to really engage in conversation. I'd felt my heart pulsing in my throat the short length of the call. And as I was hanging-up, Mom walked in. She'd asked who'd called just then. I thought about telling her it was a friend from school, calling about an assignment. But opted for the truth. And Mom hadn't been pleased. At all. Beware though -mother knows best! I told her not to worry, and headed to bed. But tired as I was, I did not sleep one wink that night.

Saturday dragged on forever -I hadn't been able to focus on the paper I needed to finish. Or on anything else for that matter. Even taking a moment for lunch had been a useless attempt at peace. Then I'd gotten ready and left the house in a rush.

The time to meet had finally arrived and I didn't know what to expect. *Linea 9* ran on our avenue. The bus stop shelter stood then immediately across from our home. I was running tight with time, so I took the first unit approaching. Seating in the back row, and upon inspecting the address I'd written down, only just realized we were meeting in the outskirts of the city -I should have inquired the reason behind it.

All day leading to this very moment, I had felt bizarrely uneasy. Now as my stop approached, I felt numb. And feared my legs would give out at any time, and that I'd fall while going down the bus' rear steps. But I hadn't. All had gone well so far.

Then the three-block stretch seemed longer than usual. And I'd felt watched -not sure why.

My mouth was dry, and my stomach queasy. I'd arrived a few minutes early, but hadn't waited long before I saw him approach. He looked about the same as four years earlier, though his features were now further marked. He was just as devastatingly handsome and perfect in all ways. Perhaps even more so now than before.

He smiled broadly and hugged me tight. And his crisp button-down shirt and delicious aftershave overwhelmed my senses, just as they had years before. And I was back in my pretty gown at fifteen, unable once again to break through the irresistible surge of manhood he projected.

Sitting at a café we talked non-stop for about five hours until we were almost pushed out and the shop doors locked behind us. He told me all about being deployed to Falklands two years earlier. He described feelings and experiences in such detail I thought he was lying through his teeth, but I eventually verified that -at least in that- what he'd said was true.

On the way back to the bus stop, the night already fully upon us, he hugged me tight once again. And always-honest me, I proceeded to tell him that I had never stopped caring for him, because when I'd seen him again, I discovered that's how I felt. But I'd cursed myself the moment the words had come out of my mouth, though there was no undoing it.

And he'd said he felt the same way (which I somehow felt was not entirely true but I didn't say *that* to his face, although I wish I had). And though he'd looked at me softly, in a very caring way, all along I felt like a lunatic in-love-with-love. My bus then arrived and he bid me farewell, promising he'd call me back.

And idiot, idiot, I-D-I-O-T me! That night I let his words sugar me up and being the fool I was, I started to dream about him. As if I hadn't been hurt enough the first time. The mere innocence (or pure stupidity) of it. Why can't our thinking brains stop our falling hearts?

We saw each other again regularly for two months, falling back into the routine of him attending family gatherings, to which he was welcomed once more, though none of it felt quite the same as it had in the past. We were both noticeably older. And different.

And one day he stopped coming without explanation. And to my surprise, I did not feel betrayed nor sad, but rather relieved at the materialization of my fears and intuition.

He owed me a couple of books he'd borrowed. To me, books were worth more than gold. And although I had a phone at home (one of the few privileged families, because Dad was a business owner), Karsten's family did not own one. There was no way for me to get a hold of him to ask for the items back, by then overdue at the library, under my name. Without a better solution at hand, two or three weeks after I'd seen him last, I made my way to his home one sunny afternoon.

Upon arrival I was received quite cordially by his mother who in a very agreeable mood had told me with great surprise in her eyes and voice, that I had grown into a beautiful, refined woman. And she had hugged me and invited me in, as if nothing had ever transpired. She'd served some tea and made polite conversation while we waited for his return, *momentarily*, as she'd put it.

And he'd arrived home shortly after, accompanied by his *fiancé*...yes you read correctly, *fiancé*, to whom I was introduced by him, in front of his mother. I was referred to as a *cousin* of sorts. His mother had looked so uneasy I thought she'd barf, not just from the situation she found herself faced with, in her own home, but because I saw with clarity that she could not stand her son's fiancé any more than she had done me some years earlier. Her eyes were almost pleading with me...to...stay??

Karsten's fiancé was younger, needier, and (pleasantly, I felt) quite unpolished.

Now, I had no title, no fancy last name, nor distinguished blood lines -I was no pearl of the first water, you may say. But neither was she. By then I'd mastered how to present and conduct myself, and how to guard what I was made of -at least to people like Mrs. Haas. I had matured, and I know I would have made my Grandpa proud.

They say that beauty is in the eyes of the beholder, and I could see this statement to be accurate. But I must give credit where credit is due -the girl had some smarts and was not swallowing what she was being fed. She'd started looking at me with such interest that he -begging me with his eyes not to spill the beans, *porque obviamente había moros en la costa* (the coast wasn't clear and danger was near)- had carefully encouraged his mother to remove her and herself from the room, allowing us a minute to talk.

He'd then closed the door and tried to desperately (and quite quickly) explain to me that he had to marry her. It couldn't be undone. To my surprise, I fought hard not to burst out laughing. Now understanding his mother's anguish and why all the sudden I wasn't so disposable to her, though she'd realized it too late.

Throughout all this, I could not help my amazement at how scarcely it hurt when discovering what he'd done. There had been shock, no doubt, but it'd been accompanied by gratitude for the fact that I was not hurt nearly as much as this girl would be, should she learn what he'd been up to. He'd used me, but in his defense, he would not be the last to do so. I met and dated several guys after him, also great looking, promising, and with as much lip, but they'd all left me with the same hollow feeling. There had been no great selection to pick from. Perhaps I was looking in all the wrong places.

Years earlier I would have fallen apart. Correction: I actually had. But this time around my pride was intact. I had already learned my lesson and he was no longer the center of my world.

I kept being reminded of a teaching Grandpa had often repeated: "No matter how tempting, do not break the rules, do not break the law, do not break your word, nor someone else's heart, and I guarantee that in the end all will be well."

I'd walked about ten blocks back to the bus stop numbed with relief that my old shoes were now filled by his fiancé. But even that numbing did not make the footwear I was wearing any less painful.

Shortly after my visit to their snobby neighborhood I sat for breakfast while reading "La Sección Social de La Gaceta" (*Socials* in our local newspaper) and had come across an announcement about a Karsten E. Haas marrying a Ms. Claudia Lomas. The very same Claudia Lomas I met in his living room and in the presence of his prejudiced mother.

I was proud the boy had never gotten even a look at my wares, nor gotten a free sampling of the goods from me -not due to his lack of asking. No siree. Though I recognize my abstinence had other roots. Truth was, in all situations I always feared the worst—it's an Italian trait embedded in me. I have always feared God. And above all (sorry God), I always feared my mother. I honestly thought that if I did what I shouldn't, I'd most likely end up pregnant, facing utter ruin…and also end up dead at my mother's hand. She was after all, l'italiana infuocato. Indeed. Italian mothers are good at a lot of things, but they normally excel in a few disciplines. Mine did so in cooking, guilt trips, and scaring the chitterlings out of you. And so, even if strictly out of fear, I was a goodie-goodie. Still am -boring but true.

Karsten and fiancé were indeed married shortly after my visit. Exactly three months after he'd reached out to me and started to actively date me again. He'd cheated on her until shortly before marrying her. For her sake, I hope he never pulled one like it again. To my knowledge they shared one daughter and three sons.

Looking back, his return had been a final disappointment.

***

Norma and I continued to attend church. Our ward was not particularly large, yet we made many good friends. I enjoyed the people and the feeling each time we sat in sacrament meetings and conferences. I also started to help out, teaching the young kids in the primary classes. Norma and I knew we were in for a long haul until we could become official members, so we might as well utilize the time intelligently. We attended Sunday meetings and any activity that did not conflict with our schedules outside of church.

The missionaries often stopped by and made it a point to speak to our parents, to see if they'd changed their mind about granting us permission to baptize. Mom hadn't. She always said we should really get to know as much as we could before asking again. She wanted to make sure we weren't just infatuated with the missionaries, who were in my age group, clean and respectful, had a dreamy accent, and more often than not, were quite the eye candy. Still, I felt there was more to them in substance. Or at least I hoped there was.

In July, new missionaries were assigned to our ward. I recall seeing Norma through the window one day -she talked to them while I studied in my room. One was quite shy -a kid from California. The other -new in the area and not so bashful- was from Utah. His front teeth shone in the sun. He had quite distinctive looking metal caps.

Mom and Dad liked them both very much, so a couple of weeks later Mom and Grandma had made homemade gnocchi and invited them over. And when asked what they'd like to drink, they had both asked for milk. Mom and Grandma had looked at them thinking they were joking, though that hadn't been the case. And later that day when they'd gone, Grandma said she was glad Grandpa wasn't there to see *that*, or he'd tell them that *in Italy* the act was punishable by five years in prison. Pasta with milk…only in (North) America!

Shortly after, that same winter, we attended Caíto's wedding, held at uncle Mocho's beautiful home. I understand my perfectionist uncle was having palpitations because people were all over the house, touching everything, and he had no control over any of it. And I know how he felt because I myself get palpitations when I have visitors.

But honestly, we could not imagine who would dare -or care to- marry Caíto, though he'd just graduated with honors as a Civil Engineer. Still, it wasn't an event that could be missed.

Expectations aside, ceremony and reception had been exquisite. And his bride had been a darling girl. She'd also just graduated, as a Biochemist. Their marriage did not last long. But long enough to result in three gorgeous children.

During the reception, Norma mentioned our church findings to my beautiful cousin Marisa. Her mom, aunt Pirucha, said she'd be interested in talking to the missionaries. The Elders had then started attending their home and teaching them, and not long after, my aunt and three cousins had joined the church. My Uncle José was not interested at first, however he also joined eventually, and even became a member of the bishopric in their small ward.

A year and a half later, my cousin Marisa married our awesome Ward Mission Leader, Walter Lemo. And, nearly a year after that happy occasion, I married the missionary of the stainless caps -best known by my family as *The Lone Ranger*. Though by then the caps were no longer, and his smile was further (much further) improved.

Kirt and I, the same age, talked a lot about many things each time he visited my parents at home, although he'd only stayed in our area for a short couple of months. I learned he'd been sent to Tucumán after spending long months in his previous two areas, where he'd gotten in trouble by breaking mission rules… (a big no-no!). Tucumán had been meant as his reforming assignment.

We had become good friends. Though not allowed to be involved (and myself being such a stickler for rules), we'd silently wished there was hope for the future, when we would no longer be subject to missionary restrictions.

He said that when he returned home, he'd make an effort to call, though at the time international calls were expensive (via satellite, and often only with operator assistance), hence could not be done frequently. He'd try to call one Sunday evening per month.

And he'd made good on his word. He called and chatted with the whole family, then with me for an extended period. I yearned to hear his voice, and when the calls finally came, a huge relief washed over me to know that his heart was still set on returning.

But the truth was that I had been protected. Too naïve and too sheltered all my life. Even through unsavory events in my younger days. And thanks to that, I struggled to tell true from phony even when my life depended on it. And I feared being duped, plain and simple.

And shortly after his first call, on a letter he'd said he was too busy to visit, and asked if I'd like to travel to the States to meet his family. He said he'd sponsor me and facilitate a visa to go for a visit and see if I'd like to stay there a while. And I was thrilled, but did not dare dream big. I could not figure how the logistics could work if he was unable to leave the States for long. Because I had no desire to leave my family and culture behind.

Things were becoming complicated. And complications were the last thing I wanted or needed in my life. And though he kept saying he would like to return to live down there, I was soon also made aware that he had too many commitments to really plan on coming to stay permanently. He had started full time at the University, a couple of part time jobs, and had a delayed contract to fulfill with the Army Reserves. Soon I started to feel even stronger that things between us may not work out after all.

Marking his first month at home, I'd received a packet from the U.S. Embassy in Buenos Aires. I could not believe this was really happening. And neither did my family. Grandma was upset and had asked me not to fall for his promises just yet because I did not know what type of person he truly was at home. And this reality had tugged at my heart strings.

I could not get all these new ideas out of my head and it really affected me when I was so busy with school and needed to concentrate on what was real in my life. But no matter how hard I fought to leave all the daydreaming behind, his words kept reeling me back into cloudland. So, as per his suggestion -and against everyone else's advice- I had gone ahead and gotten a passport.

And the letters kept coming, together with a huge box of stuff he'd been unable to carry all the way home, so he'd sent it to me from his last proselyting area. It'd taken a while to reach me but once it had, it'd felt like the biggest treasure I'd ever acquired. And I knew at that moment that I'd fallen head over hills for him, and that my naïve heart was in deep trouble. Again.

***

The fall of 1985 brought a new set of missionaries to our ward, both Argentinians. They were great service people, and Mom and Dad really enjoyed their visits. That is how one of them, an Elder Zapata from Bs.As. if I remember correctly, dared ask my parents' permission for me and Norma to get baptized. And he did not beat around the bush. And to our amazement,

Mom had agreed to it. And Dad had told us to hurry up and do it before she changed her mind.

Norma and I were baptized on June 25th, 1985 by our newest ward missionary, Elder Jesse-Dean Law, of Nampa, Idaho. He was a sweet young man. Mom hadn't wanted to attend, but Dad had come along. He'd always been supportive of us joining the LDS faith.

Over the following couple of months, Kirt and I worked tirelessly gathering all the documentation we were asked to present by the latest mailing from the embassy. Once all was submitted, we had no choice but to sit and wait for the Embassy to reach out to me to set up an appointment.

Life continued. Real life, I mean. I kept busy although my mind often wandered. Kirt called religiously one Sunday per month while we wrote to each other every day, and sent one letter per week. One letter twenty pages long, that is. International mail was slow -it took over four weeks for correspondence to reach us. Thankfully the weekly mailings were consistent, therefore the arrivals were gradual and steady. And though time went by, it did so quite slowly.

***

Nearly eighteen months after Kirt had left Tucumán, although there was no change in our commitment to meet once again someday, I started to lose hope I'd ever get the visa that would facilitate such a re-encounter. He appeared to be losing patience as well, and during one of our calls, he informed me that he'd contacted Utah's Senator Orrin Hatch about it.

And I thought that was farfetched and would hardly make a difference.

But one day shortly after, I received a huge packet from the American embassy, with a set of dates and remaining details and requirements for me to fill-in and bring along. And I had rushed to get into the restroom under the excuse of needing to shower and make it downtown for school. Instead, all I had needed was a place to be alone. To cry my eyes out. My heart was overwhelmed. I had wept under the shower, not believing this was truly happening. To insignificant ME.

That evening, I had spoken to Mom and Dad. And Mom had done the exact thing I had earlier in the day: in the middle of the conversation, she'd rushed *to shower.* And Dad had also been teary, and my heart had felt a suffocating blow. Although the plan was to initially visit Kirt and return, I wasn't convinced I was doing the right thing. The last I wanted was to cause distress to my loving family.

***

The visa appointment was two weeks out. I had to make my way to Bs.As. soon and have a complete physical by an Embassy medical appointee. I'd been provided with a three-day window of first-come-first-serve opportunity to enter the Embassy and materialize the interview.

Dad's sister Isabel heard I was looking for a chaperone to travel along, and had volunteered. She'd also volunteered to contact their brother and his family so that I could stay with them in Bs.As. Aunt Isabel would deliver me to their home and then make a hasty return to Tucumán to avoid missing too much work. She was a seamstress at a uniform factory.

And the time had come. We'd taken a train, and she'd made the long trip quite entertaining. I was glad she'd come along.

Once in Bs.As. my beautiful cousin Iris, an English teacher, accompanied me to the medical appointment and from there she headed on to work. She gave me a map showing the walking route to get on the correct buses, and how to make my way back from the station to their apartment. Buenos Aires is as big a city as any I've seen by now. I was terrified of going anywhere alone, but had no option.

My rides to the Embassy on the other side of town would be provided alternatively by Dad's brother Vichy, and by my cousin Rubén, son to Dad's sister Dalinda. The window of opportunity for the actual interview was set between 6 am and 10 am, three consecutive days during mid-August, 1986.

On the first day, I arrived at quarter to six, only to learn the line extended for blocks. My attempt had been useless.

The second day, my cousin Rubén got me there at four in the morning, but the line already reached a couple of blocks. Once again, I did not stand a chance, having waited in line under cold sleet for over five hours.

I was tired and nervous by now, anxious that my last opportunity was coming. If missed, would it mean another two years of waiting until another appointment was granted?

For the third and last day, I didn't dare go to bed. My uncle drove me over at 02:00 am and we waited in his car until people started to arrive. Fortunately, this time I was just behind the head of the line.

The Embassy did not allow lines to form on their sidewalk. All arrivals lined up on the outskirts of a park located across the street. I remember the trees. They were majestic. But it was the middle of winter in a city by the ocean, and the weather was nasty the start of this day. And the park was very dark. I was glad to see a lot of people arrive shortly after I had stood in line. I'd only felt safe then.

As daylight broke, there appeared to be dignitaries visiting. Theirs were the only vehicles allowed to enter through the tall gates around the corner. Mirrors were run under the chassis, then the fancy armored machines drove over the entrance scanners.

It was all very Hollywood, I thought. The Marine security was not only beautiful, but impressive.

As the line moved, I neared the entrance and received a place holder of sort. I recall the very moment my turn appeared on the slow changing number indicator. I was shaking. Then I was allowed through the narrow -elaborate- iron gate.

I had entered a different world.

It was midmorning already. I'd brought so much paperwork, my arms were weighed down by the files, and my elbows had almost gone numb. I walked under a flower trellis, then reached the door to the first enclosure. A Marine instructed me in broken Spanish to wait across from a faux window until called-in and invited to sit with the interviewer.

The room was huge and airy, with shiny Carrera marble floors and tall ceilings with intricate plaster work. And the windows...oh gosh, they were magnificent, and overlooked the greenest and most posh English garden I'd ever seen. The space was impeccably painted and groomed. The furnishings were sparse, but decadent. It had a very European, enchanting aura. And in the corner, imperiously staring at me, stood the United States flag.

It is worth mentioning I visited again thirty years later when accompanying my nephew to obtain a visa. Sadly, the space -at least the portion used then for public access- had been modified and expanded in such manner, it was unrecognizable.

My mind was floating in the clouds of heaven when my name was finally called. The interviewer asked so many questions, I wondered what any of his inquiries had to do with the purpose of my visa. He'd noticed and was kind enough to explain the reasoning behind his line of questioning. I was surprised at how gentle he was, fully knowing that had this been an Argentinian Embassy or public service office, the treatment would have been entirely different. Public workers in Latin

America are notorious for their arrogance and lack of decorum. Instead, the interviewer was kind, and his accent reminded me an awful lot of Kirt's.

All said and done, he had briefly left me at his desk, and upon returning, signed and stamped a few documents, asked me to sign a piece of paper, and once done he had smiled and said "Congratulations, you are approved for one entry within the next sixty days, for up to ninety days. You must marry within this ninety-day period, otherwise you must depart from U.S. soil. Keep in mind the visa process is a lengthy and complicated one. If or once you return to Argentina, there are no guarantees another will be granted, nor in a timely manner."

But somewhere around "you must marry..." I had stopped listening. He noticed this and asked if I had a question. I hurried to answer: "I had applied for a tourist visa." And he replied, "You did, and it has been denied. You have received a fiancé visa, sponsored by Mr. Kirt Butler. You can enter once within the next sixty days in the capacity of fiancé and can only remain in the States beyond ninety days if you marry him. He appears very serious about it. He has placed a lot of pressure on this office."

I had gone mute, and felt -and obviously looked- confused, because he then proceeded to tell me that he had another pressing appointment. He offered his hand in a friendly shake and wished me luck. My cue to take my leave.

Then all was a blur. I walked out of the Embassy not feeling my legs. All I could think of was how I would explain this to Mom and Dad because they'd ask to see my passport and would ask the meaning of it all. What would they think and say? Would they agree to let me go? If I didn't travel, I would not see Kirt again for who knew how long. If ever. But marry him, so soon?

I was twenty-one. An adult already (on paper, mind you) and there was nothing they could do if I decided to leave the country, temporarily or otherwise. But, did I really want to do that? I did not really feel like a true adult. And they did not deserve being hurt in that manner. It was still a time when a proper single female did not leave home with a man. Not even if promised in marriage. Even less with a stranger. A foreign stranger.

There was so much to think and plan and decide. The whole lot of it felt like a huge mess now. Had I caused all this? I'd never meant to, truly.

I returned to my aunt and uncle's place in a haze. I was worried sick about what transpired. Mom had never agreed with me having any type of relationship with Kirt. The fact was that him being so far away represented a real chance I would end up leaving, did things get serious. And now they had, and she would have as hard a time with it as I. I feared this development would be the drop that filled the glass, and Mom would lose it.

Not long after my arrival at the apartment, and while trying to explain to my aunt and cousin -who were in a frenzy and reeling with excitement, their phone rang. It was Kirt, calling to find out how it had gone. I attempted to explain to him how difficult it would be for me to make Mom understand. And suddenly I had broken down, facing the reality of what had just happened. Even worse, what was coming. I loved him. I missed him. I wanted to be with and around him. Now it was all possible! But it also meant I would have to leave behind all I knew and loved. And break Mom and Dad's heart in the process.

Kirt had volunteered to speak to her. And I let him, because I did not know how to approach the subject myself.

Mom had tried to make a point to him about the fact I had never traveled anywhere far by myself. The U.S. was too far away. I could not travel alone, and…and…and…

He told her he'd come get me. And Mom was *very* upset then, saying that she would not allow me "to leave the house, nor the town, even less the country, with *some* man. A stranger at that! What would people say?"

Kirt asked her to give him a couple of hours to seek a solution. He'd call back. When he had, he told her that I would not have to leave with him alone. He was bringing his mother along.

**

I was able to get a ticket to return home the upcoming weekend. My aunt and uncle, and cousins and spouses, came along to the station to wish me a safe trip home and the best of luck. They'd also asked me to bring Kirt along one day so they could meet him. They had been wonderful to me. Understanding, and accommodating, and overly excited over facilitating my stay, and with such success!

But the long train ride home didn't hold the enchantment of our little trips to Tafí Viejo during my childhood. Instead, the road was lonely and quiet. There hadn't been the cheerful voices, nor the yummy comforting foods and friendly games. It was tranquil, allowing me to reminisce of long-gone times. Moments I would have given anything to relive, and never -ever- leave behind.

When I arrived back and was finally home, Mom was heartbreakingly sad. Dad had tried to be cheerful about it all, but instead had also ended up tearing up. I had no idea how to make things better. I'd often lock myself in the bathroom with whatever excuse, and sob. I hated doing this to them. Even to myself. I also hated the thought of continuing to be away from Kirt, who had worked so hard to make our reunion possible.

Trying to get past this overwhelming sadness, I asked if they would allow me to freshen up the walls with a coat of paint, and Dad was happy and agreeable. Knowing I didn't have much time, I got to it right away, day and night for just over a week. I had no help, everyone continued their daily routine, while I'd stopped attending class at least for the time being. I needed to figure what came next. After we met again. I needed to think.

About ten days passed. I was home alone, in the clean-up stage of my spruce-up attempt, the day prior to their arrival into Tucumán. The phone rang. I jumped off the tall can I was using as scaffolding and picked up the receiver. It was Kirt. It was so good to hear him. He said they'd arrived a bit earlier than scheduled. Right then and there I understood how real this dream of mine had become.

The plan was for them to rent a day room in Bs. As., and catch the overnight bus to Tucumán. This would get them into our bus station next morning, allowing me just sufficient time to finish cleaning up.

I once again daydreamed as he spoke, but came out of my stupor when he asked if I could come get them. I asked at what time I should expect them. He said, "The wait is over, come on over now." I thought there was an error in his Spanglish, so I asked again, "Tomorrow at what time?" He responded, "Mom wasn't feeling well, so we took a flight instead. We are at the Tucumán airport right now. Can you come pick us up?"

My heart stopped. I still had a mess of gigantic proportions strung around the house, and I would need to shower and drive about thirty miles. And Dad was not around to give me a ride. What a pickle.

I asked him to hang tight, telling him that I'd be there in about one hour. I then rushed to my neighbor José (Yusuf), and asked him if he'd give me a ride to the airport. He agreed. I'd done "The flight of the Bumble-bee" trying to straighten up the disaster of paint cans, clean-up rugs, and rollers all over the house. I had then rushed to shower and get ready. And just as I stepped out the door and attempted locking it, Norma and Mom showed up. I told them our guests were waiting for me at the airport, and to prepare some lunch and make sure all was in order while I ran to get them. They stared and asked in unison *"Already here?"* I recognized the panic in their faces -a bit as I had felt some minutes earlier.

José and I flew through town in his fancy truck. I regretted telling him to rush because he hadn't hesitated to take off in a race against time. He then proceeded to ask why we were hurrying, and who had arrived, and…and…I simply told him "My fiancé" and avoided looking at him, waiting for reaction.

He'd laughed loudly with sincere amusement, and said *"To my knowledge you don't even have a boyfriend, how can you have a fiancé?"*

I had then proceeded to explain my predicament, making a worst muddle of the story. He'd whistled and chuckled, and told me he'd always known I was "a special one".

And I wasn't sure that was a compliment.

***

This was my first time at this airport. I had really no idea where to go, nor where to look. But because of his affluent sisters, José was well versed on how to navigate the grounds. We drove around a huge circular path past the parking lot, then approached the load/unload area.

José asked if I knew what they were wearing. Only then I remembered Kirt said he had Levi's on, and a red and yellow plaid shirt. I repeated this, mimicking Kirt's accent, making José laugh again. We started the long approach. Luckily there were very few people outside, although none seemed familiar.

José then asked me what he looked like. I said, "He is quite blonde," knowing that would narrow things a bit. In all honesty, I had only seen him in clean-cut missionary clothes, and over two years earlier. I had no idea what he'd look like as a regular individual in normal dress.

Suddenly, José said, "Well, I think I see him." Then he slowed down to a stop, and pointed to an approaching male further down the road. And I responded, "Nope, he is much younger and thinner than that guy." Famous last words…

José half-parked, half-skid along (and almost over) the curve. I hesitated for a second, but long enough for him to tell me to snap out of it and go greet him. Kirt—yes, it was definitely Kirt—started towards us, his mother in tow. My jaw dropped as this was a very different and grown-up version of the Kirt I'd known, and had been communicating with. Or so I thought.

The cute young missionary I had seen two years earlier was now a fully-grown man. He was taller, more athletic, and over-all larger. And I was surprised to notice that I appreciated all the changes. He looked like a character right out of a western film: bell bottoms (sadly, no chaps), large belt buckle, hat…the whole shebang. And his hair, dear heavens, bright gold, and shoulder length. He also sported a wiry mustache and long, bushy sideburns. I was in quite a state of shock (*and* awe, why not!). He hurried to hug and kiss me, and I was in a daze as he introduced me to his sweet mother, who stood right behind him, waiting to join the welcoming committee.

José also came to greet them and shake their hands, not understanding a peep what they were saying, but they were all smiling regardless. He helped load the luggage and then we packed like sardines into his truck for the ride back into town. Thank goodness he could accommodate us all (barely).

José was so excited to be the first to know all this, and couldn't wait to share it with everyone we (he) knew, so we'd also made the trip back in record time. And once we pulled into our driveway, Mom and Dad, my sisters, *and* the Mohamed clan had all come out in a frenzy to welcome Kirt back, and meet his mother. Everyone was ecstatic, and the news was certainly spreading fast through the neighborhood -we had all sort of acquaintances suddenly passing by to take a swift look at the Americans in our front yard. The crowd grew fast and steady.

Once finally inside and after a wonderful lunch prepared by Mom, we helped his mother to a nap. She was exhausted, and glad to be on stable ground.

Eventually, Kirt had pulled me by the hand and took me next to where his backpack had been set. He retrieved a box out of his bag, and placed an engagement ring on my finger. I nearly lost my balance, and asked if it was all real (I mean, the situation, not the ring). He assured me it was, and asked if I'd come with him when he returned. And if I'd marry him. My mind was whirling. It was too much at once to be real.

The evening of their arrival, Kirt told Mom and Dad that he would bring me to the States and that we'd marry as soon as possible. He knew this was important to them—that I did not remain single while away—unless I would be returning by myself at the earliest opportunity, no wedding bells after all. In my culture, my image would be tainted to some degree…I would have run away with a man…and been returned to sender in a used-up envelope of sort, likely C.O.D. All this according to my dramatic -but always right- mother.

That was one busy week. We were set to leave the country in seven days. This was a time for preparations and plans. Mom had exactly one week to work on a farewell of huge proportions, and to make my wedding dress. Which by the way, turned out to be the sweetest confection of voile and lace. Kirt and I made the rounds in the city, making sure to visit with people I always frequented and who I'd be sure to miss during my upcoming absence.

The following Friday evening, our Bishop Domínguez stopped by the house and gave us both a blessing, just in time for us to leave for a grand gathering of family and friends at Club Tucumán BB, the Portas' neighborhood club. The whole family had come to meet him and gathered around me and said how much I'd be missed. The feeling was one of happiness and euphoria. Everyone was thrilled for us, and Mom and Dad were so proud, though I knew that deep inside, my departure was ripping a hole in their hearts.

But even then, there were "friends" that asked me straight out: "What exactly did you do to get that man to return for you?" And the simple truth to that is: Absolutely nothing of the sort they had imagined -the exact opposite of what most girls would have done.

And I think that had made all the difference.

***

The day of our departure arrived. It was Kirt's mother's birthday, so we held a brief celebration for her, earlier in the day. Once again, there had been a parade of people at the house, as we attempted to find a moment to talk and plan and hope that my absence would not be a long one and we'd get to see each other again soon.

There had been tight and teary smiles all day, and as the evening arrived and we sat for a quick dinner before heading to the bus station, Mom and Dad bawled at times as they were hugged and comforted by everyone present. I was in such state, nearly falling apart at each turn, so I decided not to come near them for fear I would not be able to break away. I had always been their strongest child, (on the surface) and I wasn't about to let them know that I had a growing void in my heart.

Once at the station, so many folks showed up, the crowd was large and there was no spare room on the platform. And my friends were exuberantly happy and chanting farewells. I did my best to stiffen a smile and appear put together as I went around hugging and kissing everyone with genuine affection, trying to capture each face and feeling in my memory.

Our exit had been delayed a bit, but now the dreaded time had come. Our departure was announced on the speakers and imminent. I hurried to hug my sisters and could not stop my tears. Then Grandma had held my face to hers and she'd managed to say: "Oh my child…don't you dare go and forget about me." As if I ever could. And we both sobbed, grabbing each other as babies cling to their mammas when they fear a fall. Mom and Dad were next, and I found no words to express my sorrow for -literally- abandoning them. So, I'd said nothing. Only nothing would do. But I cried profoundly in their arms.

And then Kirt had reached for me, his mother already on the bus, and the drivers pressing for a prompt departure. I climbed the steps slowly, one at a time, waving as I went, looking back and around at each and every one of those humble, sweet faces staying behind; most smiling, but many shedding tears. Some were tears of excitement and wonder…but many were tears of pain and knowledge of what I would be facing in my new life, away from all I'd known.

Once onboard, Kirt gave me access to his seat by the window so that I could still see everyone and wave along as the coach positioned itself for our exit from the station. And I saw my sisters and Dad hugging Mom to comfort her. It'd been my total undoing. I felt like a monster for causing them such grief. I also then knew what great-grandma Cipriana had felt that cold day the Conde Wilfredo had pulled away from the dock in Spain. History was repeating itself.

As our expensive coach with reclinable beds and steward service moved southeast towards Bs.As., and after a fancy snack was served and the lights were dimmed, I looked over to where Kirt and his mother rested, across the aisle. They'd fallen asleep already. The seat next to me empty, I had used it to place my humble carry-on bag—my treasure chest—its contents the closest to my heart. I reached out to it and palmed the side pocket to ensure it still felt full and secure. Within it, rested a roll-up of highly selected hand-written recipes Mom had bundled up for me in a rush before leaving the house. It rested next to a tightly wrapped slice of quince tart I'd stolen from Mom's pantry just before our departure to the bus station. It was my favorite tea-time pastry. Far from hungry, but as a means of quenching my melancholy, I took a small bite, and the tears had flowed freely once again, and I'd covered my mouth tightly to avoid anyone hearing my gasps and sobs. That became another sleepless night I spent reminiscing about my growing years, my face moist with salty regret for the anguish caused to my family, and for the long-gone years I could now only relive in my dreams. And only from afar.

Early next morning upon arrival into Córdoba Province, we had stayed at a hotel during the day, and caught another coach to Bs.As. in the evening. There was yet another long stretch of road ahead of us.

We arrived Buenos Aires early next day and stayed with my aunt and uncle during the day hours. They were so excited to see me, and finally meet Kirt and his mother. I don't think they realized how grateful I would be to them (forever) for their help and support.

Then that evening we'd finally made the trip to the Ezeiza airport with plenty of time for check-in. Since this was my first ever trip on a plane, and a very long one at that, Kirt's mom suggested I wore a motion sickness patch behind my ear. And Kirt had agreed. And all had been fine at the start, but as we approached the Immigration checkpoint, between the side effects of the darn patch and my nervous state, the voice in the PA system had become a slow moan coming from a tunnel, and my eyes went completely blurry -I could not see or distinguish much. I mentioned this to Kirt, and he and his mother each held me by my arms and guided me through the rope separations in place ahead of us.

This feeling kept creeping up on me later as well, and throughout the flight. Adding to my newness at it all, and to the odd feel in my gut. I knew I was in for such change that my life would never again be what it had been. A deeply bittersweet feeling.

Throughout the flight Kirt did not say much but stayed near and made sure to provide comfort each time my tears threatened to break me down. I tried hard to prevent sentiments from overwhelming me. I expected he'd appreciate me being strong rather than a nitwit. And I felt he cared deeply. If not, the boy was putting on a heck of a show.

But I doubted he could possibly understand the priceless treasure I had just traded off for a life with him. There is no way he could have known the sheer agony I was experiencing. Could never. Would he ever? He only knew what I had held materially, which was of no significant consequence. But he had never known much about me really, my life experiences, my dreams, nor my relationships and what I held most sacred in my heart. He knew nothing really, other than what I could tell him. And tell him I had. But had he listened? Did he understand that gold is not as precious as what I'd just walked away from, thousands of miles away?

CHAPTER 12

My Promised Land

(Based on the Ocampo and Butler Archives)

We arrived in the U.S. early Tuesday morning, and were expected at LAX by Kirt's Aunt Carole, a delight of a woman. She brought us to her home in Orange County, fed us, arranged for us to rest a while, and then even took us around to visit the Los Angeles LDS Temple and the Arboretum. I met her loving husband John, her youngest daughter Angie, her daughter Melanie and her husband Mark, and some of Mark and Melanie's children. They were all warm, lovely, accommodating people.

Late that evening, we'd finally made the last leg of our trip. We'd flown into Salt Lake City where Kirt's eldest brother waited for us, mal-humored and bothered by the inconvenience, as would be the case most anytime we were around him.

Our first days in Utah were blissful as I shared moments and meals and experiences with Kirt and his family. Kirt had two older brothers and a sister. The brothers were single and still lived at home. His sister, Karen, had driven up with her family, to meet me. She and Kirt's mother, Diane, were a solid rock for me in those early days, and continued to be very good friends throughout our acquaintance. I admired them and loved them the moment we met. And do so still. Deeply and sincerely.

The first full day in town, Kirt drove us to downtown Ogden and showed me around, on our way to obtain our marriage license. We parked and walked a few blocks. Kirt laughed heartedly a couple of times when reaching a corner, he continued into the street while I remained at the curb. I was in awe of him (of everyone, really) walking freely into the path of incoming vehicles, not a care in the world as cars approached. I thought it complete insanity. He'd pulled my hand, assuring me that the cars would stop for us. Well, cars in Argentina weren't so accommodating. They only stopped occasionally, after running you over.

***

That morning Kirt and his mother had spent hours on the phone, having a tough time getting appointments at nearby temples for us. Back then, I did not speak more than (very) basic English. For my ordinances, endowment and marriage, we needed translators.

I was scheduled to receive my endowments on Friday the 19th of September, 1986. For those unfamiliar with LDS culture and customs, this is a required step prior to a marriage being solemnized in a temple. It is a religious ceremony which provides instruction and promised blessings, and through which church members make covenants to respect the sacred laws of the church revolving around eternal life, and the sanctity of marriage.

When we checked-in at the Jordan River Temple that morning, we were advised that the assigned Spanish speaking attendant who was to guide me through the sessions was ill and away for the day. The only choices were to return another day, or use the assistance of a sister from Italy, who did not speak Spanish. Returning later was not an option as we were scheduled to be married at the Salt Lake Temple the following morning. I said Italian would be as good as Spanish. And I went through the day's ceremonies accompanied by this older Italian lady who could barely walk around. She was the sweetest of souls, and we completed the ceremony hand in hand. My soon-to-be mother and sister-in-law kept asking me periodically if I *really* understood. And I kept repeating that I completely did, word for word. I had felt that Grandpa had blessed my decision to be there that day, and had been looking after me, having himself placed this dear old lady in my path.

Kirt and I were sealed for time and eternity at the Salt Lake Temple a week to the day from our departure from Tucumán. Present in the sealing room were his parents, sister and husband, and some of his aunts and uncles. My eyes were watery the entire ceremony, from emotion and heartache, fully knowing how much my family would have loved to be a part of it all, though as non-members, Mom and Dad couldn't have joined us in the sealing room.

Our ceremony was solemnized by Eduardo Balderas, the leading translator of scriptures and other LDS works into Spanish, mainly the Doctrine and Covenants, and The Pearl of Great Price. He served as the church's Chief Spanish Translator for almost fifty years, was also most responsible for translating the church's hymns into Spanish and was involved in the first-ever translation of the endowment ceremony. He conducted our wedding ceremony in English and Spanish.

This day was remarkable. Immediately after the ceremony, as Kirt's mom and sister guided me back into the dressing rooms to change into my wedding gown to then exit into the gardens for pictures, we were shortly detained and introduced to Sister Flora Benson, President Benson's wife, who was visiting the temple this day.

The wedding was too rushed to prepare for a family gathering, plus Kirt had exhausted funds on the trip to Argentina and back. A humble reception took place weeks later, on November 1st –a day we were hit with a huge windstorm that took the power out and stopped a number of folks from attending. But it was lovely regardless. A friend of the family at a printing shop had made our invitations, mom's cousin Caroline did our flowers, Uncle David DeRyke and his wife Valene (owners to Topper Bakery in Ogden) prepared our cake and much of the food, Uncle Bud DeRyke took the pictures together with Kirt's brother Keith, and photographer Mark Haines, while Kirt's young cousins assisted at the hors d'oeuvres table. It was beautiful.

But I was in for a hard awakening, never expecting I would hurt for many years before managing to control the nagging ache I carried for having left so much love and togetherness behind. My emotions always surfaced, and still do at times, throughout my time away from my *birth home*, but mostly reaching their peak around the holidays.

For many years I cried myself to sleep on Christmas and New Years' eves. What I missed wasn't easy to replace. I loved Argentina and the wonderful -modest- life my family afforded us. I loved my family. So dearly. But I also loved Kirt deeply, and thankfully we had an amazing start to our life together those early years of marriage, even though my raw heart was so bruised by the distance separating me from all I had known.

***

Prior to his trip to retrieve me, Kirt had purchased a darling tiny cottage built in 1920 in an older neighborhood of town. The house was charming and sweet. It stood shyly mid-block on one of Ogden's boroughs where back-in-the-day folks cared beautifully for their yards, which embraced all visitors warmly. Its footprint was barely large enough for our young selves and the humble few belongings we called ours then, but it sheltered us proudly as it saw us stumble through those first years; and struggle through the gigantic differences in upbringing we each brought to our union.

Ours was a marriage we had both entered with empty hands but loads of love and heaps of hope, without really knowing much of each other beyond the fact that we both ached for a life together.

That old front porch witnessed me shedding many tears. Tears of sadness and of loneliness. Of longing and hope. Tears that in the end never dried out once I came to the realization that there wouldn't ever be a return for good to what I yearned for so deeply in my very soul.

Our chats and ultimate agreement were that, once Kirt and I obtained our college degrees, we would make our way back to Argentina to raise our family. But when the time came, the turmoil and safety issues in Argentina had worsened, and it would have been insane to tear my children from a universe of opportunities to drag them back to the developing world to quench my nostalgic dreams. It would have been insane indeed. And selfish. Selfish to their futures and to Kirt's -he stood a much better chance for a promising job in the States. Selfish even to my own loved ones far away. Because where I stood, though quite alone, I would be in a better position to help should I be required to do so.

So, when life gives you lemons… (though at times I got sick of lemonade, if you get my meaning).

But in truth, life was already meaningful in different ways. And truly wonderful since our children had arrived into this world. They'd quickly sealed each void I'd felt in my heart since my sad departure. How a child can fill a heart!

I'd clung to them in thanks, at last. They were my promised blessing. The everlasting connection to all I missed. Once again, I had something truly precious and uniquely of my own.

I had gone full circle. *"Todo en su propio tiempo."*

***

My vivid memories clear pathways that send me spiraling back in time. And I return to the dear places that nurtured my childhood...

Grandma sits next to me during the sleepy siesta hours. My chair still too tall for my feet to reach the ground, while I attempt to match her speedy crocheting. She checks my work now and again, and encourages me to move along as she hums in a barely audible tone. Then a high flamenco note breaks the air. I stop and look up at her, and she smiles softly in acknowledgement, her eyes focused on her work.

And each afternoon Mom and Dad sit at the old kitchen table to enjoy their merienda. They plan, and tease, and laugh. And Dad dreams about one day opening a school to teach young boys the trade he's mastered.

But Grandma has been gone for over thirty years. And the thirteenth anniversary of Mom and Dad's passing has just gone by. Mom was ill for many years but held tight while Dad was around. Then at his sudden death, she gave up her will to remain among us, and rushed back to his side -they left this world within ten days of each other.

I owe them all so much, it is difficult to put into words. Most of all, I owe them the best childhood one can ever dream of. I won't lie though. I wonder now and then how my life would have been, had I remained home and not been so selfish as to follow my youthful dreams. As we grew up, the family's older generations hoped the younger ones would not be inclined to venture out to conquer the hardships of learning everything over in order to fit in, blend in, and succeed in a different world and society. What they'd done long before us, had really been done FOR us. So naturally Grandma had asked me on that final day at home, among tears, as a last attempt to keep me around, *"Why would you choose to do it over?"*

They knew my reasons though, and I trust they also knew that all the battles they conquered gave me the strength needed to contend with the many challenges I myself came to face in my new life. Because, even though my reason for leaving culture and loved ones behind was not politically motivated, nor financially driven but purely fairytale-ish, just as my ancestors, I paid a steep price for chasing after my dreams.

But the time flew by. After our children graduated from college, Kirt and I first waved good bye to our youngest son, now a military officer. And shortly after, destiny once again stood in front of me, and delivered yet another blow: our firstborn gathered his entire life into a backpack and headed out for a life in Europe. We knew this all meant we'd be fortunate to see them with a limited degree of regularity. Though proud of them beyond words for their choices, it hurt so much to let them go, entirely aware of the sacrifices and risks ahead. And that my heart would once again need healing, because there were no constants in life. I was destined for a journey of good-byes.

In the end, just as in the fall of 1986 I learned how my great-grandma Cipriana felt as she left Spain, thirty years later I experienced what my mother felt when I left Argentina. I can with confidence say I've gone full circle. I know with precision the feel of both, that of leaving, and that of staying behind.

I will always thank Dad, Mom, and Grandma for all the lessons taught, and for all the strength conveyed. I sorely miss them, and my life around them. I always will.

Beegees. 2013, July 08. *Bee Gees - Immortality (Live in Las Vegas, 1997 - One Night Only)*. [Video]. Format [Video file]. YouTube. https://youtu.be/bZolfKgW5Is?si=eUvIUhRZGvbf7J5C

Bibliography

Supporting articles – (all links verified active as of 14 July 2024)

Argentina.gob.ar. (n.d.) *El Hotel.* Retrieved July 12, 2024 from https://www.argentina.gob.ar/interior/migraciones/museo/el-hotel

Argentina.gob.ar. (2022, May 15). *Los primeros dos censos nacionales argentinos se conservan en el Archivo General.* https://www.argentina.gob.ar/noticias/los-primeros-dos-censos-nacionales-argentinos-se-conservan-en-el-archivo-general

ARGENTINE REPUBLIC MINISTRY OF AGRICULTURE. (n.d.). *The immigrations offices and statistics from 1857 to 1903, Argentine Ministry of Agriculture.* hellenicaworld.com. Retrieved July 12, 2024 from https://www.hellenicaworld.com/Argentina/Literature/AMA/en/ImmigrationofficesStatistics.html

Arn, C. (n.d.). *INMIGRANTES ITALIANOS EN ARGENTINA: TODA LA HISTORIA.* ItaloTribu.org, Pan American Tribu LLC. Retrieved July 12, 2024 from https://www.italotribu.org/inmigrantes-italianos/en-argentina/

Bavio, E. Valentin, J. (1898). *Segundo censo de la República Argentina, 10 de Mayo de 1895, decretado en la Administración del Dr. Sáenz Peña, verificado en la presidencia del Dr. Uriburu.* Book scanned and digitalized by Google and uploaded to the internet archive by user tpb. (2008, April 4). (Print shop, Argentinian National Penitentiary). NOT_in_COPYRIGHT (expired). https://archive.org/details/segundocensodel00censgoog

Bjerg, M. (2009). *Historias de la Inmigración en Argentina.* 1st edition. Editorial Edhasa. Cosmos Print S.R.L. academia.edu. https://www.academia.edu/32321647/Historias_de_la_Inmigraci%C3%B3n_en_la_Argentina

Bob. (2023, March 7). *Italian Immigration to Argentina.* italiangenealogy.blog. https://www.italiangenealogy.blog/italian-immigration-to-argentina/

BuscAncestros. (n.d.). *Censo de Argentina de 1895.* BuscAncestros.com. Retrieved July 12, 2024 from https://buscancestros.com/herramientas-genealógicas/los-censos/censo-de-argentina-de-1895/

Carta España. (n.d.) *Caminos del mar: Los barcos de la emigración.* inclusion.gob.es/web. Retrieved July 12, 2024, from https://www.inclusion.gob.es/web/cartaespana/-/caminos-del-mar-los-barcos-de-la-emigracion

Ciudadanía Italiana. (2020, April 26). *Inmigrantes italianos en Argentina.* ciudadaniaitaliana.com.ar. https://www.ciudadaniaitaliana.com.ar/historia/inmigrantes-italianos/

Clarín. (n.d.). *Recorrido por el Hotel de Inmigrantes, donde se alojaron muchos de quienes llegaron al país entre 1880 y 1950.* Clarin.com. Retrieved July 12. 2024 from https://www.clarin.com/ciudades/fotogalerias-recorrido-historico-edificio-retiro-funciono-hotel-recibio-inmigracion-1911-1953_5_7CCDefF.html

Cortina, A. (2022, May 11). *Santa Isabel: ¿Por qué la fábrica de Renault en Córdoba lleva ese nombre?* parabrisas.perfil.com. https://parabrisas.perfil.com/noticias/noticias/santa-isabel-por-que-la-fabrica-de-renault-en-cordoba-lleva-ese-nombre.phtml

de la Fuente, D. (1895). *Segundo censo de la República Argentina, 10 de mayo de 1895: decretado en la administración del Dr. Sáenz Peña, verificado en la del Dr. Uriburu / Comisión Directiva, Diego G. de la Fuente, presidente, Gabriel Carrasco, Alberto B. Martínez, vocales. Tomo 3.* Publicación: Alicante, Tomo 2, Biblioteca Virtual Miguel de Cervantes 2017. Buenos Aires: [editor no identificado], 1898 (Taller Tipográfico de la Penitenciaría Nacional). Obra digitalizada por Unidixital en la Biblioteca América de la Universidad de Santiago de Compostela. Universitat d'Alacant. https://www.cervantesvirtual.com/obra/segundo-censo-de-la-republica-argentina-mayo-10-de-1895--decretado-en-la-administracion-del-dr-saenz-pena-verificado-en-la-del-dr-uriburu--comision-directiva-diego-g-de-la-fuente-presidente-gabriel-carrasco-alberto-b-martinez-vocales--tomo-3/

Diario de la cultura. (2024, June 26). *Argentina, tierra de inmigrantes: La historia del Hotel donde comenzó todo.* Diariodecultura.com.ar. https://www.diariodecultura.com.ar/museos-y-artes-plasticas/argentina-tierra-de-inmigrantes-la-historia-del-hotel-donde-empezo-todo/

Digital Copy scanned by Google - Expired copywright - Public Domain. (1881, Bs.As., original). *Ley de Inmigración y Colonización de la REPUBLICA ARGENTINA, sancionada por el CONGRESO NACIONAL de 1876.* PUBLICACION OFICIAL. https://archive.org/details/leydeinmigracin00argegoog/mode/2up?view=theater

Hebrew Surnames 2019. (n.d.). *Ship Conde Wilfredo Arrivals to Buenos Aires.* hebrewsurnames.com. Retrieved July 12, 2024 from https://www.hebrewsurnames.com/ships_CONDE%20WILFREDO

Hebrew Surnames 2021. (n.d.). *LIST OF PASSENGERS SHIP CONDE WILFREDO - Arrived Buenos Aires April 02, 1910.* hebrewsurnames.com. Retrieved July 12, 2024 from https://www.hebrewsurnames.com/arrival_CONDE%20WILFREDO_1910-04-02

Iceta, V. (2021, May 23). *El desconocido linaje de Cornelio Saavedra: de un premio Nobel a un importante montonero.* noticias.perfil.com. https://noticias.perfil.com/noticias/cultura/el-desconocido-linaje-de-cornelio-saavedra-de-un-premio-nobel-a-un-importante-montonero.phtml

INDEC-Argentina. (n.d.). *Censos de Población en la Argentina.* Censo.gob.ar. Retrieved July 12, 2024 from https://censo.gob.ar/index.php/historia/

La Nación. (2020, September 17). *A 151 años del primer censo nacional, ¿cuáles fueron sus resultados?* Lanacion.com.ar. https://www.lanacion.com.ar/lifestyle/primer-censo-nacional-nid2451967/

National Security Archive, The George Washington University. (2021, March 23). *Argentina's Military Coup of 1976: What the U.S. Knew.* nsarchiv@gwu.edu. https://nsarchive.gwu.edu/briefing-book/southern-cone/2021-03-23/argentinas-military-coup-what-us-knew

O.R.O. (2014, February 28). *GLOBETROTTERS: MAGIA Y LEYENDA.* Elgrafico.com.ar. https://www.elgrafico.com.ar/articulo/0/5074/globetrotters-magia-y-leyenda

Página12. (2023, January 31). *Los datos más curiosos del primer censo de la historia argentina.* pagina12.com.ar. https://www.pagina12.com.ar/422461-los-curiosos-datos-del-primer-censo-de-la-historia-argentina

Panzera, D. for Renault. (2021, December 7). *Visitamos la Planta de Renault Argentina en Córdoba donde se fabrica la pick up Alaskan.* 16valvulas.com.ar. https://www.16valvulas.com.ar/visitamos-la-planta-de-renault-argentina-en-santa-isabel-cordoba/

Petruzzello, M. (n.d.). *Argentina Celebrates 200 Years of Independence.* Britannica.com. Retrieved July 12, 2024, from https://www.britannica.com/story/argentina-celebrates-200-years-of-independence

Pignatelli, A. (2020, September 17). *La sorprendente historia del primer censo nacional: una mayoría analfabeta, un país despoblado y más curanderos que médicos.* infobae.com. https://www.infobae.com/sociedad/2020/09/17/la-sorprendente-historia-del-primer-censo-nacional-una-mayoria-analfabeta-un-pais-despoblado-y-mas-curanderos-que-medicos/

Renault.com.ar. (n.d.). *FABRICA SANTA ISABEL, CONSTRUIMOS HISTORIA.* Retrieved July 12, 2024 from https://www.renault.com.ar/fabrica-santa-isabel.html

Rodríguez, M. (n.d.). *Immigration Museum.* welcomeargentina. com. Retrieved July 12, 2024 from https://www.welcomeargentina.com/ciudadbuenosaires/immigration-museum.html

Secretaría de Educación. (2015, November 15). *Ley de Fomento Inmigracion Europea.* educ.ar. https://www.educ.ar/recursos/128663/ley-de-fomento-inmigracion-europeanbsp

Vitale, S. (2021, September 29). *De casona aristocrática a conventillo, la multifacética historia de un emblema de San Telmo construido en 1870.* Lanacion.com.ar. https://www.lanacion.com.ar/buenos-aires/de-casona-aristocratica-a-conventillo-la-multifacetica-historia-de-un-emblema-de-san-telmo-nid29092021/

Wikipedia. (n.d.). *Argentines of European descent.* en.wikipedia.org. Retrieved July 12, 2024 from https://en.wikipedia.org/wiki/Argentines_of_European_descent

Wikipedia. (n.d.) *Fiebre amarilla en Bs.As.* en.wikipedia.org. Retrieved July 12, 2024 from https://es.wikipedia.org/wiki/Fiebre_amarilla_en_Buenos_Aires

Wikipedia. (n.d.). *History of the Jews in Argentina.* en.wikipedia.org. Retrieved July 12, 2024 from https://en.wikipedia.org/wiki/History_of_the_Jews_in_Argentina

Wikipedia. (n.d.) *Hotel de Inmigrantes.* en.wikipedia.org. Retrieved July 12, 2024 from https://en.wikipedia.org/wiki/Hotel_de_Inmigrantes

Wikipedia. (n.d.). *Italian immigration in Minas Gerais.* en.wikipedia.org. Retrieved July 12, 2024 from https://en.wikipedia.org/wiki/Italian_immigration_in_Minas_Gerais

Yahoo Search. (n.d.). *Photos of Immigrants in Argentina.* images.search.yahoo.com. Retrieved July 12, 2024 from https://images.search.yahoo.com/search/images?p=fotos+inmigrantes+argentina&fr=mcafee&type=E210US-105G0&imgurl=https%3A%2F%2Fwww.visitingargentina.com%2Fwp-content%2Fuploads%2F2018%2F09%2Finmigrantes1.jpg#id=-1&iurl=https%3A%2F%2Fwww.visitingargentina.com%2Fwp-content%2Fuploads%2F2018%2F09%2Finmigrantes1.jpg&action=click

Additional supporting videos
(all links verified active as of 14 July 2024)

Hernán Corbalán. 2008, September 25. *La Gran Inmigracion Argentina Siglo XX (Parte 1 de 3)*. [Video]. Format [Video file]. YouTube. https://youtu.be/9ccb_k4aPNk?si=OBQ2eVU9GmyVlSn0

Hernán Mazzitelli. 2018, December 06. *El hotel de los inmigrantes (Una mirada histórica)*. [Video]. Format [Video file]. Youtube. https://youtu.be/nCb0xSK5tk0?si=9WjKVuyqt9jdStm0

INDEC Argentina. 2021, May 10. *#Censos argentinos: Segundo Censo de la República Argentina – 1895*. [Video]. Format [Video file]. YouTube. https://youtu.be/Hcwsbr2Y75k?si=JSt2hq5cV2LKncbK

María Eugenia Varas. 2014, March 16. *THE INFLUENCE OF THE ITALIAN IMMIGRATION IN THE ARGENTINIAN CULTURE*. [Video]. Format [Video file]. YouTube. https://youtu.be/w72a195QpbI?si=zA9ytPAHCk_u_KBN

P. José de Jesús de Aguilar Valdés. 2020, May 20. *Montserrat – La Virgen de la Montaña*. [Video]. Format [Video file]. YouTube. https://youtu.be/A5Xf8HdzICo?si=4KRrkgywU8REqaqI

www.ingramcontent.com/pod-product-compliance
Lightning Source LLC
Chambersburg PA
CBHW020446100426
42812CB00036B/3466/J